BEYOND "HOLY WARS"

Beyond "Holy Wars"

Forging Sustainable Peace through Interreligious Dialogue

— A Christian Perspective —

Christoffer H. Grundmann

PICKWICK *Publications* · Eugene, Oregon

BEYOND "HOLY WARS"
Forging Sustainable Peace through Interreligious Dialogue—A Christian Perspective

Copyright © 2014 Christoffer H. Grundmann. All rights reserved. Except for brief quotations in critical publications or reviews, no part of this book may be reproduced in any manner without prior written permission from the publisher. Write: Permissions, Wipf and Stock Publishers, 199 W. 8th Ave., Suite 3, Eugene, OR 97401.

Pickwick Publications
An Imprint of Wipf and Stock Publishers
199 W. 8th Ave., Suite 3
Eugene, OR 97401

www.wipfandstock.com

ISBN 13: 978-1-62032-949-8

Cataloguing-in-Publication data:

Grundmann, Christoffer H.

Beyond "holy wars" : forging sustainable peace through interreligious dialogue—a Christian perspective / Christoffer H. Grundmann.

xii + 204 pp. ; 23 cm. Includes bibliographical references and indexes.

ISBN 13: 978-1-62032-949-8

1. Religion—Relations. 2. Dialogue—Religious aspects. 3. Christianity and other religions. I. Title.

BL410 G76 2014

Manufactured in the U.S.A.

The New Revised Standard Version Bible, copyright © 1989, Division of Christian Education of the National Council of the Churches of Christ in the United States of America. Used by permission. All rights reserved.

The poem "Herbst" [Fall] by Rainer Maria Rilke is in public domain.

The poem "Outwitted" by Edwin Markham is in public domain.

Contents

List of illustrations   vii
Preface   ix
Acknowledgments   xi

1   Interreligious Dialogue: Why and What for?
    —An Introduction   1

   Terror, Tears, and Traumata   1
   Politics and Religion—and Vice Versa   8
   A Changing Religious Environment Demands Religious Competence   13
   The Task Ahead   18

2   Why Is Religion so Prone to Be Hijacked by Vested Interests?   23

   Religion as Commodity in Contemporary Consumer Society   24
   What Constitutes Religion?   32
   Religion: A Short History of the Concept and Its Criticism   40
   The Concept of Religion and Empirical Religions   53

3   Tolerance, Convivence, and "Holy Wars"   60

   Tolerance, Its Historical Background and Psychological Prerequisites   61
   Convivence and Cultural Distinctiveness   71
   Convivence and Conflict Management as Political Tasks   82
   The Issue of—and with—"Holy Wars"   84

4   Dialogue, Encounter, and Dialogical Thinking   103

   Interpersonal Encounter: The Heart of Dialogue   104
   The Philosophy of Encounter   116
   Dialogical Thinking and Interreligious Dialogue   125

Contents

    5   Overcoming "Holy Wars," the Christian Contribution   130
           Minding Adequacy of Speech   132
           Embracing Others in Their Otherness   140
           Living a Dialogical Existence   157

        Bibliography   165

        Index of Names   187

        Index of Scripture   193

        Index of Subjects and Places   197

Illustrations

FIGURES

2.1 Showing the commonly applied term "religion" as a construct and its incommensurability or only partial overlapping with the central concepts in Nordic/Germanic religion, Islam, Hinduism, Buddhism, Judaism, and ancient Roman religions. 57

2.2 Showing the superimposition of the term "religion" and unarticulated presuppositions onto the empirical phenomena of religions leading to a heightened complexity which is quietly at work in any interreligious dialogue. 58

4.1 Monological-solipsistic perception of the world, its structure and resulting model of communication. 126

4.2 The basic structure of dialogical thinking and its resultant model of communication. 127

5.1 The set model, exemplified with Judaism, Christianity, and Islam. 142

5.2 The cone model, culminating in Christianity. 143

5.3 Tip of the cone model, culminating in Baha'i. 144

5.4 Tip of the cone model, culminating in Islam. 144

5.5 Tip of the cone model, culminating in Buddhism. 145

5.6 The cone model in a bird-eye's view with Judaism at the center. 147

5.7 The cone model in a bird-eye's view with Christianity at the center. 147

Illustrations

5.8 The cone model in a bird-eye's view with Buddhism at the center.   148

5.9 The plot model representing the pluralistic theory of religions.   148

5.10 Showing religious perception of other religions in Christian perspective.   149

5.11 Religious perception of other religions in Buddhist perspective.   150

5.12 Religious perception of other religions in Muslim perspective.   150

5.13 Approximation of the actual perception of one's own religious tradition within a religiously diverse situation.   151

TABLE

Forms of being-in-conversation-with-one-another   107

Preface

THIS BOOK IS THE outgrowth of a process dating back more than thirty years now when its author was teaching New Testament and Lutheran Theology at Arasaradi, the Tamilnadu Theological Seminary in Madurai, located in the far south of India. Madurai is an ancient, yet very vibrant city. It houses a major Hindu sanctuary constantly drawing multitudes of pilgrims from all over the subcontinent. When occasionally visiting the famous temple I again and again was puzzled, noticing the seriousness of piety and commitment of devotees which forbade any judgmental attitude on my part.

Several years later, when I was back in Germany, I intensified my respective studies and offered a lecture series on the topic of interreligious dialogue at my *alma mater*, the University of Hamburg. These lectures drew ever growing crowds of students, young and old. The students urged me to publish some of my material for further study, which I did in a slim volume in German (*In Wahrheit und Wahrhaftigkeit: Für einen kritischen Dialog der Religionen* [In Truth and Truthfulness: For a Critical Dialogue of Religions]).

Coming to the U.S. in August 2001, just days before the 9/11 attacks, the importance of interreligious dialogue for avoiding like confrontations became more than obvious to me, and not just to me. Yet, since tools and skills to get such dialogue going were lacking, I decided to review my previous considerations in light of these events, the result of which one finds here. While some of the ideas have been shared previously in the U.S. as well as in Europe on occasion of conferences, in journals ("Living With Religious Plurality," *Studies in Interreligious Dialogue* 192 [2009] 133–44), and with Christian and Jewish congregations, the argument in its complex entirety has never been spelled out coherently before as done here. It is my sincere hope that these reflections will aid in fostering a genuine Christian commitment to this vital task.

Valparaiso, March 15, 2013

Acknowledgments

FIRST OF ALL I would like to acknowledge with thanks and gratitude the generosity Valparaiso University has shown throughout the extended process of making this project come about. The two Provosts serving this university since the time of the inception of the book—Roy Austensen and Mark Schwehn—never doubted its importance. They rendered whatever help and support was needed and asked for by always providing the means necessary to complete this endeavor successfully, and they did so despite increasing scarcity of funds.

Special thanks, second, to my dear colleague, associate professor emerita of English Kathleen Mullen, who tirelessly worked with me to get my English in good shape. I shared with her content and ideas over and over again. Without her help and without her constantly urging me to become more explicit and clear the reading of the following pages certainly would not go as smoothly as they do now.

Third, as the insights gained in a prolonged process like this are never the product of one single person's efforts but of many in an ongoing discourse, I would also like to acknowledge thankfully the many, many people I had related discussions with, be it in person or via articles, books, and internet exchange, far too many to name here. While the bibliography gives due credit only to those whose work I used explicitly, several others are not mentioned who also did contribute to generate understanding some way or another.

And, finally, I also would like to acknowledge my indebtedness to the "cloud of witnesses" (Heb 12:1) of people living or deceased, like my parents, my theological teachers at university and seminary, parishioners and other people of faith, who raised me in the Christian faith and taught me to keep it in an ever growing religiously diverse environment.

Two final notes: (a) Square brackets in quotes indicate clarifying additions by the author; (b) all biblical quotations are taken from the New Revised Standard Version (NRSV).

1 Interreligious Dialogue
Why and What for?—An Introduction

Terror, Tears, and Traumata

THE HIGH HOPES AND great expectations with which people greeted the new millennium[1] were soon shattered, much too soon and much too gruesomely, by the terrorist attacks on the U.S. in the morning of September 11, 2001, claiming the lives of more than three thousand people from numerous nations.[2] This act not only initiated the global "war on terrorism" but wars in Iraq and Afghanistan as well.[3] It also sparked many ethnic hate crimes inside and outside the U.S.[4] When it became known that these attacks were meticulously planned by radical Islamists in the Middle East and carried out by religiously motivated suicidals who did not care for the lives of others, everyone in the secular Western world suddenly realized the actual power religion can have on the faithful, turning them into religious fanatics able to commit unspeakable atrocities.

---

1. For a visual documentation of the above statement, see the photographic documentation of millennium celebrations across the globe in The Press Association's *A Moment in Time*.

2. While *The 9/11 Commission Report* lists citizens of 77 countries who died as a result of the attacks, a report issued by the Department of State in Washington D.C. written by Carolee Walker five years later speaks of "victims from 90 countries" (see Walker, *Five Year 9/11 Remembrance*).

3. R. Clarke, *Against All Enemies*.

4. More than 600 hate crimes, which peaked in the first week after the attacks, are documented in *American Backlash*.

Beyond "Holy Wars"

The *Letter to America* written some time later by Osama bin Laden—one of the instigators behind these atrocities—stated clearly: "Do not await anything from us but *Jihad*" (i.e., divinely ordered war to defend Islam or to extend it into the non-Islamic world). And he argued: "Allah, the Almighty, legislated the permission and the option to take revenge . . . Whoever has stolen our wealth . . . we have the right to destroy their economy. And whoever has killed our civilians . . . we have the right to kill theirs . . . [P]repare for fight with the Islamic Nation [*Ummah*] . . . which is addressed by its Quran with the words: 'Do you fear them? Allah has more right that you should fear Him if you are believers. Fight against them so that Allah will punish them by your hands.'"[5] War in the name of God! Terror as an act of obedient faith justified by recourse to Holy Scripture!

However, not only were the terrorists religiously motivated.[6] The powerful response by the U.S. and its allies was so too, as became strikingly obvious when President George W. Bush in a press conference shortly thereafter equated the declared "war on terrorism" with a "crusade."[7] Even though the term crusade has lost most of its religious connotation for the American ear,[8] for others it did not, not the least due to the fact that the common Arabic translation of the term is *War of the Cross*.[9] Thus, the President's remarks, while emotionally understandable, only spurred

---

5. Bin Laden's "Letter to America," published first in Arabic on the Internet in Sept. 2001 and later, when translated into English, was made accessible by the British paper *The Guardian* on their internet site Nov. 24, 2002. Already on August 23, 1996, bin Laden published a *Declaration of War against the Americans* on the internet. The Qur'an quote refers to Quran 9:13–14.

6. This is documented beyond doubt by the *Final Instructions to the Hijackers of September 11, Found in the Luggage of Mohamed Atta and Two Other Copies*, as reprinted in Lincoln, *Holy Terrors*, 93–98.

7. Statement made Sunday, Sept. 16, 2001. See The White House, "President George W. Bush."

8. Slossen, writing about World War I (*The Great Crusade and After: 1914–1928*) in 1937 was probably the first who used the term "crusade" in the modern, non-religious sense, followed by Dwight D. Eisenhower who titled his record of World War II *Crusade in Europe*. W. Chamberlin wrote about *America's Second Crusade* in 1962, and R. Hofstadter spoke frequently of crusades in his book on *Antiintellectualism*, too (see ibid., 41, 124, 130, 338, etc.). More recent titles carrying that term are Zepezauer, *The Feminist Crusades*; and Lantzer, "Prohibition Is Here to Stay." Also, athletic teams of various universities in the U.S. identify their efforts and determination with that of "Crusaders," too, as for instance is the case with Valparaiso University, Valparaiso, IN, or the College of the Holy Cross, in Worcester, MA, and Northwest Nazarene University, in Nampa, ID.

9. See Carroll, *Crusade*, 1–14, esp. 5, 24–26.

the conflict.[10] They made use of the very same arguments as the declared enemy,[11] sending out the message that terrorist *Jihad* will be retaliated by an international *Crusade* spearheaded by the technologically most advanced armed forces in the world today. In so doing G. W. Bush and all those who applauded him in this action were following the very script of the terrorist adversaries and heeded their agenda.

Unfortunately, 9/11, 2001, was only one of the latest in the long line of so declared "Holy Wars"; and many fear that there will be more. The inglorious medieval *Crusades*—cynically now offered as an internet role-playing game[12]—come to mind first, of course,[13] but also do the taking possession of the "Promised Land" by the ancient Israelites according to the biblical book of Joshua.[14] Religiously motivated warfare also occurred in the history of Daoism in China[15] and among the various religions in India (Hinduism),[16]

---

10. See Pinkerton, "Century In, Century Out"; Carroll, "The Bush Crusade"; and Carroll, *Crusade: Chronicles of an Unjust War*.

11. "If the Americans refuse to listen to our advice . . . then be aware that you will lose this Crusade Bush began, just like the other previous Crusades in which you were humiliated by the hands of the Mujahideen, fleeing to your home in great silence and disgrace" (Guardian, *Letter to America*, penultimate paragraph).

12. The "game" (at http://www.holy-war.net/index) was first released in November 2006. It is offered as "a complex browser-based role playing game that you can *play for free*! Dive into the age of the Holy War! Take on the role of a Knight as a Christian, Saracen or Pagan and conquer or defend the Holy Land!" (original emphasis). By Jan. 2013 more than 2.3 million people had played it according to the producers of the "game."

13. See Murray, *The Crusades*.

14. For a historical-critically informed account of these happenings see now Gottwald, "Two Models for the Origin of Ancient Israel"; and Herzog and Gichon, *Battles of the Bible*.

15. The "Yellow Scarves" or "Yellow Turban Rebellion" of 184–205 CE was a religiously motivated warfare by Daoists as was the "Five Pecks of Rice Rebellion" (second to fifth century CE).

16. The "Big War" for the sake of keeping up *Dharma*, i.e., the "Law" or "Eternal Order of life" is the topic of the *Mahabharata*, which gets especially addressed in the *Bhagavad-Gita*. From the eleventh to the seventeenth century the Islamic Moguls were fought by Hindus. When the modern states of India and Pakistan were established in 1947, Muslims remaining in India came under a predominantly Hindu government, leaving India vulnerable to religious conflicts which in recent history flared up again in the destruction of the Babri Masjid Mosque in Ayodhya, Uttar Pradesh in 1992 (see Mandal, *Ayodhya*), and the 2002 massacres in Gujarat, which left 2,000 Muslims dead and forced 100,000 to flee. A comprehensive account of the ongoing tensions between Muslims and Hindus in India is given by Fernandes, *Holy Warriors*.

as they also did in Buddhism and in Shintoism (*Kaminomichi*) in Japan[17] and in Zoroastrianism in Persia, too.[18] Actually, no religion of considerable influence and size seems immune to being caught up in armed conflict.[19] They all appear to be prone to exploitation for vested interests by those who need and seek the support of genuinely committed people, be it politically, economically or personally. Tapping into the powerful source of religious commitment seems to be most desirable since it warrants enduring loyalty and radical dedication, dedication to the point of self-sacrifice as clearly demonstrated by the attackers of 9/11, which threatened to put the entire world in peril. Given these circumstances the crucial question is: How to prevent such atrocities from happening again?

To advise on a solution was one of the explicit tasks given to the National Commission on Terrorist Attacks Upon the United States created by congressional legislation in November, 2002. The commission was mandated to furnish "a full and complete accounting of the circumstances surrounding the attacks . . . [to] investigate and [to] report . . . on its findings, conclusions, and recommendations for corrective measures that can be taken to prevent acts of terrorism."[20] Completing its mandate almost two years later the commission's findings were published in one heavy volume, *The 9/11 Commission Report*.[21] After narrating first the developments of the events, analyzing in-depth the rise of the so-called "new terrorism" and evaluating the emergency responses, the *Report* reflects in its concluding chapters upon appropriate measures to inhibit recurrence of similar events.

---

17. The coalition between Samurai warriors and Zen Buddhists is well known (Nukariya, *Zen Buddhism*) as is Buddhist support of Japanese militarism. The Second Sino-Japanese War (1937–1945) was declared a *Seisen*, i.e., "Holy War" by Japanese imperial propaganda and the "League of Diet Members Believing in the Objectives of the Holy War" was formed by then-Prime Minister Konoe (see Wilson, *When Tigers Fight*).

18. Religiously motivated warfare against Jews, Hindus, and Buddhists, but also against Christians and Manicheans by Zoroastrians held sway in Persia during the early Sassanid era, that is, the third through fifth century CE. The Zoroastrian high priest (*Mobedan-Mobed*) Kartir Hangirpe (late third century) was one of its first main promoters. Religious persecution happened under the kings Shapur I, Hormizd I, Bharam I, and Bharam II. See Boyce, *Textual Sources for the Study of Zoroastrians*, 112–13; and Huyse, *Kerdir and the first Sassanians*, 109–20.

19. For a comprehensive overview on the topic, see the *Encyclopedia of Religion and War*.

20. Public Law, 107–306.

21. The public release of *The 9/11 Commission Report* took place July 22, 2004.

Chapter 12, entitled "What to do? A Global Strategy," is of particular interest here because it recommends a strategy of terror prevention held to be effective.[22] The chapter starts out with "Defining the Threat" and states: "In the post-9/11 world, threats are defined more by fault lines within societies than by the territorial boundaries between them. From terrorism to global disease or environmental degradation, the challenges have become transnational rather than international. That is the defining quality of world politics in the twenty-first century . . . In this sense, 9/11 has taught us that . . . the American homeland is the planet."[23] Like the global spread of infectious diseases or ecological disasters, terror and crime, too, have become globalized, consequently demanding a "global strategy" to counter their threat. This is to say that the world of today cannot any longer be perceived in confines of independent, isolated nation-states and economies, or as independent, autonomous cultural, religious, and ecological entities. Globalization on *all* levels and in *all* aspects of life is the reality of our time.[24]

That said and acknowledged, the *Report* identifies the particular threat of 9/11 more precisely as "posed by *Islamist* terrorism—especially the al Queda network, its affiliates, and its ideology" who "draw on a long tradition of extreme intolerance within one stream of Islam . . . motivated by religion and . . . not distinguish[ing] politics from religion, thus distorting both."[25] It maintains that "Bin Ladin [sic] and Islamist terrorists mean exactly what they say: to them America is the font of all evil, the 'head of the snake,' and it must be converted or destroyed. This," the *Report* declares, "is not a position with which Americans can bargain or negotiate. With it there is no common ground—not even respect for life—on which to begin a dialogue. It can only be destroyed or utterly isolated."[26]

Reassuring that the "Islamist terrorism" targeted is not Islam itself, the *Report* also stresses that "understanding and tolerance among people of different faiths can and must prevail."[27] However, one does not find a single word as to how such understanding and tolerance is to be cultivated,

22. Ibid., 361–98.
23. Ibid., 361–62.
24. For a concise history of this process, see Osterhammel and Petersson, *Globalization*.
25. *The 9/11 Commission Report*, 362; original emphasis. Note that the *Report* always speaks of "Osama bin Ladin." However, in the "Public Statement" on occasion of the release of the *Report* the spelling alternates between "bin Laden" and "bin Ladin."
26. Ibid.
27. Ibid., 363.

even though chapter 13 addresses explicitly the question of "How to do it?" The focus of this chapter is solely on how to prevent the growth of Islamist terrorism, how to protect against it, and how to be better prepared for probable future attacks of a similar nature. It recommends organizing government in a different way, especially the national counterterrorism forces and intelligence agencies.[28] Nothing is said about how to develop and improve intercultural communication and how to foster interreligious dialogue, the obvious failure of which gave rise to this conflict in the first place. Thus, even though the *Report* is much more elaborate than bin Laden's *Letter* the recommended actions are not very much different: responding to the situation with nothing but destruction and, thus, failing to break the vicious circle of war and revenge.

Because they ignore the need to cultivate genuine mutual understanding across cultural and religious boundaries—a competence most important in a war-stricken globalized world—these recommendations miss a critical aspect of the problem at hand. Moreover, they actually play directly into the hands of terrorists by reinforcing their determination to turn to violence. When the *Report* was released publicly on July 22, 2004, Senators Kean and Hamilton, who chaired the 9/11 Committee, elicited a public emotional response with their words, "September 11, 2001 . . . inflicted unbearable trauma on our people." They encouraged everyone in the audience "to remember how you felt that day—the grief, the enormous sense of loss . . . a deep sense of hurt."[29] They also made explicit reference to former experiences of national trauma like Pearl Harbor in 1941 and the assassination of President John F. Kennedy in 1963.[30] Recalling these events in order "not to forget" undoubtedly had an effect on the measures of action taken. It further fueled the determination to exterminate the perpetrators and their allies at all costs: by January 2013 more than 55,000 Iraqis and more than 8,000 young people of the allied forces had died as soldiers in the "war on terrorism"—more than six thousand among them Americans—besides 50,000+ U.S. soldiers seriously wounded, not to mention those of other

---

28. "How to Do It? A Different Way of Organizing the Government," in ibid., 399–428.

29. *Public Statement*, 1. See also *Trauma at Home*; and Tramontin and Halpern, *The Psychological Aftermath*.

30. Ibid., 5 ("Concluding Thoughts").

nations.³¹ The monetary cost of these wars to the U.S. alone has been $1,283 trillion by March. 29, 2011, and is projected at $1,415 trillion for 2012/13.³²

Certainly, this kind of emotionally charged remembrance and the retribution by arms has been at least as devastating as 9/11 was, to put it mildly. To keep pain and humiliation alive and seek vengeance follows the logic of retributive justice. As understandable as such a reaction may be it is counterproductive and utterly ineffective in overcoming evil and hate. Keeping pain and humiliation alive only fuels the urge for retribution and, thus, perpetuates violence. To be sure, to acknowledge trauma, pain, and tears is important for the healing of memories and for the emotional wellbeing not only of individuals but of communities and nations alike.³³ But people are ill advised to cultivate such remembrance by simply ingraining the pains of past happenings over and over again without seriously attempting to move beyond and embrace whatever future there still may be. Those who suffered the trauma are in danger of being spellbound by a disastrous past which—undeniably—inflicted unspeakable harm. Of course, one cannot avoid facing the haunting spell of horrible, traumatic events whenever these surface, no matter what triggers them. But every time these memories recur, one also has the chance to consciously work towards harnessing the pain and emotions evoked by them. If not so handled, memories and emotions tend to paralyze everyone, rekindle hatred, and provoke unpredictable reactions thereby not only making people lose the ability to change their future for the better but turning those who harbor grief, pain, and humiliation in this way into potential agents for revenge, threatening peaceful coexistence even more. In short, the way in which the "Do not forget!" is cultivated matters—indeed, especially when done publicly because public commemoration is highly political in shaping public memory and forming attitudes shared more or less by an entire population.

---

31. For the most recent updates on the figures related to operations "Iraqi Freedom" and "Enduring Freedom," see U.S. Department of Defense (http://www.defense.gov/news/casualty.pdf); Antiwar.com (http://antiwar.com/casualties); and the Iraq Coalition Casualty Count (http://icasualties.org). As of January 2013 the Government figures for U.S. casualties are 4,422 and 2,165. The official counts of wounded are 31,926 and 18,188 while the estimated overall is "over 100,000."

32. Belasco, *The Cost*, 1, 8; see also http://usliberals.about.com/od/homelandsecurit1/a/IraqNumbers.htm.

33. It is telling, indeed, that the cover of the first volume of *Trauma Psychology* shows a photograph of the gutted debris of the World Trade Towers.

Public commemoration, therefore, ought to be done in such a way which seeks to effectively overcome—not to perpetuate—terror, aggression, and retaliation.

Politics and Religion—and Vice Versa

As mentioned before, the 9/11 *Report* stated that the sudden threat to world peace was caused by "the al Queda network . . . motivated by religion . . . not distinguish[ing] politics from religion, thus distorting both." This statement thrives on an implicit notion of religion and politics appearing to be self-evident, but not shared by all. Actually, the actions of the terrorists proved this notion to be utterly wrong. Politics and religion are—and always will be—linked inseparably. To be sure, politics and religion are distinct yet they are intertwined spheres of human life in which everyone lives and acts. Indian political hero and national saint Mahatma M. K. Gandhi (1869–1948) drew attention to this linkage when he "without the slightest hesitation, and yet in all humility" remarked, "those who say religion has nothing to do with politics do not know what religion means."[34] Gandhi had experienced that anyone who aspires after Truth[35] as is the task of religion, "cannot afford to keep out of *any* field of life."[36] The long tradition of hierocracies (religiously authorized governments) in human history points to the fact, too, that politics and religion always mutually have reinforced and stabilized one another as, for instance, in ancient China and Egypt, Persia and Israel. In Japan, the emperor was officially regarded of divine descent until 1945, while the Dalai Lama as the head of the Tibetan government[37] is still worshiped as a *tulku*, that is, as a reincarnation of the godlike Buddhist *bodhisattva Avalokiteshvara*.

Acknowledging the intertwining of religion and politics is also basic for a proper understanding of interreligious dialogue. Even though modern

---

34. Gandhi, *Gandhi—An Autobiography*, 504. On this topic, see also Cavanaugh, *The Myth*.

35. Gandhi always capitalized "Truth," thereby indicating that it is not just a concept or an idea but a reality with personal qualities.

36. Gandhi, *Gandhi—An Autobiography*, 504; emphasis mine.

37. That changed in 1959 when the present Dalai Lama (the fourteenth in the tradition) fled Maoist China seeking exile in India. However, the Dalai Lama is still the head and president of the Tibetan government-in-exile (or: Central Tibetan Administration), which explains a lot of the diplomatic difficulties with China whenever other governments welcome him.

civil governments will not and cannot any longer superimpose any one particular religion or denominational version thereof on their citizens—as was for instance the established practice after the cessation of the Thirty Years' War (1618–1648) in Europe[38]—governments nevertheless still do institutionalize the celebration of their core values in quasi-religious State rituals, like the inauguration of a new President,[39] when pledging Allegiance,[40] or when celebrating national memorial days like July 4th in the U.S. or May 5th (El Cinco de Mayo) in Mexico. In totalitarian countries, too, the public shows of elaborate, disciplined mass parades and the well-choreographed festivities in honor of leaders and significant civic events in North Korea or China bear witness to the fact that secular and even explicitly atheistic governments alike cannot do without some kind of ritual akin to religion, albeit a religion of their own making, of course. However, politics and religion also blend in the life of individual people who just are concerned with living quietly and who are explicitly determined not to get involved in politics at all as is the case with the pacifist Amish and the Hutterites. Ironically, they thereby cannot avoid doing just that. Being anything but non-patriotic, Hutterites and Amish still resist the call to arms, withhold the percentage of their taxes earmarked for the Department of Defense, and are prepared to face the legal consequences; that makes them respected and authentic.[41]

Given the reciprocal stabilization of politics and religion it should surprise no one to learn that in the wake of the 9/11 attacks seasoned politicians of the secular Western world called for religious competence in political office bearers, something unheard of previously. Writing in 2006 the former Secretary of State Madeleine Albright advised: "In the future, no American ambassador should be assigned to a country where religious feelings are strong unless he or she has a deep understanding of the faiths

---

38. The *Peace of Westphalia* (*Westfälischer Friede*) of 1648 settled a conflict which was in part fought for religious reasons by Catholics and Protestants (Lutherans and Calvinists) with the formula: *"cuius regio, eius religio"* (Who owns/reigns the land, his religion [the residents have to follow]); if not, people were allowed to move elsewhere. See Repgen, *Negotiating the Peace of Westphalia*, 355–72.

39. The U.S. Presidents are all sworn in on the Bible and a special church service is part of their inauguration; see Library of Congress, "Bibles and Scripture Passages."

40. The official text of the Pledge since 1942 is: "I pledge allegiance to the flag of the United States of America, and to the republic for which it stands, one nation under God, indivisible, with liberty and justice for all."

41. See Kraybill, *On the Backroad*; and Kraybill, *The Amish and the State*.

commonly practiced there."[42] And she suggested further that the "State Department should hire or train a core of specialists in religion to be deployed both in Washington and in key embassies overseas."[43]

The paramount influence of religion on global politics had been recognized by others already earlier. In 1996 political analyst and advisor to the White House, Samuel P. Huntington (1927–2008), predicted a "clash of civilizations."[44] Analyzing the global political scenario, Huntington expected the future to be decisively determined by a more or less violent "clash of cultures" motivated essentially by ethnicity and religion. According to his analysis the growing political, technical, and economic globalization would not, after all, bring about one single unified global culture, as had previously been supposed. Rather, Huntington argued, globalization would result in an escalating, vehement competition of major civilizations. These include the Western culture of Europe and North America (along with modern Australia and New Zealand) bearing the impress of Christianity. Beside this most widely spread civilization will also stand the Islamic and the Slavic-Orthodox civilization of the former Eastern bloc, along with the Confucian-Chinese civilization of the Asian mainland, the Japanese, and the Latin American civilizations. It may be, though Huntington was uncertain on this point, that one day Africa too will be numbered as a distinct civilization of its own.[45]

To avoid bloody conflicts, all of these "civilizations" (or "cultures") have willy-nilly to manage their coexistence in a state of equilibrium. Such equilibrium, Huntington held, cannot be achieved by recourse to mental and intellectual information alone. Instead, more is required besides awareness of the highly complex, dynamic global interactions in economics, science, and politics, and of the global ecological impact new technologies have on the environment at large. To keep the world at peace today, it is of equal importance that people develop an in-depth understanding of their differences in cultures and religions.[46]

42. Albright, *The Mighty*, 75.

43. Ibid., 76.

44. Huntington was professor in the Department of Government at Harvard University. From 1977–1978 he worked as coordinator of security planning for the National Security Council at the White House. He was also a founder and for several years coeditor of the journal *Foreign Policy*. He published his basic ideas on the issue in 1993 already, but at that time still with a question mark: "The Clash of Civilizations?"

45. Huntington, *The Clash*, 21–28.

46. "For the relevant future, there will be no universal civilization, but instead a

Interreligious Dialogue

Other politicians sharing this conviction also pleaded for dialogue of civilizations in order to prevent a clash. When the Institute of Islamic Understanding (IKIM) at Kuala Lumpur, Malaysia, convened a conference "Towards a Universal Civilization" in 1997 one head of state of a Western nation affirmed that he, too, regarded the "dialogue between cultures" as "one of the most important concerns of our time."[47] And later that year one other leading politician and member of the InterAction Council, (an independent international organization of a group of retired heads of state),[48] referred to Huntington's thesis in this way:

> It is indeed highly probable that a 'clash of civilizations' . . . could happen in the twenty-first century . . . Fundamentalists on both sides, who in the global context of today play in most cases only marginal, minority roles, could possibly unleash and produce mass-hysteria on a massive scale . . . If, in facing this situation, nations and states, politicians, and the guardians and protectors of religions as well, do not learn to have mutual respect for their particular religious and cultural tradition, if people fail to balance the categorical imperatives of freedom and of responsibility toward one another, then in fact the peace between them can falter. The fabric of the international political structures and the socio-economic well-being of the peoples of the world can be extensively disrupted.[49]

It took only four years to see this doom-saying come true on 9/11/2001. Only four years later the world witnessed in shock the disastrous effects of neglecting to cultivate intercultural and interreligious dialogue. People simply had underestimated—because they had failed to understand—the importance of being in dialogue on religious matters with strangers across cultural boundaries in a globalized world. Such ignorance proved fatal on 9/11; moreover, it accelerated the momentum to plunge rational, enlightened nations—secular or not—into "holy wars" in a time where weapons

---

world of different civilizations, each of which will have to learn to coexist with the others" (ibid., 49).

47. Bundespräsidialamt, "Speech by Roman Herzog," 2. Now also in Herzog, *Preventing*, 49–52.

48. The InterAction Council was established in 1983 as an independent international organization to mobilize the experience, energy and international contacts of statesmen who have held the highest office in their own countries. For more information see their website http://www.interactioncouncil.org.

49. Schmidt, "Time to address duties!" (my translation)

of mass destruction are readily at hand and biological warfare has become reality.

To repeat it once again, religion and politics are more closely connected than is generally accepted. This insight challenges and puts critically into question the familiar assumption that religion and faith are exclusively private concerns of individuals. The radical privatization of religion in post-Enlightenment secularized modern societies has obscured the actual significance of public religion in preserving and fostering values shared in common, values around which identities crystallize and which provide cultural coherence and cohesion among an otherwise amorphous mass. The price for this neglect and the ego-worship of the autonomous, "enlightened" individual is the disintegration of society and the de-solidarization of citizens for lack of a common ethos. However, some people nonetheless do sense this loss of focus and coherence. Fearful of the threat of unruly chaos, many form or join fundamentalist and radical movements to "save" society—nay, humanity—from its own destruction and annihilation. They do so according to their particular view of what is best for all, of course. Al Queda is only one among these movements—single-minded, reckless, stubbornly refusing dialogue—and therefore a very dangerous one, to be sure. Yet "to destroy or utterly isolate" it, as the *Report* advises, only reinforces the logic of terror instead of getting at the root of it.

The grim reality of "holy wars" today reminds even the most determinedly secular person of the indispensability of interreligious dialogue. Already in 1984, years before Huntington predicted the "clash of civilizations," theologian Hans Küng said in a conference at Temple University, "No world peace without peace among religions, no peace among religions without dialogue between the religions, and no dialogue between the religions without accurate knowledge of one another."[50] Harvey Cox, who agrees with Küng in principle, though he states it less programmatically, put the issue in his own style this way:

> Multiple specters stalk the human enterprise today. We have reached a point where strife between nations and religions could lead to the final apocalypse. We need more than ever to doxologize the fragile oneness of the whole earth and all her inhabitants. Yet

---

50. Küng, *Christianity and World Religions*, 194. The above mentioned quote became later the mantra and programmatic agenda for the ambitious "Project World Ethos" and the "Global Ethic Foundation." See Küng, *Global Responsibility* and *Yes to a Global Ethic*. The URL for the "Global Ethic Foundation" headquartered at Tübingen, Germany, is http://www.weltethos.org.

Interreligious Dialogue

for men and women of faith, the sacred stories by which we hymn the unity of our species and its animal and cosmic neighbors need not be invented. Paradoxically, those stories and symbols are already embedded in the same traditions that sometimes threaten to tear us asunder. Our task is to claim these reminders of our common destiny from within the disparate sources that first gave them voice.[51]

The al Queda attacks have widely demonstrated the factual impact of religion on global politics which the politicians of the post-Enlightenment, secular Western world tended to ignore for much too long. It is, therefore, high time now to obtain an adequate understanding of what religion is all about. Living in a world of religious diversity—and who does not, in times when *none* of the nations in the world is mono-religious any longer[52]—demands some kind of religious literacy by all, at least to a certain degree, a literacy which is not confined to subject matter only but a literacy which can also competently discern genuinely religious claims from merely alleged ones serving vested, even criminal interests. To overcome religious prejudice and religious ignorance in order to keep religiously motivated violence at bay, literacy in religious matters for the sake of interreligious dialogue is a must, something now also explicitly promoted in the U.S. by the *President's Interfaith and Community Service Campus Challenge* launched ten years after 9/11.[53]

A Changing Religious Environment Demands Religious Competence

Clearly, to go beyond "holy wars" and to avoid the clash of civilizations, nations must work to dispel religious ignorance and religious illiteracy. Since religiously motivated terrorists are threatening the peaceful coexistence of peoples, religious literacy and competence are demanded urgently to keep the world at peace by engaging in dialogue. While the necessity and urgency of the task at hand—*Death or Dialogue*[54]—are well recognized by

---

51. Cox, *Many Mansions*, 18.

52. For the most recent data see the statistics on religion in the section Comparative National Statistics in the annually revised *Britannica Book of the Year*.

53. For further information, see http://www.whitehous.gov/administration/eop/ofbnp/interfaithservice.

54. *Death or Dialogue* is the arresting title of a multiauthor publication of 1990 edited by Swidler et al.

many, the particular challenges and skills required to get such a process rolling are not. This inertia has to do with numerous factors, one of which is the ubiquitous change of the religious landscape as an epiphenomenon of globalization. Even remote, isolated places today cannot but notice the change of the religious environment. Take, for instance, the U.S. where until recently religious diversity consisted mainly in denominational variations within Christianity and Judaism, besides the presence of a host of sects. Not until Congress lifted the ban on immigration from Asia in 1965 and after suffering the impact of the Arab oil embargo in 1973 did the American public at large become aware of and exposed to other religions—notably Buddhism, Daoism, and Islam. "Within a matter of decades," writes Georgetown University professor of Islamic Studies John L. Eposito,

> the demographic landscape of . . . North America has changed significantly. Though for some time the second largest of the world's religions, Islam had remained invisible on the cognitive maps of most Americans, whose first major encounters with the Muslim world were the Arab oil embargo of 1973 and the Iranian revolution of 1978–1979. However, by the beginning of the twenty-first century, Islam and Muslims represent the second largest religion in Europe and the third largest in North America.[55]

Today Buddhism ranks as the third-largest religion in the U.S., closely followed by Islam.[56]

Tourism, intercontinental migration by business people, athletes, asylum seekers, and highly skilled experts, as well as communication via new media like the internet have not only added their share in bringing about a bewildering mix of people and ideas from different cultural backgrounds and religious traditions to even the remotest places; these developments actually have accelerated the change of the religious landscape and along with it have also hastened the spread of new religious movements.[57]

Of course, information on different religions and their teachings was available to generations before, even to a broader audience on occasions

---

55. Zahid et al., *Muslims' Place in the American Public Square*, xi.

56. According to the *Pew Forum on Religion & Public Life/U.S. Religious Landscape Survey*, Buddhists of all traditions account for 0.7 percent of the overall U.S. population, while Muslims account for only 0.6 percent (see the Pew Forum at http://religions.pewforum.org/pdf/affiliations-all-traditions.pdf). For general information about Buddhism in America, see Seager, *Buddhism in America*.

57. See the books by Hexham and Poewe, *New Religions as Global Cultures*; Dawson, *Comprehending Cults*; and the informative *Encyclopedia of New Religious Movements*.

like the first "Parliament of the World's Religions" in Chicago in 1893, which featured formal public encounters between representatives of Eastern and Western religious traditions.[58] But the degree to which awareness of religious diversity has penetrated the general public today and the instant availability of broad information on points of interest for us is far beyond that of any previous era. Unthinkable decades ago that the leader of one Buddhist sect of a tiny, far away mountainous country would have met with such public welcome worldwide as has the Dalai Lama of Tibet in our time.

To be sure, Christians knew about Judaism from within their own tradition for centuries as did Jews and Muslims, too. Hindus did know about Buddhism as also did Buddhists about Hinduism. Such awareness of other religions was cultivated mainly through the texts of the respective Holy Scriptures, which were read and recited again and again. However, this did not represent any genuine knowledge of the religious other. Rather, it was highly selective, often polemic in nature, biased and one-sided. In times without means of mass communications like print media, radio, and television, and, more importantly, in times without general public education, commoners were unable to study these matters on their own. Only things most strange and curious about the cultural and religious other reached their ears, often in the form of fantastic fables, tales, and derogatory myths. Many of these would be reinforced and bowdlerized by prejudicial proverbs or sayings,[59] by distorting and humiliating images, and by songs or musical motifs in like manner.[60] Thus the foundation was laid for serious misperceptions and silly caricatures of people of other religions, oftentimes making them become scapegoats for whatever mishap which occurred. Somewhat reliable information about other religions remained locally confined and limited to a comparatively small and elite circle.

Dissemination of reliable knowledge of other religions was impaired further in former times by the fact that written texts and sacred scriptures in particular were accessible only to those who were initiated and entitled to study these, something in many religious traditions commonly denied to women, ordinary folk, and strangers until recently. For most of the time

---

58. See Seager, *The Dawn of Religious Pluralism*.

59. Ample examples, which for obvious reasons the author refrains from quoting here, are to be found in Smith, *The Oxford Dictionary of English Proverbs*, and in Simpson, ed., *The Concise Oxford Dictionary of Proverbs*.

60. See Corrigan, *Visual Polemics in the Ninth-Century Byzantine Psalters*, and Cuffel, *Gendering Disgust*. A classic case in point for music is W. A. Mozart's *Entführung aus dem Serail* (KV 384).

encounter with people of other religions was a byproduct of migration, military conquest such as the campaign of Alexander the Great (356–323 BCE) and his troops into Asia,[61] or else by way of extensive research- and commerce-related expeditions. Above all, it was in the centers of trade along major routes of commerce like the famous Silk Road[62] and in port cities that personal contact between people of other religions came about regularly. Therefore, engaging in interreligious dialogue was formerly a privilege of a certain elite only while the political authorities were less concerned about it. What the political authorities were concerned with was public order and cultural homogeneity within their territories, not really encouraging cultural or religious diversity in their respective dominions. However, during the Middle Ages political authorities in Spain for instance also occasionally organized interreligious debates as public events with compulsory attendance by the commoners, especially those belonging to the cultural and religious Jewish minority living among them.[63] The admitted agenda of many of such disputations was *not* to foster mutual understanding in dialogue but to debate with representatives of the deviant religious minority, to prove them erroneous by rational argument, and to make them join the fold of the Church—for their own true salvation.[64]

Luckily, today we have now, as people had never before, almost full and unrestricted access to nearly all the sources of religions, along with detailed knowledge of their sacred scriptures, rites, images, and holy artifacts.[65] Thus, the breadth of reliable information at our disposal allows for a more appropriate, critical appreciation of the diverse religious traditions

---

61. For a documentation of Alexander's campaigns, see Brunt, *Arrian: Anabasis of Alexander*; and Wolohojian, *The Romance of Alexander the Great*. See also the biography by Green, *Alexander of Macedon*; and O'Brien's study *Alexander the Great*.

62. See Foltz, Religions of the Silk Road. To further the cause of interreligious and intercultural dialogue the University of Florida established in 2004/2005 the "Silk Road Club" (http://grove.ufl.edu/~silkroad/constitution.html). See also the UNSECO sponsored "Silk Road Project" for the same cause (http://www.silkroadexperiences.org).

63. See the respective studies by Chazan, *Barcelona and Beyond*; Cohen, *Scholarship and Intolerance in the Medieval Academy*; and Johnston, *Ramon Llull* (1995).

64. For further in-depth reading on this issue, see the publications Tamlage, *Disputation and Dialogue*; and Maccoby, *Judaism on Trial*; besides Berger, *The Jewish-Christian Debate*; and Chazan, *Daggers of Faith*.

65. The most obvious document of this is the *Encyclopedia of Religion* with its fifteen volumes.

Interreligious Dialogue

around us and enables a well-informed, knowledgeable discussion of the topic. There is no excuse any longer for religious illiteracy today.

Yet, to become religiously literate is not just a matter of acquiring respective information about religion. What is also needed is the ability to make sense of and really understand religiously informed cultural differences. As it turns out, not only secularized societies but also populations which claim to be "religious" have actually only very little understanding of what religion is all about,[66] and this despite the fact that in the day-to-day life of our culturally and religiously diverse global society a lot has become established good practice. Restaurants and hotels, hospitals and airlines, now observe *kosher* meal preparation for Jewish guests, honor abstinence from pork by Jewish and Muslim customers, and accommodate obligatory vegetarianism of orthodox Hindu and Buddhist patrons. However, when religiously informed cultural differences become more visible in the public sphere—the dress codes that Sikhs wear the *Dastar* (i.e., turban) and Muslim women wear the *hijab* (the veil), the *chador* (long narrow face screen), or the *burkha* (covering the entire body)—issues and tensions abound.

Take the case of Ms. Lubna Hussein, a mother who wanted to accompany her children at a public swimming pool in Omaha, Nebraska, but was refused entry because she did not wear a swimsuit herself. She was dressed "modestly" in accordance with Muslim law instead, that is, with arms and legs covered. In *Lubna Hussein v. City of Omaha* the City of Omaha settled the case (2/18/2005) by permitting exceptions for religious reasons.[67] Likewise, the turban-wearing Sikhs in Great Britain are exempted from putting on a hard-hat when working on construction sites or from wearing a crash helmet when motor-biking.[68] Even such seemingly insignificant actions

---

66. On the topic of religious illiteracy in the U.S., see Prothero, *Religious Literacy*, esp. 21–25.

67. The lawsuit was filed in June 2004 by the American Civil Liberties Union of Nebraska on behalf of Lubna Hussein who came to the pool with her small daughters to watch them swim but did not intend to swim herself. She was refused entry into a public swimming pool due to her religious clothing. The city policies in place at the time of the lawsuit did not permit people to enter a swimming pool or the poolside area unless they wore a bathing suit. The lawsuit alleged civil rights violations on the basis of race, national origin, gender and religion. The City's answer filed in federal court responded the dress code rules were intended to be neutrally applicable. The City of Omaha has amended its policies now to allow a variance in dress code based on religious and/or medical needs. A copy of the dress code and request form is available online at: www.ci.omaha.ne.us.

68. Section 11 of the UK *Employment Act* 1989 exempts turban-wearing Sikhs from

as the compulsory removal of shoes upon entering Muslim residences or apartments which are also used for prayer[69] or not observing proper conduct in a teetotal taxi-cab can stir legal repercussions today.[70]

Certainly, incidents like these push people out of their comfort zone, making them feel uncomfortable and not at home any longer. Feeling disturbed by intruding strangers, many long to have it "the good old way." They resist change, and, fearing loss of control and alienation, are not willing to face the new challenges. What has been unquestionable in their daily routines, things such as dietary staples, communication in the vernacular, or conventions of dressing, have now become matters of conscious consideration, shaking the foundations of nearly everything they have been familiar with for so long. But, just as it matters how one handles traumatic experience, so too does it matter how cherished values are honored and kept alive. Values cannot be preserved by declaring them off limits from the encounter with the present. Only by engaging these in dialogue with the challenges of the times can values be kept alive and convictions retain their plausibility because those holding them dear have to critically appreciate these anew in the process of dialoging and, thus, will re-own them more authentically than before, whereas shunning dialogue spoils it all.

The Task Ahead

As has become sufficiently clear by now, dialogue is actually and practically indispensable for the peaceful living togetherness in a globalized environment for the individual as well as for the public at large, interreligious dialogue in particular. Still, some important conditions for effective dialogue

---

any requirements to wear safety helmets on a construction site. When a turban-wearing Sikh is injured on a construction site, liability for injuries is restricted to the injuries that would have been sustained if the Sikh had been wearing a safety helmet. Sikhs who wear turbans need not wear crash helmets when they ride motor cycles or scooters. They have been allowed to wear the turban as their only headgear. In accordance with the *Motor-Cycle Crash Helmets (Religious Exemption) Act 1976* passed by the British Parliament in 1976, Section 2 A "exempts any follower of the Sikh religion while he is wearing a turban" from having to wear a crash helmet.

69. This was a case in Germany in which a Muslim family refused the meter-reader of the utility company entry into their apartment, because he did not take off his shoes when entering the room which happened also to be used by the family as a prayer room; according to Islamic code, such a room may not be entered with shoes on—it would be a sacrilege. See "Rechtsstreit."

70. See "Minnesota's Teetotal Taxis," *Time Magazine*, January 29, 2009, 30.

Interreligious Dialogue

must be set. First, every such dialogue has to steer clear of any simplistic leveling. Instead, dialogue must be conducted in a truly self-critical, responsible, and reflective way honoring dissenting views. It has to address core essentials—in marked contrast to frivolous, shallow, and insignificant talk about peripheral matters—moving from everyday experiences and observations in the ordinary life of people, their "life-world,"[71] to the all-determining center of what lies at the core of their differences. Some of what follows might therefore appear to be nothing more than associative digression at first or a redundant remark only. But, in retrospect, the details will cohere and all pieces will fall into place and, hopefully, elicit the reader's comprehensive understanding.

The second preliminary condition sounds a note of caution, because no one single system will be proposed or terminologically constructed, nor will any step by step unfolding of a new or original concept be made here. Instead, since today's extreme individualism and "hyperpluralism"[72] does not allow taking anything for granted, every statement strives to be intelligible and to affirm the dialogical structure of the reflections shared. This position requires at the outset that the underlying principles on which the argument rests be clearly spelled out.

The basic principle to which the author holds in this context is the conviction that interreligious dialogue can only be pursued from within the distinctive perspective of a particular lived religion. Any other approach would so distort the situation as to destroy the subject matter. If not engaged from within a genuinely lived religion, that which is called interreligious dialogue would devolve merely into a talk *about* religion as an idea and mental construct. In this scenario dialogue would become an opinionated discourse among people of different faiths with no further in-depth consideration of the underlying, ultimate causes of the distinctive beliefs, lifestyles, and actions which give rise to their diversity in the first place. Pursuing interreligious dialogue from within a particular lived religion, in contrast, necessitates communication about matters of ultimate concern. It implies acknowledgement of existing but conflicting diverse ultimate claims as such—a stance anything *but* obvious in an age of radical

---

71. The discovery of the "life-world" as a meaningful and essential a priori of any philosophy was a principal insight of phenomenology as developed by Edmund Husserl (1859–1938) and his students; see Ricoeur, *Husserl*; Natanson, *Edmund Husserl*; and Schütz and Luckmann, *The Structures of the Life-World*.

72. The neologism "hyperpluralism" is frequently used by Gregory in his *The Unintended Reformation*; see 11, 74–75, 112, 229, etc.

relativism and pluralism. Expecting a discourse of this kind requires that all participants in the dialogue are prepared to be able to articulate and willing to share the underlying religious-cultural roots of their particular perception of life and world. Any abstract, non-situated interreligious dialogue is simply no such dialogue at all.

Advocating this principle requires also giving a full and honest account of the religious background from which the argument is advanced here. The author of these pages is a Christian theologian specializing in the study of comparative religion and an ordained minister of the Lutheran church. As such he pursues theology as an academic discipline which has to be intelligible and reasonable, able to show the meaning of its statements convincingly, even when referring to hallowed tradition and "revelation." Just so, it is theo-*logy*. At the same time, it is *theo*-logy—Christian theology—only in so far as it finds its center, the unity of its statements and reflections and their coherence in explicit reference to God who became incarnate in Jesus Christ. Theology thus understood guards against the merely emotional, purely spiritualized, immaterial, and oftentimes vaporous witty speculation about God—so fashionable nowadays—while it at the same time demands vigilant, selfless sobriety which neither gets wrapped up in mere theoretical reflection nor becomes immobilized by any kind of restricting doctrine.

With these strictures in place it indeed seems possible to approach interreligious dialogue sober mindedly and to pursue a meaningful discourse on the topic. To get this going the next chapter (2) addresses the question "Why is religion so prone to be hijacked by vested interests?" Exploring what the term "religion" actually stands for, the chapter sets off with analyzing the perception of "religion" in our contemporary open society followed by a brief survey of the history of the concept of "religion" and, inseparably linked to it, also of the critique of the concept as it developed over time. This sketch leads to the realization that any abstract discussion of "religion" does not do justice to the socio-cultural phenomena it claims to describe, namely to actually lived "religions" like Judaism or Christianity, Islam, Buddhism, or Hinduism. To demonstrate its true reality, the concept is juxtaposed with the actual self-perceptions of the various traditions.

Once this incommensurability is realized, a different approach to interreligious dialogue is asked for which is *not* preoccupied with any kind of abstract, theoretical concept. Chapter 3, therefore, introduces and discusses two empirical examples of how people manage peaceful coexistence despite significant differences in culture and religious beliefs, namely by exercising tolerance and by cultivating living togetherness, also termed convivence. After showing how these ideas and practices developed, the chapter looks at issues in resolving conflicts, especially when hostility and violent conflict loom. In this context "holy wars" past and present and their justification by religious authorities are addressed explicitly.

Against this backdrop the next chapter (4) substantiates in detail the opening thesis that peaceful coexistence in today's world is critically dependent upon the success of interreligious dialogue. It deepens the philosophical and epistemological foundations of this claim in general and the concept of dialogical thinking in particular as developed and expressed in the so-called "philosophy of encounter," familiarizing the readers with remarkable Jewish and Christian thinkers on the topic. As a result the chapter suggests perceiving of dialogue always as an interpersonal, face-to-face encounter between individual personalities, who in the case of interreligious dialogue happen not just to represent different beliefs and worldviews, but who are also seriously concerned about fostering sustainable peace in a multicultural environment.

The argument of the book reaches its climax in chapter 5, which looks into the specific contributions to interreligious dialogue by Christians. It holds that interreligious dialogue can succeed only when pursued as human communication about diverse ways of authentically relating to the Ultimate. It shows that only dialogue so perceived has the strength to foster genuine mutual understanding while intellectual arguments about religion and dialogue, however elaborate, lack such strength and power. To ground this assertion reliably the chapter introduces and critically evaluates various models of dialogue proposed in the context of respective discourses, namely the so-called exclusivistic, inclusivistic, and pluralistic models. It indicates that in contradiction to their claims and intentions, these concepts in fact do not allow for acknowledging others in their actual distinctive otherness. Instead, as well-defined models they still superimpose some kind of preconceived opinion and ideal type of "religion" on their counterparts in dialogue. The point is made that any philosophically conscious and religiously well-informed approach to interreligious dialogue must, therefore, deconstruct all such models for the sake of genuine dialogue.

The chapter, finally, alerts to the fact that in pointed contrast to the immense potential accorded to interreligious dialogue for forging sustainable peace stands the vulnerability of dialogue itself, because genuinely religious people will never fight for their cause nor will they defend it with arms. Their way to defend it is, instead, by fearlessly witnessing to the Ultimate. In so doing they unmask everyone who merely pretends commitment to an ultimate cause. Such exposure is dangerous, of course, since the powers so unmasked will seek to silence their critics one way or the other, whether by completely ignoring it, or by brute force through incarceration of its advocates or by putting these to death as was done with Jesus of Nazareth. This outer vulnerability, however, does not indicate failure of dialogue. The cross, rather, underscores the actual power of dialogue: While worldly powers and authorities could execute the one who fearlessly unmasked their claims, they were deceived to think they could kill his message. The resurrection of Jesus Christ made it clear that despite their serious efforts these powers did not succeed in quenching the witness to the living God as the truly Ultimate. Believers are called to witness as Jesus did, confidently trusting that their risen Lord and Master who has promised to be with them "always, to the end of the age" (Matt 28:20) will actually reveal himself anew as the one he really is wherever and whenever they engage in dialogue. In fearlessly living out this calling Christians not only open up to the world in every respect, they at the same time foster a culture of genuine dialogue and, thus, make sustainable peace become reality.

2 Why Is Religion So Prone to Be Hijacked by Vested Interests?

ARGUING FOR INTERRELIGIOUS DIALOGUE as one of the most important means to attain sustainable peace in today's globalized world necessitates clarification of the two basic terms, religion and dialogue. This chapter, therefore, focuses on the topic of religion, while chapter four investigates the subject of dialogue.

It is a strange phenomenon indeed to notice that so much cruelty in the world has been—and still is committed—in the name of "religion" which claims to be concerned with nothing but "ultimate truth" and with the "supreme Good." What, then, is the reason for this contradiction of claim and reality? One approach to solving this riddle is to reverse the question by asking: could it not be that these regrettable incidents are caused by people who pursue vested interests disguised as legitimate religious concerns in order to tap into the loyal commitment of unsuspecting believers for their own ends? Looking at the issue from this angle makes one ask immediately the other question, too: Why is "religion" prone to exploitation by vested interests at all?

To give a brief answer here right at the outset: religions are vulnerable to vested interests because the core of genuine believing, faith, hinges on ultimate, confident trust in the appropriateness of the cause. To use an analogy here: when we fall in love we are spirited and energized, happy, "up in the clouds." We do not ask why nor are we suspicious. We are convinced—nay: absolutely certain—that all is perfectly good and will only get better. As with love, so with believing, since believing, too, is an attitude of unconditional trust and confidence. The vulnerability lies here, because such unconditional trust can be betrayed much too easily, as also love, when disappointed, stir up strong emotions. To tap into this enormous and powerful source of radical commitment in order to use it is a temptation difficult to resist for, clearly, religious commitment warrants enduring loyalty and radical dedication, dedication to the point of self-sacrifice.

A more satisfying answer, however, requires a deeper understanding of religion. Taking as the point of departure random observations of how contemporary consumer society perceives religion, the chapter then unfolds the meaning of this term along the lines of some of its most articulate interpretations in the history of Western thought. These, proposed by individuals, mainly philosophers of their times, will show how the modern understanding of religion came about and also, why the abstract concept does *not* do justice to empirical religion and the religious traditions actually lived. This somewhat surprising, even disturbing discovery not only indicates a far-reaching, yet well-established misunderstanding; it also calls for a thorough reconsideration of the commonly held conviction that religion is merely a matter of personal choice by self-determined individuals who, accordingly, also have the liberty to deny any religious association at all.

Religion as Commodity in Contemporary Consumer Society

One of the hallmarks of a globalized world is the experience of religious plurality; however, this phenomenon of a religiously diverse society is not all that new. There has always been religious pluralism, especially in multi-ethnic civilizations such as ancient India, Greece, and Rome as well as in Russia and China. However, what *is* new today is the near omnipresence of this phenomenon and the changing attitude of people toward established religions, notably in the West. While variety of religion and religious diversity are no new phenomena, the market perspective on religion is. No longer does the appeal to hallowed, longstanding tradition and holy authority carry convincing weight for contemporary critical-minded individuals. Rather, it is one of the essential features of the secularized post-modern West that people perceive religion as a commodity to be traded or simply as negligible in their lives. If people are religiously interested at all, they shop around, searching out what appeals to them most; if they are not thus interested, people just ignore religion and leave it aside.

Why Is Religion So Prone to Be Hijacked by Vested Interests?

In 2005 a California based company published a cardboard dial chart "Wheel o' Wisdom" with the title *Choose your Religion—A Guide for the Savvy Convert*. Setting the pointer of this device to one of the choices on display like Taoism, Moonies, or Catholicism, the patron finds in cut-away windows brief information about "Potential new friends," "Perks," "Drawbacks," "Afterlife promises," and "Accessories/Paraphernalia." The company promotes this somewhat unusual "Cordless Search Engine for Life," as they call it, the following way: "Disappointed with your religion of birth? Agonize no longer—use proven techniques of comparison shopping to select just the right religion for you. Base your religious choices on things that really matter—what you'll wear, whether you can have sex, where you'll go when you die. Judge almighties and religions side-by-side with breakdowns of 30 world religions . . . With this innovative consumer's guide, now you can choose the very best religion for you."[1]

Given the company's profile one may take this with a twinkle in the eye as poking fun at the bewildering variety of religions and denominations around. However, the dial also reflects a somewhat general attitude toward religion in contemporary society according to which religion and faith seem to be nothing more than matters of personal preferences, convictions, and tastes satisfiable by what the market has to offer in order to find the best deal promising the most personal satisfaction.

A recent U.S. Religious Landscape Survey conducted by the Washington D.C. based Pew Forum on Religion and Public Life in 2008 seems to confirm this. Reporting the findings in *Time*, Jackson Dykman summarized these as follows, "Americans love to shop, even for religion. More than 40 percent of U.S. adults have changed their faith since childhood, many opting for no faith at all . . . The study found that the fastest growing religious group is people without any religious affiliation describing their religion as 'nothing in particular.' . . . Protestants remain a bare and strikingly diverse majority; the study found widespread movement among 100 variations of Protestantism. For America's faithful, it's a buyer's market."[2]

To know about options and to choose among them is, no doubt, an expression of freedom and independence, the limits of which seem defined only by personal taste and economic wherewithal. In fact, to be able to choose *is* to enjoy freedom, individually as well as politically. Writing in the

---

1. Knock Knock Who's There, Inc., Venice, CA.—the texts quoted are from the back of the said device.
2. *Time Magazine*, March 10, 2008, 41.

Beyond "Holy Wars"

aftermath of World War II and having realized the traumatic excesses of totalitarian fascist doctrine and ideology, British philosopher Karl Popper (1902–1994) declared it the explicit task and duty of politics in a democracy to ensure that no national or religious ideology take hold of the minds of citizens. Instead, politicians in a democracy have to warrant the general public freedom of choice, characterized by critical rationalism. Anyone superimposing one particular way of conduct telling others what to do is a declared enemy of the "open society." Popper held that in the "open society" which he advocated avidly, individuals confront themselves with "personal decisions" only without being given any lead as to strictures or reasonableness, in terms of content, for deciding one way or the other.[3]

Popper's liberal concept faithfully reflects the actual self-perception of modern individualistic society: It has no single common point of reference any longer and it decries any appeal to a higher authority (especially not one claimed transcendental or sacred), save the claim for the freedom of personal choice. Decisions in a democracy are, in the end, perceived as nothing but deliberate commitments of individuals and groups guided only by rational sobriety. This claim, of course, reflects the legacy of Enlightenment thinking, especially Jean-Jacques Rousseau's idea of the state as nothing but the product of a Social Contract (*contract social*) of autonomous, self-determining individuals, and it is this concept of state which makes for the epithet "secular" in secular society.[4]

Obviously such a truly secular concept of society is bound to collide with authoritarian alternatives like theocracy (as in Islam), aristocracy (as in many tribal cultures), and hierocracy (as in Tibetan Buddhism), for instance. But it is not just conflicting concepts of state and society as such which meet head-on in a globalized world. The entire attitude toward life, the whole lifestyle, is challenged, including elements like wearing a head scarf or veil, observing special holidays, and abstaining from certain kinds of food.

To put it simply: Conflicts happen because different concepts of society reflect different core values, and these conflicts cannot—and should not—be sugarcoated with deceiving niceties. However, the enlightened, rational, open societies of the West have obviously lost the capacity to understand why their way of life and behavior might appear to devoted Muslims, for instance, as sacrilegious because it violates their core values;

---

3. See Popper, *The Open Society*.
4. See Rousseau, *The Social Contract*.

the handling of the impact of the 9/11 attacks is a classic example of the inability to understand blasphemy and shows insensitivity toward faith-based religious sentiments which in turn makes Western civilizations vulnerable to "holy wars." As long as public order and cohesion is understood as being just—and only just—the outcome of mutual agreement among equals, such order is easily challenged by different ideas about state, nation, and the common good. However, to those who hold that public order is not just based on manmade agreements but transcendental, even divine in nature, ordered by God or *dhārma*, any challenge of it would be blasphemous, since whatever is sanctioned by ultimate authority demands unfaltering obedience.

Of course, the appeal to ultimate authority might be feigned by those in power and their peers; the history of human culture abounds in examples of this deception. So, every such claim has to be critically authenticated over and over again by those who appeal to such authority and hold power, a task both difficult and challenging, but something indispensable and which a prudent leadership would always want to cultivate. To simply ignore that there are numerous governments in the world who accept being ultimately bound by a higher authority not of human making, fatally exposes one to "holy wars" declared by those strictly opposed to democracy and any other form of political governance than their own. How to breach this chasm and mediate successfully toward sustainable peace?

It would be short sighted to expect education by rational, pragmatic argument to convert genuinely committed religious people. First of all, such an education would be given by those who have already decided that religion has little or nothing to do with politics. Second, genuinely committed people have arrived at their decision either by critical reflection or by internalizing an accepted way of life which makes them who they are and thus somewhat immune to change. And, third, a non-religious, pragmatic approach to politics intending to make religious people tolerate deviant attitudes totally ignores the systematic way in which secular societies keep people busily occupied with trivial concerns instead of focusing on the truly essential. This latter aspect deserves some further attention here since it is of enormous practical importance.

Entire armies of marketing strategists and information managers strive to find ever more enticing ways to make people actually believe that the magnificent array of possibilities put on display for exercising choice is at the disposal of everyone and that it is essential for life. Individuals should make ample use of the possibilities offered so to construct an identity of their own, realizing their personal self-image by showing off a distinctive life-style. However, the garish colorings of promotional materials and their shrill, obsequious tone insufficiently conceal the shadow side of a fantasy world of supposed absolute freedom and self-determination. It all points to virtual, not factual, reality, a reality which thrives on assumed affluence based on simplification, individualization, and gradual loss of touch with real life in the real world.

However, even as mere virtual reality, this kind of reductive perception of life is not without effect, and it is anything but harmless. On the contrary, advertising has great powers of suggestion to draw people into its spell, especially those who cannot detach themselves from being bombarded with impudent images and slogans arousing desires, and who are not able to see through these empty promises. Advertising, like cyberspace, clouds people's consciousness of any clear and distinct boundaries between wishes, dreams, and factual reality. Who isn't familiar with the dream house, the once-in-a-lifetime experience of a vacation? Who does not aspire to a dream job?

Everything seems to be near, within reach instantly, if only one decides—now—in favor of it. And these trivialities are then declared to be life itself. Life, thus, becomes one big motley experiment in which all the goods and wares on display can—and should, quite obviously and naturally—be tried out. This notorious "both-and" attitude along with the "You-can-have-it-all" mindset which some have dubbed the "modernization trap,"[5] is not easy to escape. So entertaining is the sham of virtual reality that it obscures any sober sense of the arduousness of everyday reality. The longer one indulges in it the more distant reality becomes. Everyone under its spell develops a growing inability to recognize, discern, and to duly face up to the real challenges of life. People thus become existentially volatile and unable to account meaningfully for the whys and wherefores of life. The tricky thing is that all of this happens quite effectively but very unspectacularly.[6]

Seduction by *la dolce vita* and distraction by the ever-present possibility of entertainment are the two key strategies in the process of desensitization to religious issues. The principles and slogans conveyed in various forms are intended to enchant the whole world and to strangle any budding critical potential. As satirist Juvenal (55/60–127?) observed, the Roman

---

5. Wahl, *Die Modernisierungsfalle.*
6. See Heidegger, *Being and Time.*

emperors anesthetized the critical potential of their citizens by keeping them fed and entertained according to the maxim *panem et circenses*, i.e., "bread and games." The program is the same still today: Anesthetize critical spirit by pampering emotional desire in establishing a marketable counterculture expressly for that purpose in which anything goes. Everything that is wanted or which seems desirable seems to be allowed. Nothing can or should be radically called into question anymore. This fundamental doctrine of the permissive, open society seems to mark the appalling level to which perception and understanding of liberty and freedom in the Western world has been lowered today. Existential alertness, in contrast, would turn against this entertainment craze by fearlessly unmasking its implicit strategies of dehumanization and unveiling its ever growing distortion of life.

The inordinate range of wares on display and the outspoken desire for radical self-determination have led to a situation which is no longer existentially manageable. Incessantly caught up in making decisions and taking chances, again and again people must weigh—and therefore determine, at least slightly critically—what is to be done here and now. Luckily though, over time one begins to form preferences which gradually form patterns of thought and action before they finally become habitual. After all, who buys a different newspaper every day? Who takes always a different route to work? Who hasn't found his or her own personal style in clothing, décor, food?

Habits are extremely practical because they aid in decision-making and make day-to-day routines manageable.[7] Habits help stem the tide of the otherwise overwhelming task of constant decision-making by keeping this challenge to a tolerable level in reducing the complexity of possible choices. The more frequently one and the same particular decision is taken, the more everyday its nature, the more likely it becomes a habit, thereby freeing and preserving strength and power for more important decisions in extraordinary situations.

However, the acid test of conscious, personal decision-making is faced in those comparatively rare situations in which one has to decide, for instance, about a career, a spouse, and a family. All such decisions have a deep and long lasting impact on the future of one's life. Unfortunately though, due to lack of experience, the uncertainty in these matters and the number of misguided decisions are disproportionately high. Yet, one does not act in a complete vacuum, because despite the fact that existentially important

---

7. Lally et al., *How Are Habits Formed?*

decisions are quite often made in personal solitude, traditional habits and religious directives and notions come into play here, however much they may have been experienced as unduly constricting or even irrelevant previously. Culturally established habits and religiously sanctioned manners provide points of orientation and—fairly—reliable guidelines in these most critical, fragile life situations. They mediate a proven way toward a stable, life-protecting and life-furthering future. In cases where there is a religious void, such guidance for decision making will be taken over by common wisdom or the more or less formal principles advocated by one's peers.

Socially sanctioned standards in the existentially relevant spheres of life are provided by cultural-religious conventions. If still plausible, these conventions effectively assist in containing the chaos which otherwise threatens. On the other hand, if cultural conventions appear unreasonable or not plausible any longer, they lose their claim to being obligatory. Consequently, then, the entire burden of decision-making rests solely on those who in the actual situation experience detachment from longstanding tradition and alienation from prevailing mores so that the burdensome impact of decision-making affects them all the more since literally everything rests on their shoulders, on theirs alone.

Every decision, however consciously made, and however painstakingly balanced and critically considered by an individual, by groups of people, or by a community as a whole, will be challenged in the long run, be it by new political or technological developments or changes in attitude. Political decisions are not stable, nor are they everywhere and in every respect binding, especially not in an open society and a democracy; the democratic principle, actually, demands constant revisions of decisions by the parliamentary process. Much more so are individual decisions. Decisions made by a single person are especially vulnerable and unstable, because they are prone to being arbitrarily revoked by the change of mind of just one individual and not shielded by a formal process of deliberation. To complicate matters further, it also holds true that once one has taken a decision, one cannot avoid being consciously aware of having done so; that is to say, such an awareness carries within itself the kernel of nagging doubt, because one could have decided otherwise and, even worse, one might have decided wrongly. In this way the consciousness of self-determining human beings is constantly plagued by final uncertainty, something not easy to get rid of, as sociologist Peter Berger has shown.[8] This fundamental unsettling

---

8. Berger, *The Heretical Imperative*, esp. 145–56.

of certainty through potential doubt is quite obviously the flip side of an unprecedented freedom of choice, but something contemporary society has to live with.

Friction and difficulties in life cannot fail to be interpreted today as the unhappy result of unfortunate earlier wrong decisions. Such decisions could, and indeed should be overturned, no matter whether they have to do with the choice of a profession or spouse, with procreation, or even with joining a particular religion. The right to return goods if they don't satisfy, long a practice for consumers, is little by little also coming into its own as legitimate *ultima ratio* for answers to fundamental, existential questions. Enduring and exploring the consequences of an earlier decision as definitely binding and with all the implications for the good or the bad was in former times taken as a challenge to maturing and personal growth, if no alternative was at hand. Today, however, the tendency is to avoid such critical confrontation with earlier decisions and with one's own biography in principle. To shield against being harmed one now tends to keep everything at arm's length, to leave the options open as broadly as possible, and, practically, to remain undecided. One is always mindful of a plan B, a backdoor escape, just in case. Thus, modern people skim the surface of life only and dispel the painfully lived experience of mistakes much too quickly. In case of conflict they almost immediately survey remaining options and look to compensate the disappointment experienced as soon as possible. However, any such turning to the market born out of disappointment or dissatisfaction with previous choices, only leads to an increased susceptibility to further disappointment in an even shorter period. Thus, the hunt for real satisfaction and meaning in life accelerates, because there always will be someone else to meet and always will there be something else to be experienced, this time promising real satisfaction, indeed. Life, thus, turns into a relentless chase after life without ever reaching the finishing line.[9]

According to sociologist Gerhard Schulze, a diagnostician of contemporary Western affluent society which he calls the *event society*, "everything which wants to establish itself in the marketplace of events has to pass through the needle's eye of being in demand. This is at the heart

---

9. This experience was pointedly captured by Latin church father Aurelius Augustinus (354–430 CE) in his autobiographical *Confessiones* 1.1, where he states, "*inquietum est cor nostrum donec requiescat in te*" (Restless is our heart until it comes to find rest in Thee). An older English translation reads "[O]ur heart is unquiet till it finds rest in Thee" (Augustine, *Confessions*, 4).

of the present day rationality of offering eventful experiences."[10] However, the "constant refinements and improvements in the quality of products . . . are not able" to even out "the drop in the intensity of the experiences advertised." All buying ever does is allow for "the events to be available, not the eventful experience itself—this must still be produced by individuals themselves and by their own self-direction . . . Enjoyment does not increase proportionally to the means used or the money spent."[11] Therefore, according to Schulze, it is "neither astounding that our society does not seem contented, nor is the escalation of expenditures with which they strive for happiness inexplicable." The once so innocent and playful approach to life has morphed today into hard and serious work. The "*homo ludens* [the playful human] plays with increasing grimness."[12]

To conclude, market perspective, autonomous self-determination, and event-oriented consumer attitudes exercise a decisive influence on all realms of life. They have an impact not only on attitudes toward the material means of life, but also on political power, authority, and control as well as—and this is the important point here—on religion, too. This situation calls for clarification of the view of religion.

What Constitutes Religion?

Although religion does not shun the public space of the *agora*, the open marketplace of commodities, ideas, and concepts, religion is in no sense essentially a consumer item. Instead, religion represents at times a highly complex sociocultural structure with an elaborated tradition of rites and doctrines demanding intensive studies as in Judaism, Buddhism, Islam and Christianity, for instance. At other times that which could be described as "religion" is amazingly plain and simple, often the case with indigenous or private religions. Religions have not been founded in an instant. Rather, religions, especially those known to us today as world religions, emerged and grew over the course of centuries representing the lived core of communal key experiences. As so-called "religions" they form a relatively coherent socio-cultural whole, which has and preserves its unity by constant reference to events regarded as constituting it, whether those are historic incidents, a prophetic revelation, a particular text or a space or a person

---

10. Schulze, *Die Erlebnisgesellschaft*, 439 (my translation).
11. Ibid., 548; see also 432 (my translation).
12. Ibid., 14 (my translation).

regarded as "holy." While such pivotal experiences differ from one religion to another, a certain commonality does exist among all of them. They all acknowledge that what they revere and worship is of definite and ultimate character and thus binding beyond doubt.

Without going into detailed discussion of the well-researched, conceptual history of the concept of "religion" now—a sketch of the subject will be given in the next subsection—let "religion" here generally be defined as the *lived relationship towards an Ultimate*. Understanding religion in this way not only allows for identifying religious phenomena beyond the sphere of culturally established religions; it also enables meaningful communication between people of different cultural-religious traditions without superimposing a distinct concept of religion. While the truly Ultimate can be thought of and experienced variously as personal, a-personal, or even transpersonal, it is this kind of "lived relationship" which leaves its mark on a follower's way of life, finding its tangible expression in lifestyles and, ultimately, in distinct cultures, not just of explicitly religious people, but of anyone else, too. Even agnostics and all those who expressly do *not* believe in anything and do *not* find religious concerns tenable, convinced that religion and faith are much too trivial to merit serious attention, relate to convictions of ultimate concern to them like Swiss novelist Max Frisch (1911–1991).[13] Where the relationship to the Ultimate is clearly articulated and reflected upon, one can speak of it in terms of "faith"; where such a relationship is not reflected upon—or hardly so—we might speak more broadly of "religiosity," and where everything is only confusedly oriented toward the longing for an experience of the Ultimate we may speak of "spirituality." The definition provided here still allows discerning what the ultimate points of reference are for an individual's life, just as something about persons becomes known by "the company they keep." Lifestyle is a sure and clear indicator of the treasured principles by which one lives. This is so quite independently of the extent to which these principles are consciously held and articulated, if indeed they are articulated at all.

However, the implicit definition of religion present in every agnostic position must itself be questioned as to its coherence and logic. After all, who says that religion has anything to do with a world "beyond"? To the contrary, discourse about belief in "redemption" and "salvation," in "heaven," "paradise," "eternity," and "hell" has actually nothing to do with feeding anyone false hopes in a better world, the perfect world hereafter or

---

13. See Frisch, *Sketchbooks*.

its opposite, which one can imagine however one likes. Instead, any serious discourse about faith and belief is intended to enable people to live in the world as it is actually experienced here and now and to learn to deal with the challenges presented by real day-to-day life—but humanely. Salvation and redemption are not made manifest outside of, but rather *in* the midst of concrete and tangible actual life. And just so the lived relationship toward an Ultimate becomes recognizable on its own.[14]

Religion most certainly has to do with reference to ultimate validity, but validity not as claiming a definite fact in the sense of absolute data, which would be unacceptable anyhow.[15] Speaking of ultimate validity merely means the unprejudiced, unbiased acknowledgement of the existence of such an unconditionally binding Ultimate to which people who are aware thereof relate, something which neither the present reality of religious diversity nor the absolute self-determination of the experience-driven individual has succeeded in altering.

Ultimate validity in the sense of "ultimate validity for me" or "for one person" or even "for a group of people" escapes value comparisons. It is sufficient unto itself and has its value in itself. It expresses itself, therefore, typically enough, in the mode of personal testimony rather than the mode of theoretical discourse or thesis statement. Paying attention to this detail is essential, because while theoretical discourse belongs to the sphere of intellectual communication with a tendency toward unfettered, nonbinding reflections in the service of critical deliberation, a personal testimony is not at just anyone's disposal. Those testifying or bearing witness to something ultimate as truly binding and valid do so in clear demarcation from other views and positions. Just so, relations of ultimate validity reveal themselves at their innermost in an entirely personal way, exposing those who hold them dear as vulnerable and open to attack, because the open presentation of the fundamental motivations for their actions and convictions makes people become predictable. Therefore, responding to such a testimony demands cautious, respectful, circumspect behavior, whether or not its content and style is to one's liking. A testimony of this kind cannot be argued with. It can either be accepted or rejected on its own terms only, or it can simply be brushed aside and ignored.

14. Scriptural references to this saying may be found in Matt 12:34: "Out of the abundance of the heart the mouth speaks." See also Matt 6:21: "For where your treasure is, there your heart will be also."

15. Concerning the analysis of contemporary society, see Luhmann, *Observations on Modernity*, esp. 44–62.

These explanations yield the logical conclusion that religious claims to ultimate validity are in fact incommensurable. This means that to compare religions side by side is impossible since it would require application of a yardstick taken either from the outside or from one particular concept of religion which is not necessarily in line with that religious tradition being actually compared. Religions cannot be compared with one another or be played off against each other. Such an approach demonstrates as great a misconception about the matter as does the post-Enlightenment secular or the pluralistic theory of religion, which in fact levels all claims to ultimate validity and thus dissolves religion by relativizing it (see below, chapter 5).

English philosopher and theologian John Hick (1922–2012), one of the early proponents of a modern theory of religious pluralism, was very aware of the fact that the pluralistic approach to religion stands or falls with the way the question of ultimate validity of religious claims is handled. He wrote:

> Perhaps the most serious objection to the pluralist hypothesis ... is that it conflicts with the absolute claims that have been made and are still being made by each of the great religious traditions. For a genuine pluralism is incompatible with any claim that there is no salvation outside the church, or outside *dar al-Islam*, or outside the *Sangha* or outside any other bounded human group, and it is inhospitable to any claim to sole possession of complete, definitive, and normative revelation or truth, a truth that judges all others even while perhaps also imperfectly reflected in them.[16]

The problem with this approach is that it does not distinguish among religious expressions as such and irreligious, theoretical reflection, or even philosophical reflection on religion. At least any such approach must be able to explain and clarify the relationship between "ultimate validity" and any "absolute claims." In terms of confessing faith in Christ, such conceptual inattentiveness leads to statements like the following: "It is clearly incompatible with a pluralistic interpretation of religion to consider Jesus Christ as the sole source of salvation. If this were the case, Christianity would ... be the religion surpassing all others, because it had preceded all others in the knowledge of the one mediator of salvation ... Jesus is ... not constitutive for, but rather representative of salvation."[17]

---

16. Hick, "Religious Pluralism," 333.
17. Schmidt-Leukel, "Was sind Religionen?," in *Fremde Nachbarn*, 31 (my translation).

Beyond "Holy Wars"

Catholic theologian Paul Knitter, probably one of the most popular theologians of religious pluralism, comments on this very matter in this way: "Christians are sensing that just as their traditional ecclesiology was an impediment to Christian dialogue, so their traditional Christology, which insists on the finality and normativity of Christ, is an obstacle to interreligious dialogue. The new environment of religious pluralism is forcing Christians to ask whether God is revealed definitively in Jesus, whether the incarnational movement of Divinity is broader than what happened in Jesus Christ."[18]

Such analysis of the multireligious situation plays with intellectual possibilities and so constructs reality—in this case religion—that it confines to the parameters of a fixed theory. Because this theory holds that "Jesus considered as the sole source of salvation" is "incompatible" with the concept, Jesus cannot, indeed, shall not be "the sole source of salvation." Consequently, a Christian claim to the universal validity of cross and resurrection of Jesus Christ cannot be made. Neither can Jews claim to belong to the chosen people of God entitled to inherit the promised land, nor can Muslims hold to the ultimate validity of the revelation of God's will in the Qur'an, nor can Buddhists claim absolute knowledge about the true essence of life and world. There cannot be such claims because there shall not be such according to this theory.

In fact, however, the problem of juxtaposing irreconcilable and logically mutually exclusive claims to validity is a problem of theory only, not a problem of day-to-day religious praxis. In actual life, these kinds of questions recede behind pragmatic, spiritual, or even mystical solutions and answers. Over and above that, one can observe a tendency within modern, highly differentiated, individualized societies of the West that people put up with one another tolerantly and make efforts to come to terms with one other.[19] Also, the religiously diverse situation nowadays encourages autarchic, enlightened individuals to cut and assemble their own religion in a kind of patchwork-like fashion determined by their own taste and preferences. They do so in an eclectic and syncretistic manner, sometimes using trappings that are otherwise part of various and different independent religious traditions and at other times creative new and original inventions; one only needs to study the proliferation of publications on esoterica and the New Age on the internet or in the bookstores.

18. Knitter, "Theocentric Christology," 144.
19. For a recent document of this, see Idliby et al., *The Faith Club*.

Yet, the pluralistic solution to the theoretical crux demonstrated is only made more difficult insofar as the commonly cherished "both-and" mode of thought is incompatible with what are, on reflection, conflicting ultimate claims. The pluralists turn an intellectual need—and in a minority situation, quite often an existential one—into a heuristic virtue. They do so by not really taking seriously these ultimate claims' all-decisive binding nature; instead, they ignore by principle the mutual exclusions these claims imply. However, such a strategy only veils the cognitive problem rather than really solving it, because ultimate claims are posed with such absolute certainty of their fundamentals that they cannot really be shaken by mere critical, intellectual inquiries. Ultimate claims resent rational discourse. They are so thoroughly and personally internalized that, to the persons affected, they are present only as undoubtedly given, not as critically and consciously known. For emotional reasons, these kinds of in-depth certainties cannot be jettisoned—if they were, one would have nothing to hold on to.

What distinguishes genuinely religious people within given empirical religions from others who just happen to cling to one by convention is that they explicitly relate to what is, for them, beyond any doubt and, therefore, not to be called into question at all. Truly religious people relate to what in their eyes cannot—and therefore should not, should never—be analyzed any further, because it has proven itself to be ultimately valid even though advocates of a pluralist view of religion are convinced otherwise in that their theory is "in logical regards *all-comprehensive* and *inescapable*, and in theological regards, *adequate*."[20] It certainly is not so. The pluralistic theory of religion dissolves the explicit self-perception of religions and thus leads itself in the final analysis *ad absurdum* by evaporating its subject matter, a consequence which its proponents seem not yet to have fully realized.

As understandable as the almost involuntary comparison of different religions in our age may be, one should not distort the essence of individual religious traditions and run roughshod over the real difficulties in comprehension, because the presence of different religions in such close proximity as today is historically—not conceptually—conditioned. To interpret a multireligious environment as a panoply of religious options is only one more instance of the omnipresence of market-oriented perceptions; it also shows lack of proper comprehension of religious matters and does not

---

20. Schmidt-Leukel, "Zur Klassifikation religionstheologischer Modelle," 163; original emphasis. See also Schmidt-Leukel, *Gott ohne Grenzen*.

represent any actual religious self-understanding. Religions do not become accessible as religions in the perspective of a competitive market setting, nor by systemstheoretical or semantic analysis. Religions "can be understood only through" themselves by grasping their very own innermost center, their "central intuition"[21] and core, their particular "basic intuition" [*Zentralanschauung*],[22] as theologian Friedrich D. E. Schleiermacher (1768-1834) once put it. Therefore, in the interest of genuine and authentic interreligious dialogue, the challenge is to present and to articulate explicitly the perception of the respective ultimate claims as such and to communicate to others intelligently the heart and core of a religion in its specificity—in sharp contrast to pluralistic relativism which so characterizes the spirit of the times. It is from here, and only from here that understanding of other religions will be succinctly disclosed, as will the entire surrounding of a culturally distinct environment. Knowledge of the non-interchangeable center of experience of an empirical religion, that is, its central intuition, illumines the manifold and distinctive aspects of its worldview, doctrine, depictions of life and the world, of the state, society, and the individual, of practical patterns of living, as well as distinctive mores and customs. Rabbi Simon Philip de Vries once explained it with reference to Judaism in this way:

> Judaism can be recognized outwardly by its peculiar features, unfamiliar and conspicuous to a non-Jew. It stands out by its Sabbath, its festivals, its worship, its dietary regulations, its ritual and ceremonies. Naturally . . . above all, there is its concept of God and its core religious thought, the most important of which is contained in the word, in the concept of monotheism. . . .
> As a people of worship . . . it [Judaism] has, like every other religion, its worldview and a valid order of life for its adherents. To be sure, in actuality it doesn't *have* a worldview—because it *is* a worldview. In it everything is contained as a unity. It comprehends creation and life as a *unit*, and indeed, in the absolute and widest sense. This worldview is a culture of its own, in which everything belonging to life, as touching and pertaining to life, has its greater or smaller share . . . in this unity. From this point of view everything is judged and considered. Its object is humanity and the human person. It is exactly as with the state and its members as it is with society in general and the life of individuals in interpersonal, social relationships. Therefore the political order is not excluded. There is also room here for criminal justice and civil

---

21. Schleiermacher, *On Religion*, 113, 104.
22. Ibid., 112.

jurisdiction. Likewise the home, the Synagogue, and ritual belong to this unity.[23]

Whoever is concerned about religions is touching upon all-comprehensive worldviews—in other words: is touching upon the pivotal concepts of worldviews and their impact on the conceptualization of life in general. Every way of life is related to this center one way or another and receives its sanction from there. This is the definite point of reference by which everything is to be measured, the center from which the circle can be completely described. If one knows about the central intuition of a religion, then one does not need an external conceptual yardstick and can much better understand the actual differences and distinctions which are indeed not merely evocative of one's curiosity and wonderment or distinctive difference, but also cause conflicts to flare up. Those striving for political power no matter what the means sometimes know quite well how to manipulate these differences and put them to strategic use. In this respect, the knowledgeable pursuit and cultivation of dialogue which is concerned precisely with the conflicting evaluations and interpretations of world and life, is itself nothing less than proactive peacekeeping.

However, a caution is in place here. One is well advised not to start dialogue with the mutually excluding claims and their content matter just mentioned, because all such claims and interpretations are secondary. Instead, it is advisable to focus in the first place on how different religions respond to and interpret existential situations. In other words, it makes sense to approach the problem of excluding ultimate claims from an existential point of view instead of a dogmatic, apologetic, or polemical one. Such an approach has nothing to do with taking a tactical advantage nor is it born out of disdain for the self-reflective tradition of, for instance, Christian theology. The existential approach recommended here does not interfere with claims to ultimate validity—neither one's own, nor the others.' Rather, this approach only transposes these claims onto the plane of human universals first before going any further in the discussion.

Practically, then, any interreligious dialogue must first of all pay attention to whether the answers given—that is to say, *lived*—within the framework of a particular religious tradition are at any point life-promoting,

---

23. Vries, *Jüdische Riten*, 314–15; italics original. (Since the English version, *Jewish Rites and Symbols*, was not available to the author, the above text, originally written in Dutch and published as separate newspaper articles [*Joodsche riten en symbolen*, Zutphen: W. J. Thieme, 1928–1932] had to be rendered from the German version; my translation.)

life-enhancing, and life-furthering or whether they are life-hindering and life-destroying, respectively, well knowing that even the perception of what "life" actually is varies significantly from one religious tradition to another. One will, similarly, have to ask whether the differing answers lived in empirical religions are plausible and comprehensible to people in general. The pragmatic existential approach as it is taken for instance in the so-called Faith Clubs[24] yields yet another advantage for interreligious dialogue. More than any other it is such an approach which promises to come to terms with the self-perception of each religion and culture. It honors religions as vital expressions of human life and recognizes each of these in their own peculiarity, neither postulating equivalence nor imposing exclusiveness.

Is there a common basis for dialogue among "religions" at all? Is Buddhism, in virtue of being a "religion," at all comparable with Islam understood as "religion," too? Is Hinduism a "religion" analogous to Judaism as a "religion"? What about the "Modern Religions" in Japan? In order to see clearly, a historically informed glance at concepts and ideas about the term religion is called for. This promises to bring the issue into sharp focus.

RELIGION: A SHORT HISTORY OF THE CONCEPT AND ITS CRITICISM

The ancient Latin term "religion" was adopted into the Indo-Germanic languages as a technical term to some extent sometime during the Middle Ages (between the fifth and fifteenth centuries) to denote the entirety of reverent expressions of life toward a variety of deities, a particular god or goddess, to several gods, or to God as proclaimed in the Bible. But already long before this happened, scholars debated the basic etymological root of the term.[25] Roman statesman and rhetorician Cicero (106–43 BCE) derived *religio* from *releger/relego* which literally translated means "to roll [a scroll] together"; "to read it anew again"; "to reconsider once more." Used as a noun, *religio* meant "conscientious consideration, mindfulness" (especially in regard to holy matters); but also "fear of god" and further "belief in" or the "dutiful and faithfully performed veneration of gods." Four centuries later, however, the Roman writer Lactantius (c. 240–320) would take issue with that derivation and explain that Cicero was mistaken because, Lac-

---

24. See The Faith Club at http://www.thefaithclub.com.

25. For the following, see especially Feil, "The Problem of defining and demarcating *religion*," 1–35.

Why Is Religion So Prone to Be Hijacked by Vested Interests?

tantius held, *religio* is not derived from *relego*, but from *religare/religo* and thus means "to re-connect, to tie up, to truss up."[26] Religion, thus, brings "relationship to a deity" to expression, an understanding similar to one later taken up, developed, and handed on by Augustine (354–430), the famous theologian of the Latin Church. For Augustine, religion is the act by which people turn again toward God whom they had forsaken previously. Religion, therefore, Augustine essentially perceived as a "turning around" and a "turning back" in the literal sense of "conversion."[27] At the same time and in addition to this meaning, when Augustine speaks about topics we today would label as "religious" he uses a variety of words like *fides* (belief), *doctrina* (teaching), *lex* (law, order, commandment), *cultus* (cult, rite, liturgy, worship), and *pietas* (sense of duty, thankfulness, piety). All of these not only signify different aspects within the meaning of what today is generally regarded as "religion," but also, at the same time, indicate connotations of meaning on different levels which flow together in the concept of religion.

In general, it can be said that in the time of the early church, *religio* would not have been understood as something in its own categorical right, as a genus, although it can be shown that throughout this time the plural *religiones* (religions) was also used. But the plural only denoted the "veneration of *many* gods" or else the "carrying out of *many* acts of divine worship"; it did not refer to a multiplicity of diverse religions. Religion as the concept familiar to us today was not popular at all, but rather, was merely one expression among several others for denoting commitment, dedication, and faithful practice in relation to a supreme being. When Christians of the early centuries spoke about their way of life—of following Christ—they always spoke about it as *fides*, that is, as "the way of faith" and "the way of life."

During the Middle Ages the term religion came to be adopted by non-Latin languages in Europe, though. In the Germanic languages it replaced, for instance, the term "*ê*" a term which meant "good—in the sense of reliable—order," "good institution," and "good, trustworthy law/rule," as can be seen in renowned poetry of these times, such as *Parzival* by Wolfram von Eschenbach (1170–1220) or the *Nibelungs* (about 1200) which speak of "*kristen ê*" or in other words, "Christian-like *ê*" and thus of the "Christian order" and "Christian rule of life."[28] However, religion as a concept neither played an important role nor had it any great significance until well into

---

26. Lactantius, *Divinae Institutiones* 4.28.3, in *Corpus Scriptorum* 19/1:389.
27. Burleigh, *Augustine*, 218–83.
28. See Grimm, *Deutsches Wörterbuch*, 14:801–2.

the seventeenth century, that is, until the beginning of the Enlightenment. The term religion is used during the centuries before, of course, but for most authors it does not carry any special weight or significance. Instead, *fides*, *pietas*, and *cultus* are of much greater importance. *Religio* in Christian Europe merely denoted the virtue of devoted service and the "veneration of God." From this meaning it became a technical term for people who dedicated themselves wholly and exclusively to the veneration of God like priests, monks, and nuns who now became to be referred to as "religious," as they are up to the present time.

A closer look at several classic advocates for dialogue from the Middle Ages and thereafter will help to show how modern the concept of religion in fact actually is. Toward the end of his life, Peter Abelard (1079–1142), philosopher and theologian of the High Middle Ages, drew up a famous "Dialogue between an (Arabian) philosopher, a Jew, and a Christian" (also known as *Collations*), in which he never speaks of "three religions" (*religiones*) because religion as an independent topic was not a reality to talk about; Abelard, rather, speaks of three different *fidei sectae* and thus of three different "faiths" or "ways of believing."[29] The same holds for Albert the Great (ca. 1200–1280) and his student, Thomas Aquinas (ca. 1225–1274) who treat what we today would call religion under the concept of *fides*, faith—as do all their contemporaries.[30] Similarly, Aquinas' younger contemporary Spanish theologian Raymond Lull (1232/33–1315/16) speaks of the *fides Iudaeorum, Christianorum, Saracenorum*, and thus of the *beliefs* of Jews, Christians, and Saracens (Muslims).[31]

A general concept of religion emerges only slowly during the Renaissance of the fifteenth and the Humanism of the sixteenth century, which later in the age of European Enlightenment in the eighteenth century would unfold its full impact. The beginning of this development is marked by a book which appeared in 1474 in Italy entitled, *De Christiana religione* [About Christian Religion]. Its author was the philosopher Marsilio Ficino (1433–1499) who headed the Platonic Academy in Florence founded by Cosimo Medici in mid-century (1459). In this book Ficino speculated about the presence of an original monotheistic religion which once was common to all human beings (*communis omnium gentium religio*), which

---

29. Marenbon, *Peter Abelard*.

30. For Thomas Aquinas, see his *Summa contra gentiles*.

31. See Lull, *The Book of the Gentile and the Three Wise Men* (*Liber de gentili et tribus sapientibus*).

in the course of time would gradually bring about the *divinitas*, the deification of the human being as the epitome of true blessedness.[32]

Still, some time would pass before the concept of religion as known today would become established, for in the age of European Humanism, too, *fides* always remained the common and dominant expression for what we call religion today. Cardinal Nicholas of Cusa (*Cusanus*, 1401–1464) entitled his treatise on interreligious dialogue of 1453, which he wrote in reaction to the Ottoman siege and bloody conquest of Constantinople by Sultan Mohammed II (April 6–May 29, 1453), *De pace fidei* [On the peace of the faiths—A dialogue on world religious peace].[33] However, for Nicholas, Judaism and Christianity alone were deemed faiths (*fidei*), not Islam. Islam, Cusanus held, represented a distorted version of Christianity, namely the heresy of Nestorianism, a conviction then current in the Latin-speaking church of the West.[34]

During the time of the Reformation in the first quarter of the sixteenth century, Judaism, Christianity, and Islam were not seen as "religions" still. Instead, everything centered on *faith*, the *proper* and *legitimate faith*, to be sure, and, therefore, again on *fides*—despite the fact that during this era the concept of "religious peace" gains in importance, denoting peace between the different *denominations* then emerging within Central Europe. However, Martin Luther (1483–1546) at points availed of the term *religio* when referring to faithful actions born out of *reverence* for God; nevertheless, he could also express the very same just as well using the terms *pietas* or *Gottesdienst* (worship). Even "Jews and Turks" (i.e., Muslims), as Luther calls them, have *fides* and *religio*, albeit he clearly holds that "*extra Christum omnes religiones sunt idola*," that is, Luther regarded "all forms of worship and religion apart from Christ" as "idol worship."[35]

Luther's junior colleague Philip Melanchthon (1497–1560) in his theological primer, *Loci theologici* (1521/1543) defined religion over against all godless *prophanitas* (profanity) as authentic and honest conversion to God, true reverence, actual faith, and the new obedience resulting from it.[36] In 1536, Swiss reformer John Calvin (1509–1564) issued his major work by the title *Institutes of the Christian Religion*. Though

---

32. Cassirer et al., *The Renaissance Philosophy of Man*, 193–214; Kristeller, *Eight Philosophers*, 37–53; Kristeller, "The Platonic Academy of Florence," 147–59.

33. See Biechler, *Nicholas of Cusa on Interreligious Harmony*.

34. See Baum, *The Church of the East*.

35. Luther, *Luther's Works*, 27:88.

36. See Hill, *The Loci Communes of Philip Melanchthon*.

he mentions religion in the title, Calvin actually does not deal with the subject of religion at all except for some interesting comments which show an intellect clearly shaped by Humanism. Calvin holds that the world naturally contains a kind of "religious seed" (he speaks of *semen religionis*) which is hindered in its sprouting by human evil. Yet, this seed still remains alive, namely through the worship of the God-fearing faithful, a worship made possible by God's grace alone.[37] Thus, according to Calvin religion is both, a particular way of worship and devotion as well as a natural potential within every human being.

Only when people started speaking of "natural religion" in the second half of the seventeenth century was the way paved for a fundamental change in the understanding and perception of religion. The phrase "natural religion" expresses a non-personal notion of a universal phenomenon which is assumed to be found among *all* human beings in *all* lands and cultures, irrespective of the particular conditions and circumstances and likened to the "laws of nature" which were discovered during this time, too.[38] According to Herbert of Cherbury (1583–1648), who is the acclaimed initiator of this discourse, every person is able to recognize through general knowledge or awareness and common sense (*notitiae communes*) natural religion by its five characteristics. These are: (1) to accept the existence of God; (2) to worship God accordingly; (3) to acknowledge morality and rightful acts; (4) to compensate for wrongdoings and sins committed by remorse and repentance; and (5) to expect temporal and eternal reward or punishment on the basis of God's grace and justice.[39] The multiplicity of religions, Herbert of Cherbury explained, stems from the allegorical and symbolical interpretation of natural phenomena by different people and likewise from the distortions of religion at the hands of religious professionals, priests in particular, who abuse religion for manipulating human fantasy and who turn religion into an instrument of domination.

Herbert's contemporary Thomas Hobbes (1588–1679) came to a similar verdict. In his *Leviathan* (1651) Hobbes acknowledges "natural seeds of religion" and holds that religions are rooted in "fear" and "uncertainty"

---

37. See Calvin, *Institutes of the Christian Religion* (1536).

38. Special mention is to be made here of the astronomer Johannes Kepler (1571–1630), who discovered and described the mathematical formula of the patterned movements of the planets, the so-called "laws of the planet movements." Mention needs also to be made of Sir Isaac Newton (1642–1726), the originator of a new mechanics defined by the "laws of nature" like movement, mass, energy, and gravity.

39. See Hutcheson, *Lord Herbert of Cherbury's De religione laici*.

which form the natural seed "of that," he explains, "which every one in himself calleth Religion; and in them that worship, or fear that power otherwise than they do, Superstition."[40] David Hume (1711–1776), however, expressed doubt concerning any possibility of rational knowledge of God at all. In his *Dialogues Concerning Natural Religion* (1779) Hume argues that, since all perception is based on sense impressions, only mathematics can assure man of anything certain, because mathematics deals with relationships between ideas and is not tied to physical senses. Religion understood as "philosophical religion of reason" has one single aim according to Hume, namely to reinforce natural impulses toward morality and justice. Religion does not have a cognitive function, in the strict sense, at all. But in its moral and ethical function it is important for the communal and social life.[41]

In France, the second center of European Enlightenment, things were seen similarly. For Voltaire (1694–1778) religion is nothing but morality[42] while for Baron Paul Dietrich of Dirre, alias Paul Thiry d'Holbach (1723–1789), religion is not even that. In his *System of Nature* [*Systéme de la nature*] of 1770 d'Holbach explains, in the same fashion as had Herbert of Cherbury more than a century before, that religion came about on account of the fear of terrifying natural events and ignorance of what actually happens in nature. This fear is fostered by fraudulent priests in the interest of amassing power, especially political power. Religion, d'Holbach held, has no content or substance in and of itself; religion, rather, is based merely on the mechanisms of self-preservation and the desire to have a God,[43] a thesis directly taken up again in the nineteenth century by philosopher Ludwig Feuerbach (1804–1872) in his anonymously published work *Thoughts about Death and Immortality* (1830; see below).[44]

Romantic French political philosopher Jean-Jaques Rousseau (1712–1778) differentiates in his foundational work *The Social Contract* (*Du contrat social*, 1762) among three types of religion. The first is a natural kind of religion, which is private and "pure," a "simple religion of the gospel" which aims at inwardly "venerating the highest God and the eternal duties of morality from within" (*religion de l'homme/religion naturelle*). The second type

---

40. See *Leviathan* 11.75.

41. See Hume, *Dialogues concerning natural religion*; Hume, *Principal Writings*.

42. *Voltaire's Philosophical Dictionary*, 259–266.

43. See *The System of Nature* at http://www.gutenberg.org/ebooks/8909. See also Holbach, *Superstition in all Ages*.

44. Feuerbach, *Thoughts*.

is "civil religion" or "public religion," which ascribes absolute authority to the institution of the state (*religion du citoyen*). Third, there is the disgusting "religion of priests," that is, in Rousseau's case Roman Catholicism (*religion du Prêtres*). These three types of religion are constantly coming into conflict with one another, because the "public religion" as well as the "religion of the priests" always particularize "natural religion" in order to make people abide by the laws of the state or observe particular codes of behavior, while only "natural religion" is really and solely true religion.[45]

Like their contemporaries in England and France, the outstanding representatives of the German Enlightenment—the philosophers Christian Wolff (1679–1754), Gottfried Wilhelm Leibniz (1646–1716), Johann Gottfried Herder (1744–1803), and Immanuel Kant (1724–1804)—view the subject of religion in much the same way. Herder for example claims in his *On Religion, Doctrinal Opinions and Usages* (1798): "Religion touches one's entire being; it inspires calm conviction. In all ranks and classes of society human beings may only be human in the recognition and practice of religion. Religion touches all human tendencies [*Neigungen*] and desires [*Triebe*] in order to harmonize them all and guide them to the right path.

"By distinguishing itself from all kinds of doctrines, religion allows each of them its own place. Religion does not, however, want to be doctrine. Doctrines separate and embitter. Religion unifies, for in all human hearts religion is but one."[46]

Herder also explains why religious life appeals to its followers: because it makes people realize that they are a "human being with human beings and for the whole human race according to the ideal [*Urbild*] of the Father of this race and according to the ideal of the Father's image, who appeared in human form [that is Jesus Christ]."[47]

Immanuel Kant, the critic of reason and perception, saw it somewhat differently. In his *Critique of Practical Reason* (1788) Kant distinguishes between religion as positive, revealed religion and religion as a means to an end or "counterfeit service"[48] [*Afterdienst*; literally, serving the anus], which is all about obtaining God's favor and, as such, has no moral value at all. But religion—and this refers to yet one other kind of religion, namely to the "religion of reason" immanent in all religion—this religion holds a

---

45. Rousseau, *The Social Contract*.
46. Herder, *Against Pure Reason*, 92.
47. Ibid., 97.
48. Kant, *Critique of Practical Reason*, 136.

moral content, which philosophy has to mine. "Pure religion," for Kant, is the "recognition of all [our] duties as divine demands."[49] Pure religion is therefore the perfection of the ethical by its relating it to the idea of God, which though theoretically void is of the greatest importance for a moral worldview. Kant in his major work on the subject titled *Religion within the Boundaries of Mere Reason* of 1794 explains this classification more broadly and in more detail.[50] In it he depicts religion as reasonable faith characterized by ethical integrity and lived out by doing what is morally sound and practically good. Kant saw this understanding of religion most clearly reflected in Christianity; however, except for Christianity and Judaism Kant knew other religions from hearsay only, or rather, only by reading, for he never traveled much and hardly ever left his hometown of Königsberg, today's Kaliningrad.

Having, thus, broadly sketched the history of ideas and concepts regarding religion up to the end of the eighteenth century, we now turn to the great advocate and defender of the uniqueness of religion in the nineteenth century, the Protestant theologian Friedrich Daniel Ernst Schleiermacher (1768-1834) and his work *On Religion: Speeches to its Cultured Despisers* of 1799. For Schleiermacher, religion is a subject matter *sui generis*. It claims a province of its own and in its own right besides philosophy and morals. Religion "is neither thinking nor acting, but intuition and feeling."[51] Religion maintains "its own sphere and its own character only by completely removing itself from the sphere and character of speculation as well as from that of praxis" showing itself "as the necessary and indispensable third next to these two as their natural counterpart."[52] The uniqueness of religion over against philosophy and morals is the emotionally charged "intuition of the universe."[53] According to Schleiermacher there is no such thing as natural religion. "The essence of natural religion" Schleiermacher points out,

> actually consists wholly in the negation of everything positive and characteristic in religion and in the most violent polemic against it. Thus natural religion is also the worthy product of an age whose hobbyhorse was a lamentable generality and an empty sobriety, which more than anything else, works against true cultivation in

---

49. Ibid.
50. Kant, *Religion within the Boundaries of Mere Reason*, 31–192.
51. Schleiermacher, *On Religion*, 22
52. Ibid., 23.
53. Ibid., 24.

all things ... Thus if you are serious about considering religion in its determinate forms, turn back from these enlightened religions to the despised positive religions where everything real, powerful, and determinate appears, where every particular intuition has its specific content and its own relationship to the rest.[54]

Schleiermacher emphasizes the fact that religion always finds expression in tangible definite forms in the empirical religions. The different religions complement each other, with Christianity outdoing the others, as it were, exponentially. This primacy occurs, according to Schleiermacher, because Christianity reflects explicitly on the fundamental principle and presupposition of every religious view, namely, that the Infinite may become visible in the finite, which implies openness, on the part of Christianity, to other revelations of a similar kind. Since Christianity has become the historical manifestation of the Infinite in the finite [that is, God as revealed in Jesus Christ] Christianity is for Schleiermacher the "religion of religions."[55]

Things look quite different for Schleiermacher's colleague from Berlin, Georg Friedrich Wilhelm Hegel (1770–1831), who in his 1821 *Lectures on the Philosophy of Religion* defined religion as the consciousness of that which is true in and of itself. This definition applies especially to the elevation (uplifting [*Aufhebung*]) of consciousness to what is truthful, to God, relinquishing one-sidedness, and abandoning the standpoint of the particular, thereby transforming human knowledge of God into self-knowledge of the human in God. For Hegel, the concept of religion represents the dialectical relationship between God and human consciousness of God. Therefore, according to Hegel, religion is not to be thought of without God.[56]

This was emphatically challenged by Hegel's student Ludwig Feuerbach who sought to derive religion from within anthropology by showing how anthropology, not theology, determined religion. Feuerbach does not inquire about the essence of religion in terms of content; rather, in exactly the same manner as did the French Enlightenment thinkers before him, Feuerbach inquired about the genesis of religion, about *how* religion might have come about. He arrived at the conclusion that religion is principally grounded in the human awareness of the infinite. In established religions,

---

54. Ibid., 110–11.

55. Ibid., 113–23.

56. See Hodgson, *Hegel*. The ambitious project of a critical edition in translation of Hegel's lectures on religion, which he delivered in 1821, 1824, 1827, and 1831 has yielded only one volume so far containing the 1827 lectures (Hegel, *Lectures on the Philosophy of Religion*).

however, this awareness has become a somewhat separate realm in itself and as such distorts reality. Construed from human desire religion refers to a fictitious, alien reality, with which it then confronts people again and in a new way from the outside, as revelation, for instance. Thus, for Feuerbach, religion is "nothing other than" projection. God has been created according to the image of man and in human likeness, a hypothesis which actually, in its essentials, had already been advanced by the Greek poet and polemicist Xenophanes (ca. 560–478 BCE) more than two thousand years earlier in his biting critique of the anthropomorphisms of the Homeric deities.[57]

Feuerbach's understanding that religion is just a human projection and "nothing more" consequently gives rise to his imperative—born out of genuine humanistic concern—to repudiate religion in order to enable true love and genuine justice to come about in the here and now for the human species (not just the human individual), which he regarded as the highest and supreme being. In his *The Essence of Christianity* (1841) Feuerbach takes on Schleiermacher (among others) who in his magisterial volume *Christian Faith* had defined religion as the "feeling of absolute dependence," more adequately rendered as the "sensation of utmost dependence."[58] In response to this definition by Schleiermacher Feuerbach remarked, "ever since feeling became the mainstay of religion, the otherwise sacred content of Christian belief fell into indifference."[59]

Karl Marx (1818–1883) not only shared in the humanistic concerns of Ludwig Feuerbach and agreed with Feuerbach's critique of religion, he also broadened the critical assessment of religion to include the sociopolitical dimension. His charge against the representatives of the predominant religions in his environment and time was that instead of preparing people to revolt in the name of humanity against dehumanizing conditions and alienation, religious representatives and dignitaries put all their efforts into calming people down so they would accept even deplorable socio-economic conditions without revolt. Marx's statements on religion (that is, Church and Synagogue) climax in the widely quoted remarks from the introduction to his early work, *Critique of Hegel's Philosophy of Right* (1844), which due to the impact it had deserves some extended quoting:

---

57. See Palmer, "*Xenophanes' Ouranian God*," 16, 1–34; and DeYoung, *The Homeric Gods and Xenophanes*, http://ablemedia.com/ctcweb/showcase/deyoung4.html.

58. Schleiermacher, *The Christian Faith*, 12, 56.

59. Feuerbach, "Introduction" to *The Essence of Christianity*, in *The Fiery Book*, 106.

> [T]he critique of religion is the prerequisite of every critique. ... The foundation of criticism is this: man makes religion; religion does not make man. Religion is, in fact, the self-consciousness and self-esteem of man who has either not yet gained himself or has lost himself ... Man is the world of man, the state, society. This state, this society produces religion, which is an inverted world consciousness, because they are an inverted world. Religion is the general theory of this world. The wretchedness of religion is at once an expression of and a protest against real wretchedness. Religion is the sigh of the oppressed creature, the heart of a heartless world and the soul of soulless conditions. It is the opium of the people.
>
> The abolition of religion as the illusory happiness of the people is a demand for their true happiness ... Thus the critique of religion is the critique in embryo of the vale of tears of which religion is the halo ... The critique of religion disillusions man so that he will think, act, and fashion his reality as a man who has lost his illusions and regained his reason so that he will revolve about himself as his own true sun ...
>
> The critique of religion ends in the doctrine that man is the supreme being for man; thus it ends with the categorical imperative to overthrow all conditions in which man is a debased, enslaved, neglected, contemptible being.[60]

The critique of religion comes to a head toward the end of the nineteenth century with Friedrich Nietzsche (1844–1900), not only because of his declaring the "death of God"[61] but also, and much more so, because of his polemics which set religion and life in opposition to one another. In *The Will to Power* Nietzsche's reflections take shape in formulas that appear to anticipate contemporary like evaluations of religion in general and Christianity in particular. "A Christian," Nietzsche notes, is "the most puerile and backward man of his age" because: "The origin of religion lies in the extreme feelings of power, which, being strange take men by surprise ... Religion ... [is] an example of the 'altération de la personalité' [change of personality]. A sort of *fear*, *sensation* of *terror*, also a feeling of inordinate *rapture* and *exaltation*. Among sick people, the *sensation of health* suffices to awaken a belief in the proximity of God."[62]

Nietzsche further held that man

---

60. Marx, *Critique of Hegel's "Philosophy of Right,"* 131–32, 137.
61. Nietzsche, *The Gay Science*, 181.
62. Nietzsche, *The Will to Power*, 114–15; italics original.

has never dared to credit *himself* with his strong and startling moods, he has always conceived them as "*passive*," as "imposed upon him from outside": Religion is the offshoot of a *doubt* concerning the entity of the person, an *altération* of the personality in so far as everything great and strong in man was considered *superhuman* and *foreign*, man belittled himself, he laid the two sides, the very pitiable and weak side, and the very strong and startling side apart in two spheres, and called one "Man" and the other "God" ... Religion has lowered the concept of "man"; its ultimate conclusion is that all goodness, greatness, and truth are superhuman, and are only obtainable by the grace of God.[63]

In *The Antichrist*, also from 1888, Nietzsche becomes even more outspoken:

> How can anyone today still submit to the simplicity of Christian theologians to the point of insisting with them that the development of the conception of God from the "God of Israel," the God of a people, to the Christian God, the quintessence of everything good, represents *progress*? ... When the presuppositions of the *ascending* life, when everything strong, brave, masterful, and proud is eliminated from the conception of God, when he degenerates step by step into a mere symbol, a staff for the weary, a sheet-anchor for the drowning; when he becomes the God of the poor, the sinners, and the sick *par excellence* and the attribute "Savior" or "Redeemer" remains in the end as the one essential godly attribute—just *what* does such a transformation signify?[64]

Nietzsche is further convinced that the "Christian concept of God ... is one of the most corrupt conceptions of the divine ever attained on earth ... God degenerated into the *contradiction of life*, instead of being its transfiguration and eternal Yes! God as the declaration of enmity against life, against nature, against the will to live ... God—the deification of nothingness, the will to nothingness pronounced holy"![65] Against the "will to nothingness," this "nihilism," as he himself designates it, Nietzsche sets in opposition the "will to power." He sketches this will to power in his *Zarathustra* as the declared belief in "willing to live," in strength and laughter and therefore in the virtues of the "higher man" or "superman" (*Übermensch*) to whom he pays tribute.[66]

63. Ibid., 115–16; italics original.
64. Nietzsche, *The Portable Nietzsche*, 583–84.
65. Ibid.
66. See his *Thus Spake Zarathustra*.

Beyond "Holy Wars"

Thoroughly in line with this strand of critique are Austrian psychologist Sigmund Freud's (1856–1939) reflections on religion, too. Interpreting religious behavior as a representative of scientific medicine as it came to flower and from within a medical therapeutic perspective recalling his experiences with the treatment of people suffering from hysteria, Freud was curious about how it is that human beings have become religious at all. Freud situates the question of religion within the larger framework of general anthropology and human culture. Holding that culture is expression of the sublimation of drives, Freud uses religion as the example to illustrate how such satisfaction gets achieved.[67] Starting with the conviction that religious praxis (piety) with its routines has similarities with the behavior of compulsive neurotics (compulsive repetitive behavior stemming from fear of failure), Freud sees religion as the expression of infantile desires for wish-fulfillment. The experience of the helplessness of individuals over against nature and society incites, according to Freud, the human longing for security and for an omnipotent father, with whose help wish-fulfillment and justice can be achieved. Thus in religion, pleasure and desire have generated their own reality, a reality over against which people show ambivalent behavior, living it out in a love-hate relationship (the so-called "Oedipus complex") unable to escape the will of an almighty father. Consequently, Freud issues a call to overcome such an infantile stage. Human beings ought not to remain infantile. Growing into a mature personality means to leave the idea of an almighty father behind. Self-emancipation from religion is something people can and should be able to accomplish, provided they figure out these connections correctly. In Freud's conception, a really mature, healthy person is above being religious. To be religious is a clear symptom of illness.

Finally, in comparison with Nietzsche and Freud, philosopher Ernst Bloch's (1885–1977) critique of religion seems almost like a step backward into ideas thought long overcome, because Bloch takes up Lactantius' etymology of *religio* in order to criticize it on the basis of a materialistic dialectic. Religion is "merely *re-ligio*," a backward oriented "binding-back,"[68] and thus, a regressive, uncritical "turning back" and "being tied back" to (false) authorities. Bloch criticizes Christianity, which to him is always Christendom, by availing himself of a concept of religion understood in the

---

67. See his three principal writings on this topic, namely *Totem and Taboo*, *The Future of an Illusion*, and *Moses and Monotheism*.

68. Bloch, *Atheism in Christianity*, 62.

Why Is Religion So Prone to Be Hijacked by Vested Interests?

spirit of Marxist historical materialism. He, however, attacks religion—in clear distinction from Marx—not with the aim of eliminating religion as such, but rather, with the aim of infusing religion's regressive and repressive manifestations with a progressive messianic vision. Biblical religion should be messianic, progressive, breaking forth into an open future; it should be an agent of hope and as such criticize everyone and everything not fostering hope. Bloch writes, "Where hope is, there is religion, but where there is religion there is not always hope: not the hope built up from beneath, undisturbed by ideology . . . [H]ope is able to inherit those features of religion which do not perish with the death of God. There are such features—for, contrary to all pure facticity, the *Futurum* of hope was thought of as a property of God's being, and one which distinguished him from all other gods."[69]

Religion thus understood would battle alongside the self-disclosing God (as it happened to Moses in the burning bush according to Exod 3:14), against any god who is domesticated and controlled by the ritual and dogma of ecclesiastical hierarchies and authorities of the state.

Bloch's view of religion marks the completion of the discourse on the concept in Western thought. Except for variations on ideas previously outlined, nothing really new or substantially different has emerged thereafter. Thus we have in some way returned to the point of departure, insofar as Bloch's definition of religion as "tying or turning back to" is somewhat akin to Cicero's etymological attempt for *religio*. Discussion about religion, however, still remains as controversial as it has ever been, carrying with it today a broad spectrum of connotations though, which are discretely present in every discourse about it in one way or another.

The Concept of Religion and Empirical Religions

As just noted, various concepts of "religion" have been promoted throughout the history of ideas in Europe, especially since the Enlightenment. However, all these concepts are defective to some extent because they distill only certain aspects of actually lived religion as essential. Nonetheless, despite these shortcomings the discourse about religion stimulated the establishment of an entirely new field of study.[70] Today departments

---

69. Ibid., 266; italics original.

70. For the history of the development of the discipline of comparative religion, see Capps, *Religious Studies*.

of religious studies, departments for the study of the history of religions and for comparative religion abound in the world of academe. Numerous specializations have grown up, including the study of the philosophy, psychology, and sociology of religion(s) as well as of religious geography, aesthetics, and ethnology.[71] This scholarly academic approach takes religion as a given cultural fact and—in distinction from the philosophical attempts at definition previously discussed—makes *religion* the object of empirical research, molded after the pattern of other academic disciplines. In the course of such studies it soon became clear that reference to a personal God is far from being constitutive of all religions. The concept of God or a personal idea of God plays a significant role only for a particular group of religions (the so-called "theistic religions"), but by no means for all. Religion, therefore, cannot be tied inevitably to the assumption of one God or to deities at all. Besides the monotheistic religions like Judaism, Christianity, and Islam the term religion also refers to socio-cultural systems marked by the worship of multitudes of deities like certain Indian religions (Hinduism); it also accommodates non-theistic traditions like Buddhism, Daoism, and Confucianism. Those who still hold onto the idea of religion as a personal relationship with God are simply giving evidence of the theistic or monotheistic context (most often Christian, Jewish, or Muslim) of their interpretation of religion.

People today live in a religiously heterogeneous world with transcultural mobility and transcontinental communication on rapid increase. Thus, one no longer can achieve an understanding by unilateral dialogue with one's own intellectual and cultural heritage and tradition. What is required instead is a new approach to understanding culture and religion. Some scholars have attempted to manage the ever increasing complexity of this challenge by raising the level of abstraction at the expense of attention to practical detail and the way in which empirical religions are actually lived. While every incremental degree of abstraction increases possibilities of interpretation exponentially, the definite, concrete and tangible contours of the socio-cultural phenomena are smoothed away, sometimes to the point of becoming unrecognizable. It is, therefore, not surprising to find the following definition of religion: The "concept of religion [refers]

---

71. For a comprehensive survey of the subject matter, see the multivolume *Encyclopedia of Religion*.

to the construction of patterns of meaning and concepts, which for the human being opens up the whole of reality—emotionally, cognitively and functionally."[72]

As for empirical religions other than those sharing in the cultural-intellectual history of Western Europe (notably Judaism and Christianity), what complicates matters of interreligious dialogue further is that in other "religions" any concept of religion as such does not figure at all. For instance, Indian religions commonly subsumed under the term Hinduism (such as Shivaism, Vishnuism, Shaktism) use the Sanskrit word *dhārma* to signify their basic concept, while the term *pūjā/pooja*, which designates the ritual act of Hindu worship today, was occasionally also used in a more general sense earlier on. *Dhārma* above all means "order" in the sense of "cosmic law." *Dhārma* understood as "cosmic order," "cosmic law" is, evidently, *sanātana dhārma*, "eternal law." But the term *dhārma* also oscillates among many other meanings like "duty," "caste duty," "legal system," "offering," "justice," "essence," and "virtue."[73] In Buddhism, on the other hand, the same concept, *dhārma*, which in Pali is *dhamma*, signifies above all the teaching of the Buddha, the Thatagatha himself. Interestingly however, Buddhism lacks a concept of religion and shows no interest in one, because Buddhism is mainly concerned with the perception of the true essence of world and life, the correct perception of which have been revealed in the *dhamma* of the Buddha who compared his teaching to a vehicle—namely a raft.[74] From there, the Sanskrit word *yana*, meaning "vehicle," "raft," comes to function like a Buddhist equivalent to "religion." *Yana*, however, covers only a fraction of what is implied in the general concept of religion, specifically the actual religious life. Just what, then, does one communicate about in an "interreligious dialogue" with Buddhists?

In Islam, too, no exact identical concept of religion is to be found. The two terms used to signify the entirety of religious expressions of Muslim life are *milla* and *din*. These terms, however, pose problems in various respects. Both are loanwords into Arabic from other languages with partial, not completely unambiguous etymology. While *milla* stems from Aramaic (a Semitic language) and, as a rule, signifies the concrete "religious community" at a given place, the more frequently used *din* is Persian in origin.

72. Kerber, *Der Begriff der Religion*, 11 (my translation).

73. See *dhārma* in Monier-Williams, *Sanskrit–English Dictionary*, 510–11.

74. See Garfield, *The Fundamental*; Walshe, *The Long Discourses of the Buddha*; Fronsdal, *The Dhammapada*.

It is not possible to determine etymologically beyond doubt whether *din* derives from *dayn* (meaning "guilt," or "credit") or from *dana li* (meaning "to submit"). Thus *din* can take on entirely different overtones, such as "custom," "directive," "reprisal," "judgment," "obedience," "submission," or "tradition." In theological discourse among the Muslim theologians, the *Ulama*, *din*, as a rule, signifies the divine institution which hands down the faith and doctrines, while at the same time pointing the faithful to good works. Closely observing *din* leads to salvation in this world and the next, for or against which all those subjects who are endowed with conscious reasoning can deliberately decide. *Din*, therefore, appears to denote "religion" in its broadest sense.[75]

In Judaism the term *b^erith* serves as the central concept, one most likely considered the equivalent of "religion." But this term, too, is contested etymologically. Quite specifically, *b^erith* means "the making of a covenant sealed by an offering" on Sinai, through which, by the power of God's election, Israel became the "people of the covenant," the "people of God." But in a broader sense *b^erith* signifies, as well, a somewhat nonspecific "covenant," a "regulation," an "agreement," a "solemn pledge," and again more specifically, the "right leading" by means of the commandments,[76] and, thus it shares nothing really in common with other "religions."

The following sketch will be useful to help visualize the incommensurability of empirical "religions" when trying to honor and represent their respective identities faithfully. It clearly shows that the central concepts of various religions are not compatible with each other, as they overlap in certain fields of meaning only and only to a certain degree. If, therefore, "religion" is discussed and "interreligious dialogue" advocated, then one should always remain conscious of the underlying intellectual construct and its distortion of lived reality. Practically speaking, it has to be expected that Muslims, Hindus, or Buddhists, to name just a few, will be somewhat suspicious of the concept on the basis of which dialogue is called for, because this concept is a brainchild of Western intellectual tradition, not theirs. That is not to say that for that reason the call for interreligious dialogue should be dismissed. To acknowledge the historical and cultural distinctiveness of the concept of "religion" only leads to a heightened awareness of potential difficulties to be reckoned with in interreligious dialogue.

---

75. See *The Encyclopaedia of Islam*, 5, 431ff.

76. See *Theological Dictionary of the New Testament*, 2:106–24; *The Encyclopedia of Judaism*, 1:136–51.

Why Is Religion So Prone to Be Hijacked by Vested Interests?

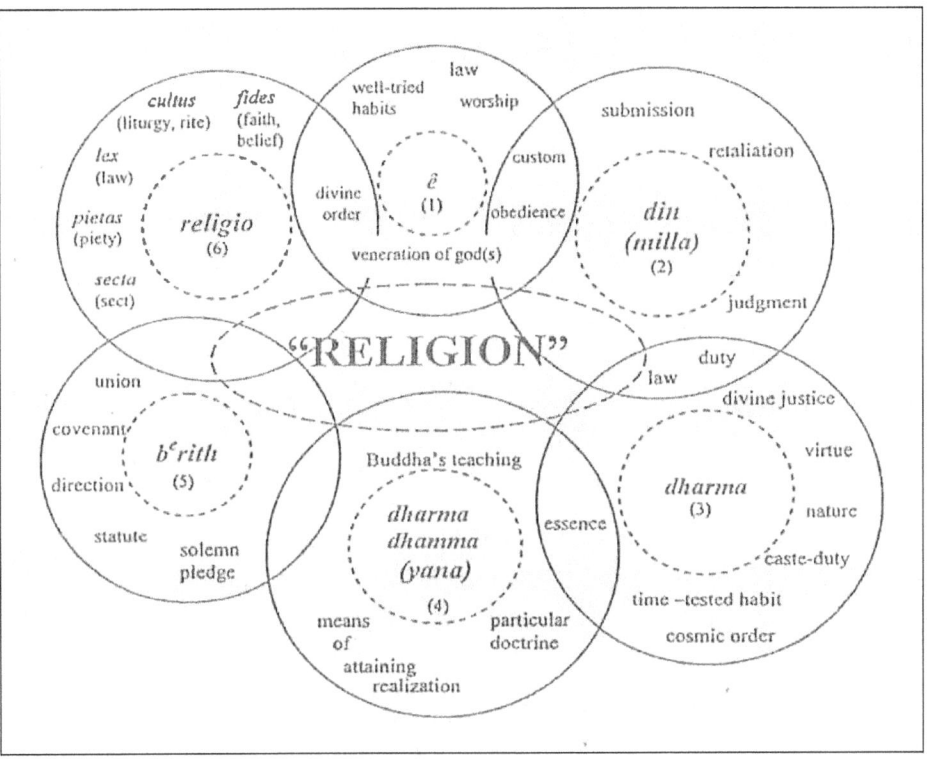

Figure 2.1: Showing the term "religion" as a construct and its incommensurability or only partial overlapping with central concepts in Nordic/Germanic religion (1), Islam (2), Hinduism (3), Buddhism (4), Judaism (5), and ancient Roman religion (6).

The unbiased, sobering recognition arising from how the facts of the case are depicted in figure 2.1 has far-reaching consequences for the further exploration of our topic. Once it is noticed that whenever talking about interreligious dialogue the terminology does not do justice to actual reality—in this case the spectrum of religious life, ideas, and identities of many other civilizations around the globe and throughout the centuries—the first step must be to compensate for these incongruities somehow thoughtfully and critically. Doing so one will quickly ascertain that the cognitive challenges this poses will loom even larger, because in addition to the absence of conceptual homogeneity among different empirical religions, numerous divergent conceptions about just what falls under the respective terms like *dhamma*, *dhārma*, *din/milla*, or *b⁰rith* will also surface, making

Beyond "Holy Wars"

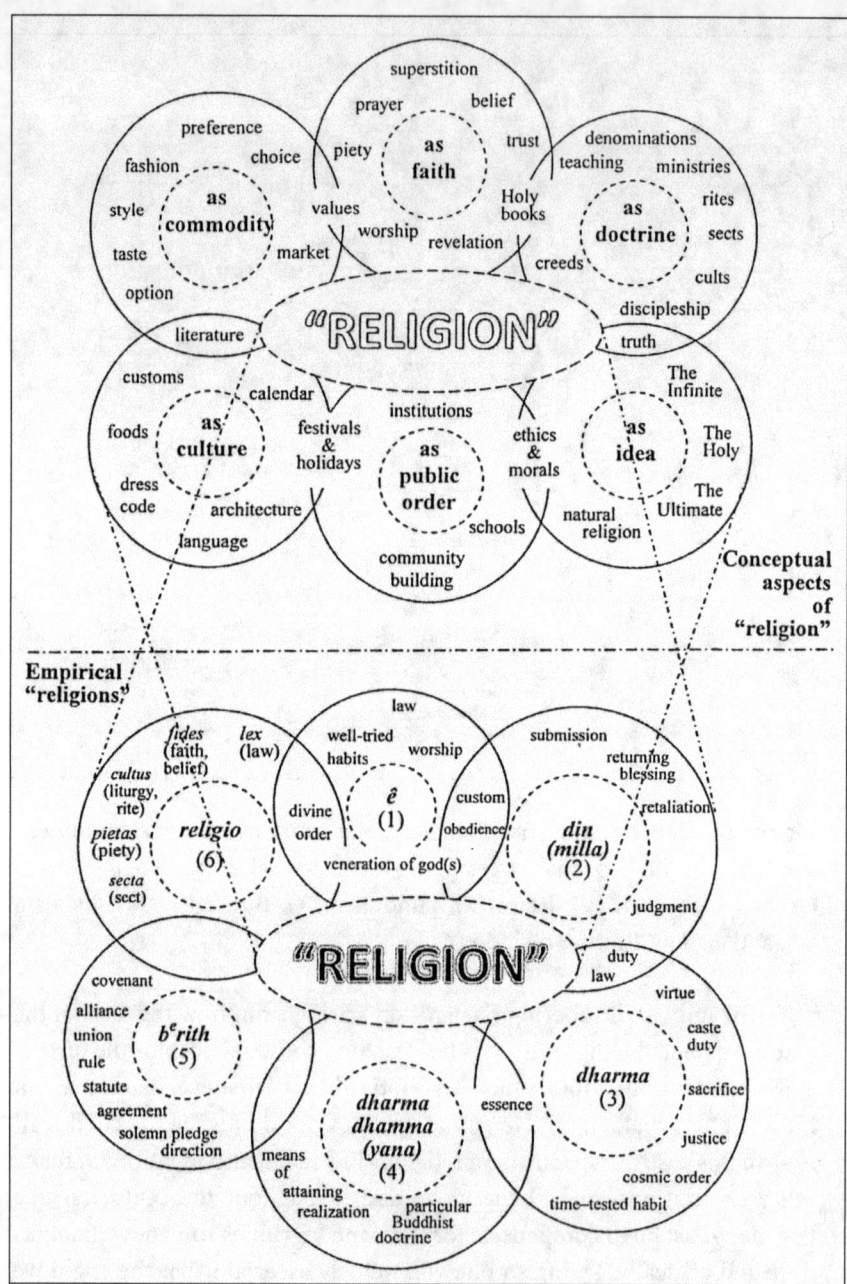

Figure 2.2: showing the superimposition of the term "religion" and the many unarticulated presuppositions onto the empirical phenomena of religions leading to a heightened complexity which is quietly at work in any interreligious dialogue.

the true complexity of demarcations no longer straightforward and clear but blurred. The more complex structure of such a conversation is made visible in figure 2.2 which shows to some extent the enormous theoretical as well as practical demand of the task ahead. Recognizing this complexity highlights the vital question of whether it will be at all possible to engage in interreligious dialogue in such a way that true understanding and meaningful communication take place.

3 Tolerance, Convivence, and "Holy Wars"

Having come to an understanding of why conventional terminology fails to do justice to religion—distorting it rather than getting at the heart of it—we now turn away from terminological concerns. Leaving clear-cut definitions behind we will continue to pursue the quest for interreligious dialogue by looking at concepts of how people have managed their peaceful living togetherness despite observing culturally diverse paths of life. The following chapter looks, first, at tolerance and at the political and legal as well as the mental, emotional, and psychological qualities required for tolerance, because awareness of the conditions of its possibility will guard against intolerance.

The subsequent section familiarizes readers with *Convivência*—a term now adopted into English as convivence—meaning "living togetherness" or "peaceful coexistence." This concept is advocated today by many as a promising approach to manage conviviality in multi-cultural environments. However, in order to avoid ideological shortsightedness this claim will also have to be scrutinized by looking at its potential for resolving conflicts, which finally leads explicitly into the crucial discussion of "holy wars." The close examination of incidents in which people staged "holy wars," breaking off convivence despite all appeals to tolerance, results in the discovery of the lack—even the complete absence—of dialogue, the topic of the succeeding chapter.

Tolerance, Convivence, and "Holy Wars"

Tolerance, Its Historical Background and Psychological Prerequisites

Even though they did not speak of tolerance the way we do today, some ancient sovereigns fostered and practiced like virtues for obvious reasons. This is especially true for those monarchs who reigned over a multi-ethnic populace. One of the most renowned of such rulers was the Indian king Ashoka the Great (304–231 BCE) who had his official edicts cut in stone on tablets and pillars for public display throughout his vast kingdom, which stretched from today's Afghanistan in the West to regions beyond Bangladesh in the East and far to the South of the subcontinent to nearly all of today's India. More than thirty of these so-called rock edicts have been found to date, among which the twelfth is of special interest here. In it Ashoka states,

> there should be growth in the essentials of all religions [*pūjā*, meaning: worship, adoration, reference, honor; often translated as "sect"[1]]. Growth in essentials can be done in different ways, but all of them have as their root restraint in speech, that is, not praising one's own religion, or condemning the religion of others without good cause. And if there is cause for criticism, it should be done in a mild way. But it is better to honor other religions for this reason. By so doing, one's own religion benefits, and so do other religions, while doing otherwise harms one's own religion and the religions of others. Whoever praises his own religion, due to excessive devotion, and condemns others with the thought "Let me glorify my own religion," only harms his own religion. Therefore contact between religions is good. One should listen to and respect the doctrines professed by others. The . . . king . . . desires that all should be well-learned in the good doctrines of other religions . . . And the fruit of this is that one's own religion grows and the *dhamma* [the teaching of the Buddha] is illuminated also.[2]

The importance of leniency toward people of other religions (or of other ways of worshipping the Ultimate) King Ashoka came to realize only after having fought numerous bloody imperialistic wars, which he regretted bitterly when becoming a Buddhist.

Another ancient emperor charging his subjects with the duty to respect people practicing different faiths than the officially established one

---

1. So according to Sen's translation in *Ashoka's Edicts*, 94.
2. Livius.org. Ashoka's Rock Edicts.

in the Empire was Constantine the Great (ca. 272–337). With his Edict of Milan of 313,[3] Constantine granted toleration to Christians and unspecified "others" who had suffered persecution in the Roman Empire before, noticeably so under Diocletian. Constantine ordered the property of the persecuted to be restored, thereby paving the way for future Christian dominance in the West.[4]

Later, in medieval Spain for instance, Jews, Christians, and Muslims lived side by side for several centuries (711–1492) quite peacefully, not all the time, but most of it. A pragmatic approach and prudent governance by different rulers helped them to manage their coexistence without speaking of "tolerance." The articulated concept of religious tolerance gained significance only in the second half of the sixteenth century when it first denoted the legally protected concessions and permissions granted by emperors and rulers of sovereign states in Europe to people practicing a different religion—such as Judaism or Islam—than Christianity. This represented a remarkable improvement over practices in previous centuries insofar as up to then it was the sovereign of a given area who decided about the faith to be practiced in the respective territory: One state—one religion. This was so because the general perception held that religion is a practiced way of a given "faith" lived; therefore, anyone challenging the given way of life posed a threat to public order. Religion was mainly a public affair, and any individual's non-compliance disturbed communal coherence and the social life at large.

It was the Protestant Reformation in sixteenth-century Europe that brought about a major change in this respect insofar as it now became practice to grant tolerance to non-compliant subjects who could not or would not—for the most part, but not always, on grounds of conscience—adhere to the locally established religion. This meant that recalcitrant subjects were not persecuted any longer but, instead, could leave their place of residence legally and relocate in a region where their way of believing was accepted practice; yet, those enjoying such tolerance had to leave their estates and any other non-movable property behind. This was, for instance, the fate of the French Reformed Protestants, the Huguenots, during the sixteenth

---

3. The *Edict of Milan* (313), issued by both the Emperor Constantine Augustus (West Roman Empire) and Licinius Augustus (East Roman Empire), granted Christians and others the rights of religious observances of their own throughout the Empire. See *Edict of Milan,* http://www.fordham.edu/halsall/source/edict-milan.html.

4. See MacMullan, *Christianizing.*

and seventeenth centuries[5] and also with the English Nonconformists and Dissenters in the seventeenth century, some of whom would later become the Pilgrim Fathers.[6]

However, prudent governments soon realized that they had to accommodate dissenters somehow if they were not to lose manpower, skills, and brains. Exercising a kind of connivance first by simply ignoring their existence worked for some time. But once dissenters gained broader support and became a people's movement, the political challenge to authority became obvious and some rulers—in Rome as well as in France—responded by granting so-called "Edicts of Toleration."[7] These edicts, while all too frequently broken, established the principle of official recognition of religious diversity and, later, of the freedom of conscience. Religious freedom, in those days and for all practical purposes, meant nothing more than, as mentioned already, freedom to emigrate from one's native principality and relocate to other territories where one's particular form of practicing the faith was not contested. Yet, in the course of the radical changes that finally led to the formation of nation-states in the mid-nineteenth century, this understanding of religious freedom and tolerance became fundamentally revamped. Today the right to personal religious belief and freedom of conscience is regarded as a basic human right claiming global validity since 1948 by its inclusion into the Universal Declaration of Human Rights. The eighteenth article of this declaration reads, "Everyone has the right to freedom of thought, conscience, and religion; this right includes freedom to change his religion or belief, and freedom, either alone or in community with others and in public or private, to manifest his religion or belief in teaching, practice, worship and observance."[8]

---

5. The so-called "St. Bartholomew's Day Massacre" of 1572 (beginning Aug. 23 and lasting to the end of September) claimed the lives of at least 30,000 Protestants and triggered the massive exodus of Huguenots; see Crouzet, *Les Guerriers de Dieu*; and Holt, *The French Wars of Religion*. For more general information on Huguenots see VanRuymbeke et al., eds., *Memory and Identity*.

6. See Miller et al., eds., *The Puritans*; and Heimert et al., eds., *The Puritans in America*. As to the designation of the first settlers as "Pilgrim Fathers," which owes its origin to a memorial speech delivered on occasion of the bicentennial in 1820 by Daniel Webster, see Kammen, *Mystic Chords of Memory*, 64.

7. "Edicts of Toleration" were granted the early Protestants in France in 1562 (*Edict of Saint-Germain*) and in 1598 (*Edict of Nantes*), which settled the first era of the French wars of religion. See Holt, *The French Wars of Religion*, 50–75, 153–72.

8. Text at United Nations, *Universal Declaration of Human Rights*, http://www.un.org/Overview/rights.html.

Beyond "Holy Wars"

Beyond the political and legal aspects of tolerance just outlined, the philosophically inspired "tolerance movement" is of special interest here. The said movement is represented by thinkers like Thomas More, Baruch Spinoza, John Locke, and Gotthold Ephraim Lessing who reflected at length and in great depth on the actual content of tolerance, both its degree and quality. They thereby affirmed other religions as genuine alternatives to Christianity which had so far dominated the public life of European cities and countryside.

One of the earliest advocates of this kind of thinking was the English statesman Thomas More (1478–1535). In his classic dialogue on political philosophy, *Utopia* (1516), the populace of the fictional eponymous island, organized along strict communal lines, is allowed to entertain whatever religious perspective they want, provided people are equally tolerant of one another. That More valued tolerance as essential to the wise governance of any state can be seen from statements like these: "There are different forms of religion throughout the island, and in each particular city as well."[9]—"For it is one of their oldest institutions that no man's religion, as such, shall be held against him."[10]—"There is no subject on which they are more careful of jumping to conclusions than this matter of religion."[11]—"So nothing is seen or heard in the churches that does not square with all the creeds. If any sect has a special rite of its own, that is celebrated in a private house; the public service is ordered by a ritual which in no way derogates from any of the private services."[12]

A century later, Dutch philosopher Baruch Spinoza (1632–1677) contemplated similar ideas in his anonymously published *Tractatus Theologico-Politicus* (*Theological-Political Treatise*, 1670), which had an enormous impact. It soon became the principal text of the tolerance movement,[13] its *Magna Charta*, so to speak. Spinoza argued that since "it is impossible to deprive men of the freedom to say what they think" people should be granted the freedom to air whatever their views if one likes it or not "without detriment to public peace, to piety, and to the right of the sovereign, but

---

9. Thomas More, *Utopia*, 72.
10. Ibid., 74.
11. Ibid., 77.
12. Ibid., 79.
13. See Windelband and Heimsoeth, *Lehrbuch*, 367.

Tolerance, Convivence, and "Holy Wars"

also that it [this freedom] must be granted if these [i.e., public peace, piety, political sovereignty] are to be preserved."[14]

Next comes John Locke whose Latin *Epistola De Tolerantia* [*A Letter Concerning Toleration*, 1689] had a similar effect, especially on ideas regarding government in the times of the French and American revolutions.[15] Locke advanced the principle that the two free associations of state and church should be kept as separate entities, because this separation warrants freedom of conscience. Church and state fulfill different tasks: The state has to care for the wellbeing of its citizens while the church has to care for the eternal wellbeing and salvation of all people.[16]

The literary and philosophical discourse on religious tolerance reached its zenith a further hundred years on with philosophical poet Gotthold Ephraim Lessing's (1729–1781) drama *Nathan, the Wise* (1779). Set in Jerusalem at the times of the medieval crusades, the play stages telling interactions among a wealthy Jew, Nathan, and his family; a Christian crusader who happened to rescue Nathan's adopted daughter from execution; and Sultan Saladin (1137–1193), the well-educated Muslim statesman and then sovereign of Palestine. Knowing that Saladin needs funds, Nathan visits the palace to make an offer. But before the ruler is willing to trust the offer, he puts Nathan's loyalty to the test by demanding an answer to a question concerning religion.

> Saladin: "What faith, or moral law, has most appeal for you?"
>
> Nathan: "Your Highness knows, I am a Jew."
>
> Saladin: "And I a Musselman [Muslim]. The Christian stands between us.—Of these three religions only one can be the true one."[17]

Nathan replies citing the famous Ring Parable, known since the Middle Ages.[18] In summary it runs like this: A royal family of the East once owned an opal ring which bestowed on its bearer the love of God

---

14. Spinoza, *Complete Works*, 571–72.

15. Locke, *A Letter Concerning Toleration*. Sometime later, in 1690 and 1692, Locke did publish two more "Letters of Toleration," this time in English, without developing the argument much further.

16. It should, however, be noted that Locke was not willing to grant such freedom to atheists, who, in his mind, could never be good citizens at all.

17. Lessing, *Nathan the Wise*, 230.

18. See the outstanding contribution by Niewöhner, *Veritas sive Varietas*.

and men. Handed down from father to the dearest son, it once came to a father of three sons unable to decide which one was his most beloved. So, secretly, he had two identical replicas of the ring made, replicas of such quality that it became impossible to distinguish the original, and caused the issue of three conflicting claims to genuineness. Hearing this story Saladin is disappointed.

> Saladin: "The rings!—Don't trifle with me!—I should think that those religions which I named to you might be distinguished readily enough, down to their clothing; down to food and drink!"
>
> Nathan: "In all respects except their basic grounds.—Are they not grounded all in history, or wit, or handed down?—But history must be accepted wholly upon faith—Not so?—Well then, whose faith are we least like to doubt? Our people's, surely? Those whose blood we share? The ones who from our childhood gave us proofs of love? Who never duped us, but when it was for our good to be deceived?—How can I trust my fathers less than you trust yours? ... —Can I demand that to your forebears you should give the lie that mine be not gainsaid? ... The same holds true of Christians. Am I right?[19]
>
> Well then! Let each aspire to emulate his father's unbeguiled, unprejudiced affection! Let each strive ... in bringing to the fore the magic of the opal in his ring! Assist that power with all humility, with benefaction, hearty peacefulness, and with profound submission to God's will!"[20]

In the final scene of the play all who once regarded one another as enemies embrace—the Jews, the Christians, and the Muslims—bringing to a powerful ending this great drama of religious tolerance. Lessing, thus, advanced the concept of religious tolerance, helping it become a common heritage of Western thought, even though sometimes much diluted and compromised.[21]

While one can rationally agree to accept tolerance as a political and personal virtue one should also be aware of the fact that humans are prone

---

19. Ibid., 233.
20. Ibid., 235.
21. It should be mentioned, however, that the drama when first premiered in 1801, twenty years after Lessing's death, in a revision by Friedrich Schiller, met with a mixed reaction. It was felt that it was much more a drama to be read than to be staged. It became a standard text in high-school education though. On the topic of the idea of tolerance in America, see Zagorin, *How the Idea of Religious Toleration Came to the West*.

to entertain intolerance much more easily, as psychiatrist and philosopher Alexander Mitscherlich (1908–1982) repeatedly has pointed out. In 1951 Mitscherlich published a first article on the topic entitled *I do unto you as I do unto myself—The psychology of tolerance*. In it he emphasized that "every demand for tolerance, however urgent or even if argued for ethically, has to explain itself anew, giving an accounting of actual human nature, or rather the essence of being human, if it is not to become fruitless or to fall on deaf ears."[22] Tolerance is according to Mitscherlich not a natural gift but a conscious attitude and disposition toward the environs and surroundings. Inasmuch as it involves the disposition to accept something that is alien to me, tolerance expresses deliberate acceptance and acknowledgement of the limitations of my own power, capabilities, and insight. It comes into play "where fear of insight is endured, where individuals have the courage to follow their tendency to be open toward the world beyond their perception of what is for the time being an alien world which they want to understand and comprehend, but which always also implies discovering it *in themselves*."[23] Tolerance is an "obligation in relation to something much greater," because it enables one to realize "the greater fullness of existence (*Dasein*) by unfolding the plenitude of ways it is ordered." Tolerance can only "be cultivated where fear and anxieties are quelled, and not where these have been intensified in the course of time."[24]

Some twenty-five years later Mitscherlich returned to the topic again when publishing in 1974 *Tolerance—Rechecking a concept*. In it he defined tolerance as "humanity's discovery about itself, which tends to fall permanently into oblivion—a discovery about the human capacity to exercise discretion, which it cannot take for granted as being at its disposal at any time."[25] The potential of tolerance "reaches exactly as far as the critical capacity of the individual and a culture were able to ... develop." An attitude of tolerance "brings to expression a typically human freedom to choose," which "to some extent saves from aggression," that is, that very impulse which in the end leads to intolerant behavior. The exercise of individual tolerance, Mitscherlich says, succeeds or fails the moment "that the warn-

---

22. Mitscherlich, *Gesammelte Schriften* [Collected Works] 5:419; see ibid., 5:410–28. See Forst, *Toleration in Conflict*. Forst belongs to the third generation of the "Frankfurt School" of sociology, of which Mitscherlich was one of the founders.

23. Ibid., 427; original emphasis.

24. Ibid., 423.

25. Ibid., 437.

ing sign of anger has become perceptible." Thus "individual courage" is the prerequisite of tolerance "along with a relatively strong ego, which allows one to behave in a level-headed fashion in the face of signs of danger."[26]

Any appeal to tolerance becomes unrealistic and fictitious "where the intensity of the aggressive drive is denied and the effort necessary to wrest some concession which will gratify the desires, either by a different route (sublimation) or by . . . offering the ego the possibility of critically intervening . . . is greatly underestimated."[27] The realistic basis for tolerance, therefore, is the "resolution to defend oneself" because "only those whose own achievements are deemed worth defending will be able to gain a serious comprehension of the life-world of others."[28] Such an attitude is not without its dangers, of course, for it exposes tolerant people to the reprisals of the intolerant for having ventured to call into question every previously valued claim to validity in the name of a greater whole, which sounds to the intolerant like a betrayal and a threat, or, we may add, to the religious like blasphemy.

This sobering insight into actual human nature is illuminating for any realistic appraisal of dialogue, too. It makes us reckon with the fact that however insightful and understandable the demand for tolerance, tolerance is prone to founder on the impulses to aggression, which are hard to keep under control by mere rationality. Tolerance expresses a strong position granted out of an assured, uncontested, and sovereign freedom. It generates a self-confident attitude, which may be rooted in a still unshaken confidence in the stability of public order, in rationality, or in the power of love among others. Tolerance might also be grounded in a still-unchallenged stronghold of moral certainty and political superiority, something which in our global age seems nearly impossible to maintain much longer. In any case, certainty and security condition the possibility of tolerance. Where certainty and security are lacking, or have never been able to develop in the first place, or where they have been shaken to their foundations, not only are sovereignty, freedom, and liberality threatened, but tolerance, too, is in danger of withering away or of—suddenly—turning into intolerance. While such change may be sudden, it does not occur by accident if one factors in the psychological considerations outlined above.

26. Ibid.
27. Ibid., 440.
28. Ibid., 454.

Tolerance, Convivence, and "Holy Wars"

To put it more simply, good intentions and goodwill alone will not warrant disposition for dialogue nor will they succeed in achieving sustainable peace in a religiously diverse environment. Instead, they can turn quickly into self-deception and wrong judgment, calling to mind the proverbial danger that "The road to Hell is paved with good intentions." However, it is not as though good intentions in themselves ought to be scoffed at, since they articulate that the enlightened will give room neither to aggression nor to hostility against potentially threatening strangers. Still, how can one avoid the danger of self-deception?

Self-deception cannot be corrected in monological isolation. Correction of self-deception happens, rather, through the initially uncomfortable, sometimes even painful experience of gaining new insights by being challenged in encounters and dialogues with others. Others will question why and what this and that means, they will argue, and they will challenge, necessitating an articulated response by those being thus questioned. These oppositions make them consciously aware of what gives rise to the concerns of others, thereby leading them to realize their own self-deception and wishful thinking. As uncomfortable as the challenges of this kind of dialogue are or might be, weighing them honestly is the only safeguard against deceptiveness. Real knowledge and insight are never gained solipsistically; they require verification and challenge by others.

Having become aware of this aspect, something else needs to be considered here, especially when pondering interreligious dialogue, because in interreligious dialogue one might encounter people who refuse to engage in dialogue. They do so with really good, reasonable grounds. A deeply religious motive for refusing to enter into such dialogue is to avoid blasphemy, to circumvent godless utterance, and to shun fellowship with unbelievers and infidels.

A report by an anonymous Spanish Muslim of the thirteenth century will provide some illustration. This person had been invited to participate in a conversation about religious matters with learned people from other faiths in Baghdad, the capital of the then Abbasid Caliphate, which in 1258 was captured by the Mongols, who sponsored such events. The pious Muslim disclosed in a letter to his friends,

> I have been ... to their gatherings twice, but have been quite wary of going a third time.—Why?—Just hear it, the first meeting was not just attended by Mohammadans of all sects, orthodox, heterodox. But present, too, were Parsi (the worshippers of the fire),

materialists, and atheists, Jews and Christians, in short, infidels of every kind. Each of these sects had its speaker, who had to defend its views. When one of these dignitaries entered the hall, everyone rose respectfully, and no one sat until that dignitary had taken his place. As the room was nearly filled, one of the infidels began to speak, "We have assembled in order to discuss . . . You are all aware of the basic guidelines, you Mohammedans may not bring arguments against us on the basis of your scriptures or that are supported by the sayings of your prophet, since we don't believe in this book nor do we believe in your prophet. Everyone present shall only appeal to grounds derived from human reason."—These words were generally greeted with cheers, and you, my friends, will understand that after having heard this kind of talk, I was no longer pleased to return to these meetings.[29]

Deep religiosity and unbroken loyalty to one's own religious tradition can therefore readily lead to straightforward rejection of interreligious dialogue, an attitude also alluded to in Psalm 1:1 which counsels the pious not to be among those who "follow the advice of the wicked," and "sit in the seat of scoffers." And the Apostle Paul, likewise, admonished the congregation in Corinth, "Do not be mismatched with unbelievers. For what partnership is there between righteousness and lawlessness? Or what fellowship is there between light and darkness? What agreement does Christ have with Belial? Or what does a believer share with an unbeliever? What agreement has the temple of God with idols?"[30]

Despite a firm conviction that interreligious dialogue is the only way to achieve sustainable peace in a multiethnic environment, one has nonetheless to honor such an attitude, too, while at the same time clearly indicating that one is seriously interested in understanding *why* such encounter would be regarded as blasphemous. This question offers those who shun dialogue the opportunity to explain themselves, actually making them enter into dialogue without even noticing it. However, to honor the genuinely religious attitude which avoids contact with infidels must be part and parcel of good dialogical practice. Dialogue cannot be forced upon people; dialogue has to be willed by people without fearing to join infidels, scoffers, and blasphemers. How to overcome this fear? An answer might be found in the modern concept of convivence.

---

29. Quoted in Kremer, *Geschichte der herrschenden Ideen des Islam*, 241–42 (my translation).

30. 2 Cor 6:14–16.

Convivence and Cultural Distinctiveness

The term *convivencia*—initially rendered into English as "living togetherness"—was first used in 1948 by historian Américo Castro (1885–1972) as a descriptor of the everyday living and working togetherness of Jews, Christians, and Muslims in medieval Spain.[31] *Convivencia* does not just describe a situation; rather, it is seen as the outcome of a conscious effort toward successful management of living togetherness in a culturally diverse environment, because *convivencia* is the *"accion de convivir."*[32] Today convivence has become an accepted neologism in English, owing its present popularity to the late Brazilian educator and theorist Paulo Freire (1921–1997).[33] Freire emphasized that unconditional *convivência* of people in power with the oppressed, powerless masses is necessary to establish genuine mutual trust. Only such a situation allows detecting what is borne communally, so that unbearable situations might be effectively opened for transforming actions.[34] Convivence thus understood stands for unconditional, unprejudiced living togetherness in a non-hierarchical, non-stratified community. In this sense convivence is akin to philosopher and cultural critic Ivan Illich's (1924–2002) use of the term *conviviality*.[35]

Later—in 1986—the term came into theological use, too, namely through an article entitled *Convivência: A principal pattern for ecumenical coexistence today* by German missiologist Theo Sundermeier, in which he argued that living in attention to one another across diverse backgrounds has to become the priority of all ecumenical efforts. Mutual differences ought not to interfere with peaceful daily living in multireligious surroundings;

---

31. Castro, *The Spainards*, 584. For a description of the living-togetherness of Jews, Christians, and Muslims in Medieval Spain, see Monecal, *The Ornament of the World*.

32. *Diccionario enciclopédico Espasa*, 379.

33. Several "Paulo Freire Institutes" committed to keep his legacy alive have been established around the globe, for instance in Spain, Malta, Israel, Finland, South Africa, and the USA (at the UCLA).

34. See Freire, *Pedagogy of the Oppressed*; *Education for Critical Consciousness*; and Horton and Freire, *We make the road by walking*.

35. Illich, *Tools for Conviviality*. In the Introduction (ibid., xxiv), Illich defines his use of the term explicitly in this way: A society, *"in which modern technologies serve politically interrelated individuals rather than managers, I will call 'convivial.'* After many doubts . . . I have chosen 'convivial' as a technical term to designate a modern society of responsibly limited tools. In part this choice was conditioned by the desire to continue a discourse which had started with its Spanish cognate" (original emphasis). For a similar more elaborate statement, see ibid., 11.

instead, these should offer an opportunity to share in learning by helping one another and by celebrating life together. Only in this way will a new communal experience emerge which, correspondingly, will effect change of consciousness. People will, thus, the longer the more turn away from preconceived ideas about what is right or wrong and arrive at a new openness toward emerging ideas and concepts. Theological insights, too, are no longer to be deductively derived from pre-established fixed systems only; rather, they have to grow out of an unprejudiced, uninhibited life in community with significantly different others, because only in this way will they bear the impress and authority of life actually lived.[36] "The truth itself," Sundermeier argued, calls "for *convivência*" for in this way truth "allows itself to be discovered."[37]

However, to think that convivence will work all by itself is a mistake, for in the everyday, practical lives of people of different religions, potential sources of friction abound, frictions which come to light most clearly in matters of mores and customs, in matters of observing different festivals and holidays tied to differences in hallowing time, and above all, in the different languages spoken; in short, in cultural differences. To gain an understanding of these challenges for convivence we now look a bit more closely into ways in which the cultural otherness of strangers finds expression.

Most conspicuously, being alien or "other" is perceived first of all in different ways of appearance. This does not just refer to the color of skin or facial trait, but also to styles of dress and attire. The colorful robes and garments that seem so exotic and charming when one vacations in far-away lands change character back home. In winter in Minnesota, for instance, garments such as the Indian sari, the Mexican sombrero, and the Arabic head veils immediately mark their wearers as different, even possibly threatening. With the ancient Romans we seem still to believe that clothing makes people.[38]

---

36. Since publication of the said article, convivence became a popular household term in the literature of the field and a key concept in contemporary thought, within both the theology of religions and missiology. This is particularly true in connection with the development of a "Hermeneutic of the stranger" (*Hermeneutik des Fremden*), which focuses on the analysis of life shared with those who are culturally different. It consciously grants equal dignity to everyone in a diverse society, not minding their various religious and ethnic backgrounds. See Becker and Feldtkeller, *Mit dem Fremden leben;* and Park, *Konvivenz*.

37. Sundermeier, *Konvivenz*, 99 (my translation); see also Sundermeier, *Convivence*, 68–80.

38. See El Guindi, *Veil: Modesty, Privacy and Religion*; Eicher, ed., *Dress and Ethnicity*.

Tolerance, Convivence, and "Holy Wars"

The breadth of international cuisine available nearly everywhere in the Western world today is striking—Indian, Chinese, Thai and Middle Eastern, Ethiopian, Mexican, and Indonesian. Yet not everyone realizes that the fare typical of each is often determined by definite religious dietary regulations which concern not only the style and manner of preparing food (as for instance in Judaism—kosher, or for Indian religions—Shiva food) but also the diet itself.[39] For example, one will not find the meat of "unclean animals" on the menu of Jews and Muslims, which in practical terms means the abstinence from pork and for Hindus abstinence from beef. Hindus of higher castes will all be vegetarians and eat "Shiva food." Likewise, Sikhs, orthodox Muslims and Buddhists decree abstinence from fermented drink and drugs, while in "shamanistic" religions, in contrast, intoxicating drink is essential to the celebration of the religious rites, as in the Mesoamerican Peyote cult[40] or the Vedic *Soma* sacrifice.[41]

Alongside differences in dress and food, ways of hallowing time, festivals, and calendars also vary from culture to culture reflecting each culture's basic temporal ordering of life. While holy sites and sanctuaries like temples, churches, synagogues, or mosques provide spatial orientation for the faithful, the calendar identifies periods to be observed and remembered in a community. However, a calendar does not simply order units of time like days, weeks, or months. A calendar functions as a kind of compass, a map in the ever flowing stream of time. It provides basic orientation for the life of a community as well as for its individuals.[42] Religious calendars in particular orient life around vital salvific events regarded as essential for life and therefore important to be remembered throughout ages. For Jews these events are creation and the covenant at Mount Sinai; for Christians it is the resurrection of the crucified Christ; while for Muslims it is the foundation of the Islamic community, the *Umma*, when Mohammed left Mecca to take refuge in Medina (*Hijra*). From these events each religion determines its particular rhythm of time, hallowing certain periods as festive while declaring others as times of public mourning and fasting, and again others for public worship and prayer. It is around these pivotal periods that all

---

39. See "Religion and Food"; Bynum, *Holy Feast and Holy Fast*; Sack, *Whitebread Protestants*.

40. Hultkrantz, *Shamanistic Healing*, 142–46.

41. See Wasson, *Soma*; and Stall, *Agni*.

42. The fascinating story of how religion structures time (inclusive of time management) is a research topic in its own right, see *Religion and Time*.

the other, more ordinary days of life are ordered, in each cultural-religious tradition in a somewhat different way.[43]

Observing a particular kind of calendar from early on makes perceiving time this way second nature. Yet one sometimes has to break this order, for instance when one has to abide by a strictly secular schedule dominated by the quantity of hours worked in order to comply with a work contract. One other reason necessitating adjustments would be the requirement to devise a common schedule for schools and community events in a religiously diverse setting. To do so without compromising one's own tradition demands some intellectual effort in order to reconcile conflicting claims, which is always purchased at the expense of relativizing one's own attitude towards the ordered structure of lived existence. This creates special problems for interreligious marriages and families.[44] Just here where tolerance and convivence must especially prove themselves, as in arranging weddings, deciding about procreation, and childbirth, observance and celebration of anniversaries, and, most importantly how to handle dying, death and burial, tolerance and convivence quickly come up against their limitations. There is no "both-and" approach to existential matters like the ones mentioned, leaving only highly complicated logistical maneuvering. Yet these compromises can have a negative effect on the quality time families share. For there to be genuine quality time together, one has to set priorities; and since preferences are at stake in these vital events of life, personal as well as cultural identities get challenged.

Yet, besides outer appearance, food, and calendric idiosyncrasies, the most obvious experience of being a stranger is in the language. How unsettling is it when everyone around speaks a language one cannot fully understand. Of course, one can communicate with hands and feet and come to some understanding, and obviously one can also communicate by means of gestures and pantomime. This is obviously also true of music, which has, with a certain appropriateness, been called "the universal language." Still, music is not just music, nor are gestures simply gestures; for body language and aesthetics are culturally determined, too. To experience this difference one may just listen to the *Ragas* of India with their strange harmonies or to the rhythms and melodies of Native American chanting or watch the different way of gesturing across cultures.[45] As long as one cannot understand

---

43. Richards, *Mapping Time*.

44. See for instance An-Na'im, *Inter-religious Marriages among Muslims*; and Rosenbaum and Rosenbaum, *Celebrating Our Differences*.

45. A simple gesture like pointing has been studied across cultures by cultural

the spoken word or as long as one's own speaking is not understood by others, one neither feels comfortable in trusting others nor can one expect their complete trust. The experience of remaining on the outside of the world of others in terms of language is painful and feeds suspicion. Language is world-mediating and thus *the* key to any culture; it opens up and conceals understanding.

Religions, too, are tied to languages. Actually it is this language base which accounts for the most decisive differences between religions, at least the so-called world religions. For example, the authoritative texts of Indian religions, the *Vedas*, are written in Vedic and Sanskrit, while those of Taoism and Confucianism are in Chinese; the scriptures of Buddhism, the *Tipitaka*, are written in Pali and Sanskrit while the holy book of Islam, the *Qur'an*, is written in Arabic or, to be more precise, in Qur'anic Arabic; the languages of the holy scriptures of Judaism, the *Tanakh*, are Hebrew and Aramaic, while Greek became the language of the *New Testament*, and Latin the medium of the Christian *Bible*. Even though most devotees are unable to read the holy scriptures of their own tradition in the language of their original composition—save the experts trained from among them—these texts, nonetheless, bring about a perceivable unity and cultural identity in that they are regularly used in ritual formulas and prayers which are part of all significant ceremonies of the religious life. For instance, passages of Holy Scriptures are recited as appointed readings in worship, the Torah in the Synagogue, the Gospel in the Christian liturgy, and the Qur'an during Friday prayers at the Mosque. By their constant repetition these texts bring about an identity which is impressed on individual believers over the course of time. Just so these texts by the force of repeated recitation contribute to the formation of a collective memory which is only in part a matter of the content of the texts as such. The way in which collective memory gets formed and inculcates identity is also by metaphors and images aroused in recitation of Sacred Scriptures, images and metaphors that are truly world-mediating. Even a translation can have great significance as, for instance the King James Version of the Bible which still retains a measure of its former authority in the Anglican and Episcopal churches and in English-speaking Protestantism across the globe, not because of any textual superiority (though myths of such do exist) but because of its centuries-long use. Although newer translations have supplanted it, the vast impact on literature by the King James Version has made it a common cultural

---

anthropologists whose findings have been published by Sotaro Kita in 2003 by the title *Pointing*.

heritage in the English-speaking world. The same holds true with Martin Luther's translation of the Bible into German.[46]

Once again, language is world-mediating. To be more specific, language is world-mediating not only by means of designating things in and of the world, but much more so by means of its grammar and syntax, its idioms and metaphors. These, too, provide information, albeit on a secondary level. Syntax communicates meaning about how things relate to each other, about the relationships among human beings and about their relationship to their environment, their life-world. This occurs because language actually grows from a subtle network of relationships as such: every speaking is information about something for someone and is thus aimed in its essence towards mutual relationship and sharing. Every language, however, emphasizes different aspects as essential and thus shapes and conditions its speakers' perceptions and experiences of the life-world. Even though such shaping happens for the most part unconsciously it has a lasting impact on mind and perception. In actually speaking a language, one does appropriate and re-own the world, the world at large as well as one's own personal world. This happens in actual speaking which avails of words in a distinctive way. Therefore, to speak (a language) is in fact active participation in the process of world-making.

In everyday usage language functions essentially as an instrument for sharing information and giving directions. In the realm of global communications marked by economic and logistical efficiency, specialized terminologies develop which are, however, unintelligible for the non-expert. Language thus used is concerned with normative unambiguity only. It avails of neologisms, acronyms, and a corresponding polyglot grammar in order to convey information as precisely as possible, a precision defined by mutual agreement of experts only. But such standardization of language—and any technical language is a standardization—is attained by a process of weakening connotation and fading out overtones; therefore, it results in atrophy of language and, consequently, of world perception, too. Words become denuded, stripped of their historically complex plenitude of meaning and their culturally specific connotations. Thus, while a certain perception of world still can be ascertained by technical language, admittedly only a very limited one, this language has barely anything in common any longer with living, vibrant everyday speech and nothing at all with the depth and associative richness of poetic language or religious texts. As German

---

46. The best proof of this for the English is the *Oxford English Dictionary*, and for the German, Grimm and Grimm, *Deutsches Wörterbuch*.

Tolerance, Convivence, and "Holy Wars"

philosopher Josef Pieper (1904–1997) once said, "Word and language, in essence, do not constitute a specific or specialized area; they are not a particular discipline or field. No, word and language form the medium that sustains the common existence of the human spirit as such. The reality of the word in eminent ways makes existential interaction happen."[47]

What language really is and how it actually mediates world can best be studied by looking to the poets, the crafters of language and words. Poets ably compress the words and syntax of their language until it sings. This pricks up the ears and enables those who can hear and see to perceive their world with new eyes. Take, for instance, the little poem "Fall" by German lyricist Rainer Maria Rilke (1875–1926) in which he shares his experience of that season and what it arouses in him. To best appreciate the poem's music, read it side by side with an English translation by me:

HERBST	FALL
Die Blätter fallen,	The leaves are falling,
fallen wie von weit,	fall as from afar,
als welkten in den Himmeln	as if in heavens' distant gardens
ferne Gärten;	withered;
sie fallen mit verneinender	they fall with gestures of negation.
Gebärde.	
Und in den Nächten fällt	And in the nights the heavy globe
die schwere Erde	does fall
aus allen Sternen	out from all stars
in die Einsamkeit.	into the loneliness.
Wir alle fallen.	We all do fall.
Diese Hand da fällt.	The hand up there does fall.
Und sieh dir andre an:	And watch the others,
es ist in allen.	it's in them all.
Und doch ist Einer,	And yet, Someone is there
welcher dieses Fallen	who holds this falling
unendlich sanft	so gently loving
in seinen Händen hält.[48]	in his hands.[49]

---

47. Pieper, *Abuse of Language*, 15.
48. Rilke, *Ausgewählte Werke*, 114.
49. My translation.

Beyond "Holy Wars"

Not only the music of the deftly placed words makes up the charm of these lines, nor only their rhyme. Just as much, the images evoked by falling foliage which impart the lively impression of what Fall and Autumn are—Autumn as a season of year, as a season of life, and as a particular life-experience. The poem connects chiefly with or speaks chiefly to those who have an experience of Autumn, whose years in temperate climes have made them familiar with it, whereas those who know only dry and rainy seasons may find it more difficult to grasp. Against the description of universal falling Rilke sets his matter-of-fact certainty of the presence of God watching over the world ("And yet, Someone is there who holds this falling"), thus affirming the Judeo-Christian worldview of this poem. Just so, language is world-mediating; and in every culture in turn, quite differently.

Taking this reflection one step further: Language mediates the world, but more than that, language also engenders the world. The priestly creation account in the first book of the Bible, Genesis, is clearly aware of this. God creates the world by his word, "Then God *said*, 'Let there be light'; and there was light" (Gen 1:3). "And God *said*, 'Let there be lights in the dome of the sky, to separate the day from the night; and let them be for signs and for seasons and for days and years . . .' And it was so." (Gen 1:14). "And God *said*, 'Let the earth bring forth living creatures . . . And it was so'" (Gen 1:24). Or, more briefly stated in Psalm 148:5, "He [God] commanded and they were created." Add to this beginning the profound insight of the prologue to John's Gospel, "In the beginning was the Word, and the Word was with God, and the Word was God . . . All things came into being through him, and without him not one thing came into being. What has come into being in him was Life, and the life was the light of all people" (John 1:1–4).

Alluding to this magisterial text of the world-creating power of the word, the poet Johann Wolfgang von Goethe (1749–1832) placed the following monologue in the mouth of Doctor Faustus, the main character of his drama by the same name. The well-educated, seasoned scholar Faust reflects in this way at the very opening of the play,

> It says: "In the beginning was the *Word*."
> Already I am stopped.
> It seems absurd. The *Word* does not deserve the highest prize.
> I must translate it otherwise if I am well inspired and not blind.
> It says: In the beginning was the *Mind*.
> Ponder that first line, wait and see,
> lest you should write too hastily.
> Is mind the all-creating source?

Tolerance, Convivence, and "Holy Wars"

It ought to say: In the beginning there was *Force*.
Yet something warns me as I grasp the pen,
that my translation must be changed again.
The spirit helps me. Now it is exact.
I write: In the beginning was the *Act*.[50]

Every translation, even of a sacred text, is a rendering into a significantly other view of life and world, as this prominent Goethe text makes clear. In the drama Goethe Germanizes the Greek root word *logos* (λόγος) meaning "word," "statement," "reason," but also "mind" to demonstrate the hermeneutical issues of translating. This kind of interpreting, which unfortunately is "not every man's skill,"[51] is of greatest significance for interreligious dialogue too, because other religions represent other worlds of language and experience. To be seriously concerned about using adequate terminology in any such dialogue expresses the earnest desire really to understand the others' perception of world and their way of articulating it, and not rashly gloss over what might not fit one's own presupposition.

Because different languages represent different worldviews, it will not be sufficient to analyze and understand language in a strictly functional way.[52] Interreligious dialogue requires mastery of language, preferably more than just one, but that would be asking too much of the average citizen, and of many experts, also. However, the mastery of language in dialogue across cultural divides has been an expected requirement from ancient times. In early Christian polemic, for instance, we find Jews lamenting the lack of familiarity with Hebrew on the side of their Christian accusers.[53] Similarly, from the diaries of the Dutch Franciscan Willem Rubruck (ca. 1210–1270) who traveled to the court of Mongolia's Great Khan Möngke in Karakorum (near today's Kharkhorin) in the years 1253–1255 to plead for the Christian cause we learn that Rubruck was at pains to hire a good translator for interpreter in the religious conversations with the Khan to avoid unnecessary misunderstandings.[54] Further, people participating in medieval religious

---

50. Goethe, *Faust*, 153; italics original.

51. Luther, "On translating," in *Luther's Works*, 35:194.

52. For the functional approach to language, see Webster, *Continuing Discourse on Language*.

53. See for instance the remark in the article on "Disputation and Polemics," in *Encyclopaedia Judaica*, 6, 79–103, esp. 84, with its criticism of Justin Martyr's *Dialogue with Trypho*.

54. See Rubruck, *The Journey of William of Rubruck*; and Jackson, *The Mission of Friar William of Rubruck*.

debates elsewhere—in Spain, Syria, Persia, China—continually lodged the complaint that dialogue partners did not really understand the arguments presented because they possessed insufficient knowledge of the languages in which the authoritative scriptures were written.[55] Thus, for example, in one of the reports about a conversation between a Muslim ruler and representatives of the Christian minority in Syria we read,

> [The] illustrious Emir did not accept the (words) of the prophets [which the Christian Patriarch had interpreted for him], but rather asked him to show on the basis of Moses that Christ is God ... The illustrious Emir asked this to be shown him from the very same book and our Father [Jacobite Patriarch John III of Antioch, 846–873] showed it to him in all the Greek and Syrian Books without error ... The Emir called a Jew, who was around and whom they prized on account of his knowledge of scripture, and he asked him whether it was really so written literally [in Hebrew] in the law [Pentateuch].[56]

In a tragically influential polemical treatise of Spanish Dominican Raymond Martini (c. 1220–1286) on exegetical issues contested by Christians and Jews, the author, who was well trained in Semitic languages, explicitly makes note of and underscores the quality of his arguments by boasting of his mastery of the language of the Jews and publishing his book bilingually in Latin and Hebrew. Martini wrote,

> In what remains, as concerns citing an authoritative text, I intend to follow at all points a text rendered from the Hebrew and not the Septuagint [i.e., the Greek version of the Old Testament] or another translator; and, what will seem a sign of yet greater presumption, I will not show any veneration for Hieronymus [the translator of the Bible into Latin] and will not avoid a bearable unsuitability of the Latin language, in order to render the truth of matters, as they are among the Hebrews, word by word, as often as it can be made certain. In this way, then, a broad and spacious way of escape will be cut off, for the Jews will no longer be able to say, the truth is not proved this way among them, as our people will show according to my translation.[57]

---

55. For respective reports, see *Friars and Jews in the Middle Ages*.

56. Suermann, "Orientalische Christen und der Islam," 124 (my translation). See also *Christian Arabic Apologetics*.

57. Martini, *Pugio Fidei*. The quote is taken from *Pugio* "Proemium" (Preface) 10, quoted in Ina Willi-Plein, *Glaubensdolch und Messiasbeweis* (my translation). See also Chazan, *Daggers of Faith*.

Tolerance, Convivence, and "Holy Wars"

Finally, a more recent piece of evidence documenting the importance of mastering the original language of holy texts for interreligious dialogue should also be mentioned here. It is the remarkable, monumental project of the two Jewish philosophers, Martin Buber (1878–1965) and Franz Rosenzweig (1886–1929) to produce a new German translation of the Old Testament, a "true Germanizing" as they called it. Introducing the project Buber and Rosenkranz say,

> Even the most significant translations of the Bible that we possess [reference is made to Martin Luther's translation] . . . do not aim principally at maintaining the original character of the book as manifested in word choice, in syntax, and in rhythmical articulation. They aim rather at transmitting to the translators' actual community . . . a reliable foundational document. They accordingly carry over the *content* of the text into another language . . . as if the spirit could be found elsewhere than in its concrete linguistic configuration, and could be delivered to other times and places otherwise than by a faithful and unprejudiced imitation of that configuration; as if the general understanding acquired at the expense of that initial linguistic concreteness would not necessarily entail a general misunderstanding, later, if not sooner.[58]

Begun in 1921, it took sixty years to complete the ambitious project, the result of which is an entirely unique rendering of the OT with numerous neologisms, making it not an easy read in German. Rosenzweig and Buber, however, never had the intention to provide a smooth translation. They, rather, only wanted to stay as faithful as possible to the world, culture, and connotations of the original biblical Hebrew, thereby showing the limitations of successful communication across diverse cultural backgrounds.[59]

To sum up, all that is called culture—customs and mores, the way of hallowing time and space, and, most importantly, the languages spoken—challenge the peaceful living togetherness of people in a global society. Surprisingly though, despite the fact that potential sources of friction abound, clashes do happen comparatively rarely. In general, multicultural, even multireligious, societies succeed more often than they fail because on the local level people are much more concerned with pragmatic solutions of day-to-day problems than with maintaining cultural identities or doctrinal purity. Yet, not all do. There always will be custodians of cultural

---

58. Buber, "On word choice in translating the Bible," in *Scripture and Translation*, 74; original emphasis.

59. See Rosenwald, "On the reception of Buber and Rosenzweig's Bible," 141–65.

identity and holy tradition—self-declared or not—who demean pragmatic solutions as betrayal of principles and defilement. When they find a hearing and succeed in garnering support, the danger of fiery storms of hatred and violence looms large.

Convivence and Conflict Management as Political Tasks

The Limits of Social Cohesion: Conflict and Mediation in Pluralist Societies is the telling title of an extensive report to the Club of Rome by the Bertelsmann Foundation containing the findings of sociological studies spanning several years and a total of eleven countries on this matter.[60] Drawing practical conclusions for how to handle normative conflicts in diverse communities, the report comes to a very interesting conclusion that feeds into the immediate context here. The report states that there are actually only three kinds of possible models of negotiations or mediations in cases of conflict.[61] The first, called the "imperative" type, relies on the authority of those who are in control and have power. This type does not rule out suppression of the opinions, more or less informed, of individuals, minority groups, or those who deviate from society at large. The second, called the "pragmatic" type, holds to the possibility of negotiation at roundtable talks and other structured dialogue between representative elites. Their distinctive strategy is to consciously set aside normative questions for the sake of implementable compromises which, however, have a high probability of *not working* when the decisions made affect deep-rooted norms. In such cases, the "third and most difficult type of mediation" namely "dialogic mediation" has to be attempted, since dialogic mediation addresses "normative differences head-on" and seeks "not just a pragmatic but an ideational compromise."[62]

According to Peter L. Berger, who headed this project and authored the summary findings, the lack of other expedients requires reference to "methodological lessons... from the experiences of interreligious dialogue" even if conflicts on the international and global plane are at stake.[63] The dialogical type of negotiation is admittedly by far more difficult than the "im-

60. *The Limits of Social Cohesion.*
61. For the following, see especially ibid., 364–72.
62. Ibid., 367.
63. Ibid., 368.

perative" or "pragmatic" type, if only for the amount of time it consumes. But it is the only type of genuine negotiation, Berger holds, because it alone engages in "dealing with everyone's otherness without simply seeking the least common denominator."[64] To concede the difficulties of the dialogical type of negotiation is not to speak against it; in fact, these difficulties only prove the complexity of normative conflicts, which, if not adequately addressed, have the potential to jeopardize every agreement accomplished. This applies to the societal cohesiveness of a given nation as much as it does to the stability of international order. Consequently, to search and strive for appropriate structures of negotiating conflicts is of enormous practical significance in politics, just as it is for interreligious dialogue.

Genuine openness and *savoir-vivre*, which are so necessary for tolerance and convivence, are not at all commonplace. Only few are aware that tolerance and convivence are achievements and the precious gift of a long, conflict-ridden process of political, intellectual, and cultural wrestling. To a generation raised in an environment where tolerance is practiced—at least most of the time—convivence may appear so natural that any talk about it might sound quasi-trivial or somehow moralistic. But this is to misjudge the case, because everything simply taken for granted remains without proper appreciation as long as it is not put in jeopardy. Only when there is some inkling of what is about to be lost, does one begin to suspect the preciousness of the achievement. Therefore, if the permissive openness people in the free world enjoy today is misjudged as something self-generating and not seen as the fruit of freedom, democracy, and affluence—and also and not least as an outcome of the Christian perception of a world worthy of protection—then tolerance and convivence lose their distinctive contours immediately. They become blunt, leveled-out principles, which will sooner or later fall into oblivion out of sheer forgetfulness, the danger of which the epigram adorning the main entrance to the imposing City Hall at Hamburg, Germany, reminds everyone. It reads "*Libertatem quam peperere maiores digne studeat servare posteritas*," which means "*May posterity diligently strive to preserve the freedom gained by those before.*"[65] This epigram powerfully reminds everyone entering city hall to be aware of the cultural achievements he or she enjoys.

64. Ibid., 370.
65. A photograph of this epitaph can be accessed at Rathaus Hamburg http://en.wikipedia.org/wiki/File: Hamburger_Wahlspruch_%28Rathausinschrift%29 .jpg.

Beyond "Holy Wars"

In fact, the danger that basic cultural and political accomplishments will sink into oblivion is much more acute than generally perceived. The permissive openness of the open society is by the very reason of its openness most at risk and susceptible to demagoguery and anomie when intolerant groups not shunning the use of weapons take recourse to terror to push their agenda on society at large. Radical groups in conflict with the larger community around are well enough known and as ignominious as they are famous, as al-Qaeda and the Japanese Aum sect, to name just a few. Their activities endanger much more than the lives of humans harmed in the actual terrorist attacks. The activities of these and likeminded groups[66] imminently threaten the continued existence of freedom and permissive openness for they provoke restrictive political and economic measures, which, unfortunately, are, then, mostly of a reactionary, fundamentalist nature. It is this nature which poses the actual far-ranging danger of terrorism. Thus, the strength of modern, open societies is at the same time what puts them at risk most. To curb this danger people have to remain conscious of the cultural achievements, notably of tolerance and hospitableness in a convivential surrounding, by staying consciously aware of it through dialogue and public discourse about the very foundations of the open society they enjoy. Actually, dialogue is in itself already an expression of and an exercise in tolerance because it not only allows but critically affirms other ways of life when seeking understanding while at the same time it heightens awareness of the basic conditions of its very possibility.

The Issue of—and with—"Holy Wars"

The touchstone for all discourse on tolerance and convivence is how well it brings accord with those whose acts and thinking cause friction and conflict with society at large. Not only do totalitarian states have great difficulties on this point and, therefore, professionalize eavesdropping and establish networks of secret informers, but hierarchically led institutions—churches and other religious associations in particular—have serious problems too. Their policing of deviationists, whom they call heretics, gave rise to numerous persecutions, executions, and "inquisitions,"[67] while their influencing

---

66. For a comparatively recent survey of theses, see *Encyclopedia of Terrorism*.

67. See Berkhout and Russell, *Medieval Heresies*; Given, *Inquisition and Medieval Society*; Shannon, *The Medieval Inquisition*; Roth, *Conversos, Inquisition, and the Expulsion of the Jews from Spain*. In the thirteenth century anti-Maimonidean Jews in southern

Tolerance, Convivence, and "Holy Wars"

political authorities and public opinion often irritated pragmatic reasoning and motivated waging "holy wars."[68] The power of any religious establishment so to do rests with the nature of religious claims, which appeal to a higher good and an ultimate authority beyond and above. As sociologist Niklas Luhmann has observed, "No other social functions system [except religion] can convey the conviction and can make communicable that what we do is in the final analysis good."[69] Indeed, throughout the ages religions and the guardians of faith have justified going to war as a noble task worth every sacrifice.

The most prominent religious document advocating war against those who put the proper order of the world in peril is the *Bhagavad-Gita*, an excerpt from the celebrated Indian epic *Mahabharata*.[70] The *Gita*, sometimes also called "The New Testament of Hinduism,"[71] depicts the critical moment in the annihilating battle of Kurukshetra (fought probably around the tenth century BCE) in which one of the chief commanders of the army of the Pandavas, Prince Arjuna, contemplates calling off the fight with his kinfolk, the opposing Kauravas who had violated *dhārma* by not handing over gubernatorial authority to their cousins as was their duty. Arjuna's charioteer Krishna, however, an embodiment (or *avatar*) of the principal Hindu deity Lord Vishnu, admonishes him not to violate *dhārma* himself, that is, not to ignore his duty as warrior and also, not to "sorrow over men you should not be sorry for." Krishna explains his counsel thus: "The wise are not sorry for either the living or the dead" for "the man who knows him for what he is—indestructible, eternal, unborn, without end—how does he kill whom [him] or have who [him] killed?"[72] The *Gita* teaches the attainment of radical disinterestedness and detachment as solution to the ethical

---

France asked the Christian Inquisition to assist in their prosecuting heretics. In Islam Abbasid Caliph al-Ma'mun in 218 AH/833 CE declared a *Mihna*, that is, a testing of particular individuals concerning their view of whether the Qur'an is created or not. The response was not without consequences. Measures were taken against those who rejected the doctrine of the createdness of the Qur'an, including dismissal from public office, imprisonment, and even flogging. The *Mihna* was ended in 861 by al-Ma'mun's nephew al-Mutawakkil (see Cooperson, *Al-Ma'mun*).

68. See Murphy, ed., *The Holy War*; Nolan, *The Age of Wars of Religion*.
69. Luhmann, *Observations on Modernity*, 62.
70. See van Buitenen, *The Bhagavadgita in the Mahabharata*. The time when the Gita was written is still a matter of much debate among scholars who suggest as wide a range as the fifth century BCE to the fourth century CE.
71. Nikhilananda, *The Bhagavadgita*, v; Rosen, *Essential Hinduism*, 107.
72. Van Buitenen, *The Bhagavadgita* 24[2].10–15 (75).

dilemma of war, thus reassuring Arjuna that only when he remains "unconcerned" and stays focused on his duty (*dharma*) as warrior will he be set "free from all evils" since he fulfills *dharma*.[73] In closing, the *Gita* narrates that all "mounted their chariots and arrayed their ranks . . . sounded their drums and cymbals by the hundreds . . . and roared forth with their various battle cries."[74] In the end, only twelve highly praised "heroes" out of several hundred thousand survive this eighteen-day epic battle.[75]

While a devastating battle of rival kinship clans in northwest India in the far reaches of history provided the content of the epic, it is obvious that the main topic of the *Bhagavad-Gita* is the war between righteousness (*dharma*) and unrighteousness (*adharma*). It clearly proclaims the message that anyone concerned about *dharma* has to join in the struggle for *dharma* in order to fulfill *dharma*, because the world and social order will collapse and turn into chaos without proper preservation of *dharma*. Thus, it is the human life which is the battle ground for the upkeep of *dharma*. Such spiritualization and ethicization of warfare, while understandable in order to arouse uninhibited determination, nevertheless cultivates at the same time a subtle "holy war" attitude, especially if it holds true that action and inaction are to be regarded the same, that the truly wise "are not sorry for either the living or the dead," and that it really does not matter if someone kills or gets killed, as the *Gita* teaches. Such impartiality makes the content of human exploits irrelevant, relativizes ethical concerns, and provides arguments for disregarding potential sacrifices and victims.[76]

Another religion in which the "holy war" between good and evil figures prominently is Zoroastrianism, named after its prophet Zoroaster (Zarathustra). It emerged in Ancient Persia during the sixth/fifth century BCE and is still alive in Iran and elsewhere;[77] the Parsees in India are one

---

73. Ibid., 40[18].65 (144–45).

74. Ibid., 41.95 (155).

75. Rajagopalachari, *Mahābhārata*, 183, estimates the figure at 3.94 million, which, however, appears to be far too much, considering the population at that time in north India.

76. For a recent illustration of this statement, see Fernandes, *Holy Warriors*.

77. The number of Zoroastrians living in Iran today is estimated to be 0.1 percent of the population of 75,276,000, that is 75,276 according to the most recent statistics (see *Britannica Book of the Year 2012*, 628). This, however, conflicts with the figure given in the context of "Comparative National Statistics: Religion" in the same source where the number of Zoroastrians for Iran alone is claimed to be 1,780,000 (ibid., 796), while the *Megacensus of Religions 1900–2011*, given in the same source (ibid., 300–301), mentions only 198,500 Zoroastrians worldwide.

of its most prominent adherents today.[78] According to the *Zend-Avesta*,[79] the oldest collection of sacred texts of Zoroastrianism, Ahura Mazda is the highest god. He is the uncreated creator and the sustainer of truth, *asha*. He is wholly wise, supporter and guardian of justice, benevolent, good, and the friend of every just person on earth. While he is not omnipotent—he allows for and honors the free will of humans—he is omniscient and constantly challenged by his rival, Angra Mainyu, the principal evil spirit, the source of all misery and sin. Angra Mainyu, though uncreated as well, is not an equal to Ahura Mazda, but a constant source of concern for him, diligently watched and fought until total destruction.

Both deities created armies of likeminded spirits, angels, and demons (*yazatas* and *daevas*) as their envoys assisting the principal opponents in their cosmic struggle. It is these spirits who communicate with ordinary people, urging them to join one side or the other willingly. Zoroastrians, the followers of the "Good Religion" (or the "Religion of Good Conscience"[80]) are called to join in the cause of Ahura Mazda by cultivating "good conscience" amidst all adversity, by always entertaining "good thoughts, good words, and good deeds," confident that their fight for the good will be finally victorious.[81] Everyone bears responsibility not only for his or her final destiny as an individual but also for the future fate of the entire universe, because in the end there will be a bodily resurrection of all for judgment, a judgment which is decisive for definite annihilation or for life everlasting. Everything a person does in his or her life is therefore of critical importance. Each individual has to be mindful of this responsibility when joining in or withdrawing from the battle for the good, a radical enhancement of ethical obligation, indeed.

The call to a metaphorical warrior life resounds in the New Testament, too. The first letter of Peter, for instance, charges the faithful, "Discipline

---

78. See Taraporevala, *Zoroastrians of India*; and Hinnells, *The Zoroastrian Diaspora*.

79. The texts of the *Zend-Avesta* are readily available at AVESTA Zoroastrian Archive http://www.avesta. org/.

80. See Masani, *Zoroastrianism: The Religion of the Good Life*. It is interesting to note that the Zarathushtrian (!) Assembly at Buena Park, California, has been formed to restore the "Good Religion" of Zarathustra. See http://www.zoroastrian. org/articles/The_Good_Religion_and_Zoroastrianism.htm.

81. The Zoroastrian concept of the final renovation of the universe for the good by Ahura Mazda, *Frashokereti*, is detailed in a ninth-century text only, called *Bundahishn*, not in the much older *Avesta*; see Boyce, *Zoroastriana: their Religious Beliefs and Practices*; Moazami, "Millennialism, Eschatology, and Messianic figures in Iranian Tradition."

yourselves, keep alert. Like a roaring lion your adversary the devil prowls around, looking for someone to devour. Resist him, steadfast in your faith" (1 Pet 5:8–9). Christians should "lay aside the works of darkness and put on the armor of light"; they should "put on the Lord Jesus Christ, and make no provision for the flesh, to gratify its desires" (Rom 13:12, 14). Similarly, the members of the congregation at Ephesus should ready themselves for fighting the adversary by dressing with armaments like Roman soldiers. They are advised to

> Put on the whole armor of God, so that you may be able to stand against the wiles of the devil. For our struggle is not against enemies of blood and flesh, but against . . . the cosmic powers of this present darkness, against the spiritual forces of evil in the heavenly places . . . Stand therefore, and fasten the belt of truth around your waist, and put on the breastplate of righteousness. As shoes for your feet put on whatever will make you ready to proclaim the gospel of peace. With all of these, take the shield of faith, with which you will be able to quench all the flaming arrows of the evil one. Take the helmet of salvation, and the sword of the Spirit, which is the word of God. (Eph 6:10–17)

While texts like these undeniably mirror the socio-cultural circumstances of their times, they also keep alive the valuable religious insight that striving for the good, striving to do the right thing at the right time, is not an act one can ever become simply accustomed to or comfortable with. All endeavors for the good will always meet with opposing forces which have to be overcome, one after the other and one at a time. How can waging "holy wars" this way be deemed inappropriate? Such a summons is not an expression of religious bellicosity or spiritual militancy. On the contrary, it appeals to a necessary sobriety since every genuine struggle for spiritual life is experienced oftentimes as a fierce battle or a tough athletic competition (as also frequently alluded to in the New Testament).[82] To liken the human struggle to battle brings instantly to mind the serious nature of the cause, the requisite dedication, and the resolute determination of those engaged therein. Human life perceived as the decisive battlefield of the war between good and evil, righteousness and unrighteousness, is not just a dramatic

---

82. See 1 Tim 6:12; 2 Tim 4:5 (combined with the metaphor of military fighting like a "soldier of Christ" in vv. 3–4); Heb 12:1; with close association to "struggle," see 1 Thess 2:2; Phil 1:30; Col 2:1. The Greek term used in all these instances is ἀγών (agon), the technical term for sportive competition like a race. The term for actual war would be πόλεμος (polemos).

metaphor; it reflects the gravity of the struggle for succeeding or failing as a *human* being. At the same time, the battlefield metaphor also expresses the experience of the dangers, difficulties, and challenges faced by everyone joining in this effort. Whoever has come to realize that life is gained only by overcoming serious odds in the face of evil forces and death won't mind being likened to a warrior.

The Holy Scripture of Islam, the Qur'an, admonishes the faithful repeatedly to "struggle in the way of God."[83] The verb used is *jāhada*, meaning "to struggle [earnestly]," "to strive [seriously]," and also, "to fight for the faith."[84] The "fight for the faith," known as *jihād*[85]—commonly though not adequately translated as "holy war" or "war for the faith"—includes but goes beyond actual warfare. Actually, *jihād* is the Qur'anic term to describe the all-comprehensive struggle for a God-fearing life. Sakena Yacoobi, the foundress of the Afghan Institute of Learning—a women-led organization supporting underground home schools for girls during the time of Taliban reign[86]—used the term in this way in her plenary address on occasion of the Parliament of the World's Religions meeting at Melbourne, Australia, in December 2009, by plainly stating: "Life is *jihād*."[87] Muslim mystics, the *Sufis*, and others speak of a "lesser" and a "greater" *jihād*, teaching that armed warfare for Islam is the "lesser" and the struggle against the self the greater *jihād*.[88] Muslim jurists, the *Fuqaha*, distinguish among four ways in which the obligation to engage in *jihād* may be fulfilled, namely by heart (combatting the devil), by tongue (speaking the truth, teaching Islam), by hand (doing the right thing, preventing the wrong), and by sword.[89]

Scottish Islamologist W. Montgomery Watt has sketched in a highly instructive article on "Islamic Conceptions of the Holy War" the development of the idea of *jihād* from the times of the Qur'an to the early twentieth century.[90] He comes to the conclusion that the

83. See Surah 2:218 (215); 5:54 (59); 8:74 (75); 9:19 (19); 29:69 (69), etc.

84. See Kassis, *A Concordance of the Qur'an*, 587–88.

85. The noun appears four times in the Qur'an, Surah 9:24 (24); 22:78 (77); 25:52 (45), and 60:1 (1).

86. See Yacoobi, "Women Educating Women in the Afghan Diaspora."

87. *Make a World of Difference*, 18.

88. See Schimmel, *Mystical Dimensions of Islam*, 112. See also Cook, *Understanding Jihad*, 32–48; and the "Documentation of 'Greater Jihad' Hadith," at Living Islam, http://www.livingislam.org/n/dgjh_e.html.

89. Khadduri, *War and Peace in the Law of Islam*, 51–138.

90. See Murphy, ed., *The Holy War*, 141–56; and Bonney, *Jihād*; Cook, *Understanding Jihad*.

Beyond "Holy Wars"

> Islamic conception of the jihād or "holy war" developed gradually out of the circumstances in which the [first] Muslims found themselves in their Arabian environment... The original linking of the Islamic religion with fighting was thus the work of Muhammad's pagan opponents who by their measures against the Muslims put the latter in the position of having to fight for survival... In a certain sense, then, it may be said that Muhammad gave to the pagans of Arabia a choice of "Islam or the sword."... For Jews and Christians in the first place, and then for Zoroastrians, Buddhists, and even Hindus, another status was possible, namely that of "protected minorities."[91]

Members of "protected minorities," that is, adherents of religions with a body of sacred scriptures of their own or, as the Qur'an calls them "people of the book,"[92] were secondary citizens in the world of Islam, to be sure, but they were accepted and tolerated. A tax for their protection was levied on them and they were not to be fought against since they, too, honored God's revelation in scripture.

However, during the seventh and eighth centuries, the time of Islam's rapid extension beyond the Arabic peninsula, Muslims faced challenges not addressed by the Qur'an. This brought about a new body of tradition called the *Sunna*, which is second in authority only to the Qur'an and serves as the main source for its interpretation. The *Sunna* consists of accords of the "habitual" or "standard [good] practice" of the Prophet himself as handed down by his companions and eyewitnesses of his words, actions, and approbations (*Hadith*).[93] Within this tradition the concept of *jihād* developed along the lines of outspoken bellicosity in justifying wars of conquest, because, according to the *Sunna*, the world is divided into "the house of Islam" (*dar al-Islam*) and "the house of war" (*dar al-Harb*).[94]

However, to restrain excesses of brutality and plundering and to curb territorial and material greed, certain criteria for the proper conduct of "holy wars" and "holy warriors" (*ghazi* [pl. *ghazawāt*] rather than *mujahid* [pl. *mujahideen*], but never 'jihadist') eventually emerged. The *Imam* or *Caliph* as the head of state in his duty to watch over religion has to declare war

---

91. Murphy, ed., *The Holy War*, 145–46.

92. See *Encyclopaedia of the Qur'an*, 4:36–43. The term occurs in Surah 2:62; 3:64; 3:113–15; 29:45 (46).

93. See Brown, *The Canonization of al-Bukhari and Muslim*; and Musa, *Hadith as Scripture*.

94. See on this topic Murphy, ed., *The Holy War*, 152; and Cragg and Speight, *The House of Islam*.

against those who have refused to become Muslims despite being invited to join. The Commander of *jihād*, the *Emir*, has to carry out *jihād* according to best military practices, being mindful of not violating *Sunna*.[95] This basis implies several conditions: 1. that *jihād*—which in principle cannot be declared against Muslims—should not be called for if there is no chance of success; 2. that *jihād* is not lawful unless unbelievers have first been offered the opportunity to join the faith; and 3. that *jihād* has to be stopped once Islam or the status of "protected minority" has been accepted by the people being fought against. If unbelievers resist the invitation, three options remain: to make a truce (but for up to ten years only), to reach an agreement for paying a ransom, or to kill all males and sell their families into slavery. Warriors of the faith, *ghazawāt*, should be concerned about upholding and promoting Islam only, purely desiring that unbelievers become Muslims and not seeking wealth or fame. If they lose their life during *jihād*, they become martyrs who enjoy special merits and in the hour of death enter paradise immediately.

Regardless of this tradition, history is full of examples of *jihād* against fellow Muslims, too,—in Africa, Arabia, India, and Asia[96]—and of several calls to *jihād* for political interests of the people in power rather than for Islam itself.[97] To make matters more complex, factions within Islam such

---

[95]. So according to tenth-century Muslim legal scholar al-Mawardi (973–1058) in his treatise *Al-ahkam as-sultaniyya* (*The Ordinances of Government*). Since 1996 the title is available in a handy English translation.

[96]. Muslims fought against Muslims in Africa in the Sudan when Muhammad Ahmed Al Mahdi declared *jihād* against the Ottoman rulers, declaring all Turks "infidels" (Holt, *The Mahdist State in Sudan*). Saudi Wahhabists waged *jihād* against Shiites in Iraq in the early nineteenth century (1801–1802) and gained control of Mecca and Medina in Saudi Arabia in 1803/04 (DeLong-Bas, *Wahhabi Islam*, 2004). In India Mughal Aurangzeb (1618–1707) called for *jihād* against Shi'a Muslims and other heterodox groups (Richards, *The Mughal Empire*, 1993), as also did *Emir* Abdur Rahman Khan in Afghanistan in 1892 (Monsutti, *War and Migration*, 2005). In China it was during the Dungan Revolt (1862–1877) that the Turkic Uyghur Muslims under Yaqub Beg declared *jihād* against the Chinese Dungan Muslims (Kim, *Holy War in China*).

[97]. As was the case with Sultan Essad Effendi, Sheikh-ul-Islam, the head of the department of religious affairs in the Ottoman Empire, who on November 14, 1914, called the *Ummah*, that is, the entire Muslim community, to wage *jihād* against Russia, Britain, France, Serbia, and Montenegro by getting involved in what became World War I, a call which was not heeded because it was fought in co-operation with non-Muslim allies and deemed as a war of aggression by other Muslims (see Peters, *Islam and Colonialism*). The so called "Fulani Jihad" in Western Africa of 1804–1810 fought by Usman dan Fodio (1754–1817) was a military conquest of Fulanis against the Hausa in the region of today's Cameroon and Nigeria, followed by numerous other wars in Western Africa also called

Beyond "Holy Wars"

as the *Kharijites*, a radical sect emerging in the late seventh century, taught armed *jihād* as the sixth pillar of Islam, a conviction also held by some *Sunni* scholars and the militant Egyptian Islamic Jihad still today.[98] On the other hand, warfare in the name of God is strictly prohibited to the Twelve-Imam Shi'ites until the return of the Hidden Imam,[99] while members of the *Ahmadiyya Muslim Community* (founded in India in 1889/1914) regarded by many as non-Muslims, are declared pacifists.[100] All this is to show how impossible it is to construct a general statement with regard to *jihād*. The term contains multiple interpretations in the course of the history of Islam across a variety of cultures and peoples—far too many and far too multifaceted to allow for the simplistic equation of *jihād* with (armed) "holy war."

There has been considerable debate over how much the conception of *jihād* has influenced the idea of crusade,[101] a term coming first into general use via Latin *crucesignatus* [literally "one who is marked with the cross" when vowing to go to Jerusalem] during the thirteenth century.[102] Moreover, to wage war in the name of the "Gospel of Peace" for the "King of Peace" appeared absurd and irreconcilable to Christians, at least up until the eve of the First Crusade. Warfare "was far from having the Church's blessing and approval: it stood under its condemnation. Far from being a legitimate service in the name of Christ, the profession of arms was not really fitting for a Christian man."[103]

Yet, warfare has been a topic of reflection within the Church at least since the fourth century when the Roman Empire turned Christian, namely through the writings of St. Augustine, which exerted a huge influence on medieval theologians and canonists. Appropriating a terminology used by

---

"jihad" (see Waldman, *The Fulani Jihad*, 333–55).

98. See Esposito, *Unholy War*, 62–63; Kenney, *Muslim Rebels*, 19–54.

99. Momen, *An Introduction to Shi'i Islam*; *The Twelver Shia in Modern Times*.

100. See Friedmann, *Prophecy Continuous*.

101. See the discussion in Noth, *Heiliger Krieg*, 136–46; and Murphy, ed., *The Holy War*, 103.

102. For *crucesignatus*, see Markowski, *Crucisignatus*, 157–65. For the history of the term *crusade*, see *Oxford English Dictionary*, 1221. The English *crusade* comes into universal use in the English speaking world as late as in the middle of the eighteenth century only. The Latin *cruciata*, the French *croisade*, the Spanish *cruzada*, and the Italian *crociata* are much older. For a comprehensive picture of the crusades, see Murray, *The Crusades*; and Tyerman, *God's War*.

103. Cowdrey, "The Genesis of the Crusades," in Murphy, ed., *The Holy War*, 17.

Tolerance, Convivence, and "Holy Wars"

Cicero already in 44 BC,[104] Augustine upholds the idea of "just war" under the condition that it fulfills the following criteria: first, war has to be the *ultima ratio*, that is, the last means resorted to when every other attempt at resolving an issue has failed; second, that war is declared by a legitimate authority; third, that it is fought for a just cause; and, finally, that the means and weapons used are acceptable.[105] While Augustine wanted to curb bellicosity, not stimulate it, and while he did not ponder "holy war" at all, it is nevertheless through him that the concept of "just war" found a place within Christian theology, even though it lay dormant for centuries.

A principal change in the Latin speaking Church's attitude toward warfare took place during the papacy of Gregory VII (1073–1085) who assigned aristocratic, knightly warriors a place in the salvific ministry of the Church. He wanted them to become *milites Christi*, soldiers of Christ dedicating their swords, virtues, and skills to the service of Christ at the command of the vicar of Saint Peter in office. Besides their personal sanctification the knights should attend with devotion to their ordinary business of wielding arms in defending Christendom and promoting godly order among people. Whoever dies in battle dies, after all, in a "just war" and his reward is the certain forgiveness of sins.[106]

Once the Pope gave lay warriors of noble descent a genuine share in the mission of the Church by declaring as meritorious the use of arms for the sake of Christ, the call to activate this power did not wait for long. Approached in 1095 by then Byzantine Emperor Alexios I Komnenos (1048–1118) to help fight the Seljuk Turks who had taken Jerusalem in 1070 and by 1092 had conquered nearly all places of ancient Christianity in the Near East threatening the extinction of the Christian Byzantine Empire, Pope Urban II (1035–1099) on occasion of the Council of Claremont later that year called on the knights to "take up the cross" and embark on a

---

104. The principal texts are *De Officiis*, of 44 BC, and the earlier *De re publica* (54–51 BC).

105. The main text is Augustine's *De Civitate Dei contra Paganos* (*The City of God against the Pagans*), especially books XV and XIX. Written during the years 413–426 it was an attempt at explaining the conquest of the city of Rome by the Visigoths in 410 and to show that Christians are not responsible for it. Writing more than eight hundred years later, and well aware of the first crusades, Thomas Aquinas (1225–1274) defines the "just war" as a war that is waged with the intention to further the good and/or to prevent evil (*intentio recta*) against those who deserve it on account of a definitive guilt (*auctoritas principis, justa causa*). On the whole issue, see Russell, *The Just War in the Middle Ages*.

106. Robinson, *Gregory VII and the Soldiers of Christ*, 169–92; Murphy, ed., *The Holy War*, 104–5.

pilgrimage to the Holy Land to secure the route to and reclaim the site of the Holy Sepulcher at Jerusalem, forcefully if need be.[107] "*Deus vult*," it is "God's will"! The call found a broad hearing due in part to the fact that the Council offered indulgences for the participants by promulgating: "If any man sets out from pure devotion . . . to liberate the church of God at Jerusalem, his journey shall be reckoned to him in place of all penance."[108] This call and promise led to what was later labeled the "First Crusade" (1096–1099), an armed pilgrimage which despite heavy losses, sacrifices, and poor leadership surprisingly achieved its goal. The trek through non-Christian Seljuk territory was safeguarded by establishing "crusader states"[109] staffed and cared for by members of the newly emerging class of Christian military orders,[110] and, much to their own surprise, Fatimid-ruled Jerusalem fell in 1099. The Christians were quick in interpreting this victory as God's intervention on their behalf and thus—even in the face of acts of unspeakable cruelty—as godly justification of the entire enterprise.[111]

---

107. Riley-Smith, *The First Crusade*; Cowdrey, in Murphy, ed., *The Holy War*, 11–12.

108. *The Councils of Urban II*, quoted by Cowdrey in Murphy, ed., *The Holy War*, 23.

109. These were the County of Edessa (1098), the Principality of Antioch (1098–1268), the County of Tripoli (1109–1289), and the Kingdom of Jerusalem (1099–1291).

110. The military orders combined religious devotion with military virtues by taking on the vow of fighting for the sake of Christ in addition to the three classical monastic ones, which are: poverty, celibacy, and obedience. The first of these was the Order of St. John (also known as Knights Hospitaller), which emerged in 1099 from a brotherhood dedicated to the care of pilgrims to Jerusalem in the Amalfi hospital on site. The second was the order of Templars (*Pauperes commilitones Christi Templique Solomonici*; 1118–1312), and the third worth mentioning here was the order of the Teutonic Knights (*Ordo domus Sanctæ Mariæ Theutonicorum Hierosolymitanorum*), founded in 1190 at Acre. First, it was an order for caring for sick pilgrims, but, like the Hospitallers earlier, it soon became a powerful military order that became instrumental in expanding Christianity in the Baltic regions of Northeastern Europe. For a detailed survey on these orders, see Forey, *The Military Orders*.

111. "It is not surprising that the crusaders were astonished or that they became convinced that the enterprise in which they were engaged really was God's own, that they were experiencing his omnipotent interventionary power, that they really were his chosen people and that their dead were martyrs. It was natural for them to relate all of this to scripture, above all to the trials and triumphs of the Israelites" (Riley-Smith, *The First Crusade*, 154). For reports of the committed cruelty, see *The Siege and Capture of Jerusalem 1099*, http://www.fordham.edu/halsall/source/cde-jlem.html. See also Foss, *People of the First Crusade*, 159–228. The cruelty also affected Jews in Europe who suffered under fierce riots; see: Chazan, *European Jewry and the First Crusade*; and Cohen, *Sanctifying the Name of God*.

Tolerance, Convivence, and "Holy Wars"

Less than fifty years later, after Turkish Muslims reconquered the city of Edessa in 1147, the Papacy issued a new indulgence-bearing call for armed pilgrimage to the Holy Land. This call was powerfully supported by the influential Cistercian Bernard of Clairvaux (1090–1153), the former teacher of then Pope Eugene III (1145–1153).[112] Even though there was competent military leadership by two crowned heads of state, the venture suffered defeat and turned into a nightmare. It disillusioned many early advocates of the cause and sparked growing criticism of what only from then on would be termed "crusades."[113] At the same time, however, the failure in the East increased the determination of the church in the West to pursue "crusading" further, at least until the fall of the city of Acre in 1291, the sole remnant of the last remaining crusader state, the so called former Latin Kingdom of Jerusalem. Simultaneously, the popes became more generous in awarding crusaders' indulgences to everyone defending Christendom or papal politics—be it on the Iberian peninsula against Muslims and Jews (Reconquista, ending in 1492), in the Baltic region against Slavs (Wendish Crusade, 1147), or in France against Christian heretics (Cathar/Albigensian/Waldensian Crusades, 1209–1229)[114]—thereby not only perpetuating religiously motivated warfare but also cultivating a belligerent sentiment against people of other faiths and against nonconformists.

Crusades, then,—very much like *jihād*—are far too complex phenomena to warrant sweeping statements. In the beginning they were not imperial wars; they were, rather, military expeditions of pious feudal knights who sought forgiveness of sins by joining the movement to reclaim and secure the ancient Christian sites for the Church requested by the emperors. The Muslims, who termed these expeditions "Frankish (*Franj*) wars" or "Frankish invasions" because French chevaliers often represented the majority of the troops, did not really feel seriously threatened by these skirmishes in

---

112. See Phillips and Hoch, eds., *The Second Crusade*; and Gervers, ed., *The Second Crusade*. In 1146 Bernard published a circular letter to Archbishops and Bishops of France and Bavaria promoting the call to arms. When the enterprise failed miserably Bernard wrote an apology for his engagement in it in 1149/1152 (see Saint Bernard, *On Consideration*, 1908). Noth has pointed to remarkable parallels between passages of the Qur'an and sermons seeking support for the expedition to the East by Bernard (see *Heiliger Krieg*, 143–44).

113. See Throop, *Criticism of the Crusade*; and Flahiff, *Deus Non Vult*, 162–88.

114. For the Reconquista, see Watt and Cachia, *A History of Islamic Spain*; and O'Callaghan, *Reconquest and Crusade*. For the Slavish Crusade, see Christiansen, *The Northern Crusades*. For the Albigensian/Cathar crusades, see Strayer, *The Albigensian Crusades*; and Graham-Leigh, *The Southern French Nobility and the Albigensian Crusade*.

Beyond "Holy Wars"

Ottoman and Fatimid borderlands.[115] Yet, the idea of "crusade" and the attitude of "crusading" left their mark not only on the Church,[116] but also on the mindset of an entire culture, as perceptively noted by James A. Brundage, "So long as Europeans derived their cultural identity largely from their self-identification as Christians, the Church was able to exercise considerable control over warfare . . . As cultural identifications have changed, however, the remnants of the older categories of warfare have become increasingly dangerous and misleading. The holy war served particular purposes in a specific social and cultural environment. In modern society its vestiges probably do more harm than good."[117]

Jewish rabbis, too, were—and still are—debating whether war waged on religious grounds is justified and permissible. Wrestling with the Biblical tradition which bears testimony to ancient Israel's merciless wars of conquest and extermination in the name of God,[118] the Talmudic discussion distinguishes between a war commanded by God, *milchemet mitzvah/ milkhemet mitzwah* (occasionally also termed *milchemet chovah/milkhemet hovah*) in which everyone has to participate even on *Sabbath*, and a war fought at the discretion of the political authority in power, *milchemet/*

---

115. See Athamina and Heacock, *The Frankish Wars*; C. Hillenbrand, *The Crusades: Islamic Perspectives*; Maalouf, *The Crusades through Arab Eyes*; and Gabrieli, ed., *Arab Historians of the Crusades*.

116. As for instance in the institution of the Inquisition in Spain, Portugal, and Rome, the Christian conquest of Latin America in encountering the Aztec and Inca cultures, the treatment of dissenters by the Church of England, and many mission activities of more recent days as is, for instance, clearly reflected in book titles, like *The Christian Occupation of China: A general survey of the numerical strength and geographical distribution of the Christian forces in China*, published by Stauffer et al. on behalf of the China Continuation Committee, Shanghai. The language of war used in many calls to mission is also very much deceiving as is the name of mission initiatives like "Campus Crusade for Christ."

117. Brundage in Murphy, *The Holy War*, 125.

118. See especially Deut 20:16–18: "But as for the towns of these peoples that the LORD your God is giving you as an inheritance, you must not let anything that breathes remain alive. You shall annihilate them . . . so that they may not teach you to do all the abhorrent things that they do for their gods, and you thus sin against the LORD your God" (see also Deut 3:6; 7:1–2). "Now go and attack Amalek, and utterly destroy all that they have; do not spare them, but kill both man and women, child and infant, ox and sheep, camel and donkey" (1 Sam 15:1–3; see also 1 Chr 4:42–43; Josh 6:17; 10:28–40; Deut 25:19). Herzog and Gichon give an overview and military analysis of these and other texts in their *Battles of the Bible*. See also Rad, *Holy War in Ancient Israel*; Niditch, *War in the Hebrew Bible*. For a more recent struggling with these texts, see Lamm, "Amalek and the Seven Nations," in *War and Peace in the Jewish Tradition*, 201–38.

milkhemet reshut, which allows one to refuse serving in it.[119] While most rabbis categorize only the biblical wars of old against the Amalekites and Canaanites as "divinely ordered" and others argue that the Talmudic tradition intends to inhibit going to war at all because the declaration of "discretionary," "permissible," or "governmentally authorized" wars is made dependent, among other provisos, on the approval of the Sanhedrin—the highest Jewish court, which dissolved in 358 CE[120]—still others disagree and declare the contemporary struggle of the secular State of Israel in Palestine as *milkhemet mitzwah*. Those who hold this view advise their partisans, "Open your eyes! Know the enemy and his goals. Fight back hard. Smite the enemy and deter him. By such means, G-d's name will be sanctified on Earth."[121]

What is interesting, though, is to notice that, despite cherished tradition, "Rabbinic Judaism largely avoided discussion of holy war for the simple reason that it became dangerous and self-destructive" for a minority people living under foreign rules and amidst cultures not their own. "The failed 'holy wars' of the Great Revolt [66–70 CE, also called the First Jewish-Roman war] and the Bar Kokhba Rebellion [123–135/136 CE] eliminated enthusiasm for it ["holy war"] among the survivors engaged in reconstructing Judaism from ancient biblical religion."[122] However, the great medieval philosopher, Torah-scholar, and physician Moses-ben-Maimon (also known as Maimonides or Rambam, 1135–1204) developed some kind of a concept of "holy war," most probably occasioned by discourses on *jihād*. This influence is not surprising since Maimonides spent all his life in the Jewish diaspora—in Spain, Morocco, Palestine, Egypt—wrote in Arabic, and was also court physician to Sultan Saladin.[123] In the last book of his

119. See Inbar, "War in Jewish Tradition"; Goldberg, *Swords and Plowshares*; Schiffman and Wololwelsky, eds., *War and Peace in the Jewish Tradition*.

120. See Rabbi D. Hartman, "Rabbinic Limitations on War," http://www.myjewishlearning.com/beliefs/Issues/War_and_Peace/Peace_and_Nonviolence/Limitations_on_War.shtml. As for the institution of the Sanhedrin, its history, and the several attempts to revive it, see "Historical Overview," Thesanhedrin.org, http://www.thesanhedrin.org/ en/index.php/ Historical_Overview.

121. So Rabbi Dov Begon, "We are waging a milkhemet mitzwah," Israelnationalnews.com, http://www. israelnationalnews.com/Articles/Article.aspx/6412. See also Rabbi Meir Kahane, "Parashat Ki Tetzei: Holiness in Times of War," meir-kahne.angelfire.com, http://meir-kahane.angelfire.com/kitetzei.html.

122. Firestone, "Holy War in Modern Judaism?," 954; original emphasis.

123. Davidson, *Moses Maimonides*; Kraemer, *Maimonides*; and Shapiro, *Studies in Maimonides and His Interpreters*.

Beyond "Holy Wars"

multi-volume code of Jewish law (*halakha*) called *Mishneh Torah* written during the years 1170–1180, Maimonides tackles the duties of a king of the Jews—the "Messianic king," to be sure[124]—whose "deeds shall be for the sake of heaven. His purpose and intent shall be to elevate the true faith and fill the world with justice, destroying the power of the wicked and waging the wars of God. For the entire purpose of appointing a king is to execute justice and wage wars as 1 Samuel 8:20 states: 'Our king shall judge us, go out before us, and wage our wars.'"[125]

Before declaring a war (*milchemet reshut*) the king is bound to offer peace to the people Israel wants to subjugate—save some[126]—by asking them to pay tribute, accept an inferior state of citizenship, and abide by the seven Noahide laws.[127] If they refuse this offer the king may legitimately proclaim war provided the Sanhedrin approves. He then has to appoint and properly install a priest of war (*meshuach milchamah*) for the task of identifying among the conscripted those entitled not to serve like those having bought a vineyard and have not yet enjoyed its first crop or having just been engaged to a fiancé. These people he has to dismiss from the army by sending them back home. After having done so the war-priest has to encourage and motivate the remaining troops for battle.[128] Opting out of the draft is permissible only in a *milchemet reshut*, not in a *milchemet mitzvah*.[129] However, for Maimonides *milchemet mitzvah* does not refer to the

---

124. *Mishneh Torah, Sefer Shoftim, Melachim uMilchamot*, chapter 4, halacha 8, according to the translation by E. Touger at Chabad.org, http://www.chabad.org/library/article_cdo/aid/682956/jewish/Mishneh-Torah.htm.

125. Ibid., chapter 4, halacha 10.

126. "No offer of a peaceful settlement should be made to Ammon and Moav, as Deuteronomy 23:7 states: 'Do not seek their peace and welfare for all your days.' Our Sages declared: Although it is written: 'Offer peaceful settlement,' does this apply to Ammon and Moab? The Torah states: 'Do not seek their peace and welfare.' Although it is written Deuteronomy 23:17: 'He must be allowed to live alongside you in your midst,' does this apply to Ammon and Moav? No, the Torah forbids 'their welfare.' Even though we should not offer them a peaceful settlement, if they sue for peace themselves, we may accept their offer" (ibid., 6, 6).

127. These are: avoidance of idolatry, murder, theft, sexual immorality, blasphemy, abstaining from eating flesh of animals still alive, and establishing just laws for the community; see Barre, *Torah for Gentiles*; and Dallen, *The Rainbow Covenant*.

128. *Mishneh Torah, Sefer Shoftim, Melachim uMilchamot* 7, 1+2.

129. In "a *milchemet mitzvah*, the entire nation must go out to war, even a groom from his chamber, and a bride from her pavilion" (ibid., 7, 4).

Tolerance, Convivence, and "Holy Wars"

wars waged once against Amalekites and Canaanites only, but to each and every "war fought to assist Israel from an enemy which attacks them."[130]

Maimonides' younger contemporary, Catalan Rabbi Moses ben Nahman Girondi (also known as Nahmanides or Ramban, 1194–1270), himself a famous Torah teacher, philosopher, and physician,[131] took serious issue with Maimonides' stance on discretionary wars (*milchemot reshut*) especially with regard to the conquest of the Promised Land. Nahmanides held that to conquer and settle Israel, the land given to Abraham, Isaac, and Jacob, is a standing divine order, a commanded war, *milchemet mitzwah*, which binds every Jew in every generation.[132] This conflict set the tone of a vivid, still ongoing debate between Jewish religious activists, especially religiously orthodox Zionists who are convinced that the resettlement of Israel by Jews will hasten the coming of the Messiah, and those who hold that such interpretation of Holy Scripture is cultivating a highly questionable notion of "holy war" which is diametrically opposed to the core tenets of Judaism.[133]

The various discourses on "holy war" within the different religious traditions just surveyed certainly reflect the reality of the threat of annihilation faced. The discourses surveyed obviously attempt to reconcile the reality of actual warfare with the religious teachings, the respective cultural standards, and the cherished norms of what is deemed to be good and appropriate. Thus, such discourses mirror efforts of not getting lost in chaos by arguing for the cause of war as a means to achieve the ultimate good. It is, however, noteworthy to realize that none of these traditions speaks of "holy war" as such. Every religious tradition uses specific and distinct signifiers instead, like *jihād, crusade, milchemet mitzwah*, upholding *dhārma*, fighting the cause of Ahura Mazda, conquest by *dhamma*. Thus it becomes obvious that "holy war" is a generalizing interpretative term for a broad

---

130. Ibid, 5, 1. Maimonides, however, made it clear elsewhere that he understood the fights against Amalek and the Canaanites as fights against idolatry and immorality as is obvious from his answer to the "Positive commandment 187" in his *Book of Commandments* of 1497 (see *The Commandments*). In his *The Guide for the Perplexed* (*Moreh Nevukhim*; originally written in Arabic, too) he mentions that, because the Amalekites and Canaanites are no more, the command applies to the eradication of idolatry (Maimonides, *The Guide for the Perplexed*, 77–78.).

131. See N. Caputo, *Nahmanides in Medieval Catalonia*.

132. Firestone, "Judaism: Medieval Period," 246.

133. See the insightful analysis of Firestone in "Holy War in Modern Judaism?" 954–82. See also Firestone's "This War is about Religion," http://www.shma.com/2001/12/this-war-is-about-religion-and-cannot-be-won-without-it-our-own-house-needs-order/.

range of phenomena which oscillate, as seen, between moral admonitions to individuals and calls to arms of entire populations, between encouragement for personal discipline and spiritual warfare but also support of annihilation and extermination of enemies. People sometimes fought "holy wars" to defend their cultural-religious identity and to protect innocents in danger of being slaughtered; but "holy war" terminology was—and is—also still used today to justify terrorism. What is common across the board, though, is that "holy war" implies radical commitment and determination to fight for an ultimate cause, something not realized in a new interpretation of "holy wars" which defines these as just being "warfare for ideas."[134] Yet, this construal cannot account for the utter determination of those who engage in it, nor can it explain their willingness to commit horrendous cruelties. Who is willing to die for an idea only? Instead, every "holy warrior" is convinced that the battle fought is justified beyond doubt and worth every sacrifice, so that brutal acts of hatred seem to be justified, too, which, however, would defy any claim to holiness. But resolute determination closes the mind and effectively inhibits any sober mindedness, and it appears that this is precisely what those want to achieve among their following who declare "holy-wars." Those strategists fear nothing as much as the demoralizing effect of critical consciousness among their following.[135]

---

134. Cowdrey in Murphy, ed., *The Holy War*, 11.

135. Maimonides's *Mishneh Torah* may be cited as one text of interest here because he addressed this issue in *Sefer Shoftim, Melachim uMilchamot* 7, halacha 15, with these words: "To whom does the phrase 'Is there a man who is afraid or faint-hearted?' refer? The phrase should be interpreted simply, as applying to a person whose heart is not brave enough to stand in the throes of battle. Once a soldier enters the throes of battle, he should rely on the Hope of Israel and their Savior in times of need. He should realize that he is fighting for the sake of the oneness of God's Name. Therefore, he should place his soul in his hand and not show fright or fear. He should not worry about his wife or children. On the contrary, he should wipe their memory from his heart, removing all thoughts from his mind except the war. Anyone who begins to feel anxious and worry in the midst of battle to the point where he frightens himself violates a negative commandment, as it is written (Deuteronomy 20:5): 'Do not be faint-hearted. Do not be afraid. Do not panic and do not break ranks before them.' Furthermore, he is responsible for the blood of the entire Jewish nation. If he is not valiant, if he does not wage war with all his heart and soul, it is considered as if he shed the blood of the entire people, as ibid., 20:8 states: 'Let him go home, lest he demoralize the hearts of his brethren like his own.' Similarly, the prophetic tradition explicitly states: 'Cursed be he who does God's work deceitfully. Cursed be he who withholds his sword from blood.' Jeremiah 48:10 In contrast, anyone who fights with his entire heart, without fear, with the intention of sanctifying God's name alone, can be assured that he will find no harm, nor will bad overtake him. He will be granted a proper family in Israel and gather merit for himself

Tolerance, Convivence, and "Holy Wars"

Every declaration of war indicates a failure of communication in attempting to solve a precarious situation *humanely*. War perpetuates hostility and bloodshed; it does not solve the problems it purports to address. Moreover, to declare a war as "holy" is contradicting itself since it ennobles an unholy act, arrogating to itself supreme authority and demanding ultimate commitment; that is the reason the term appears here in quotation marks throughout. The very moment violence flares up, safeguarding and shielding threatened life take top priority, of course. The immediate reaction by armed resistance appears well justified, but it comes at the price of choking off dialogue. If there is no resistance to violence except violence, human life becomes hell. Until the direct threat is over and genuine human communication reemerges again, one has to fear for the worst. The best, therefore, would be to eliminate perilous situations altogether by fostering a robust culture of dialogue within society from early on, because such an attitude will preempt any serious consideration of taking to arms for settling conflicts at all.

Of course, there might come times when in defending what one cherishes most, one will have to make sacrifices for the sake of life, including risking or even giving up one's own life. But to be conscious of these existential risks neither endorses violence nor does it approve victimization.[136] Such an attitude, rather, reflects a clear sobriety about the reality of violence: recognizing that "holy wars" and intolerance pose real threats, it does not give in to it. At the same time people entertaining fostering dialogue are also aware of the fact that to ignore aggression or suppress violence will not render these ineffective. Instead, only when explicitly addressed do violence, aggression, and hatred become accessible for rational discourse. Once these are raised to the level of consciousness, one becomes enabled to appropriately intervene and deescalate perilous situations in genuinely *human* ways of problem-solving.

In contrast, declaring war is submitting to pressures exercised by powers of various kinds—military and ideological, economic and psychological.

---

and his children forever. He will also merit eternal life in the world to come as I Samuel 25:28–29 states: 'God will certainly make my lord a faithful house, for my lord fights the wars of God and evil will not be found with you . . . and my lord's soul will be bound in a bond of life with God.'" The same holds good with Krishna's advice to prince Arjuna in the *Bhagavad-Gita* and others.

136. On the discussion of religion and violence, see Girad, *Violence and the Sacred*; Bromley and Melton, eds., *Cults, Religion, and Violence*; and Cavanaugh, *The Myth of Religious Violence*.

Beyond "Holy Wars"

However, dialogue—in this case most probably multilateral diplomacy on various levels—must never be suspended even if war is going on. Those who would mediate must pursue diplomacy and dialogue all the more in order to keep the damage at bay and seek whatever communication between opponents might still be possible. Sometimes this will not be much, but the little that can be achieved plays a decisive role in opponents' coming to their senses by realizing that the declared "enemies" are human beings like themselves. As the next chapter will explore more extensively, the only truly humane alternative to warfare is to seek dialogue.

4 Dialogue, Encounter, and Dialogical Thinking

CHAPTER 2 HAS ESTABLISHED that the terminology commonly used to describe religious phenomena and diversity is inadequate. The preceding chapter, however, has emphasized that despite this admitted limitation there is need for explicit articulation of significant religious differences so that convivence may succeed. In response to both the inadequacy of terminology and the need for communication about religious phenomena, what emerged as the means best suitable to do justice to both is dialogue—that is, finding adequate means of communication about religious matters and fostering mutual trust. This chapter further qualifies the nature of dialogue, probing its heart and uncovering the power of its practice.

The first section examines dialogue in itself: its nature, dynamic, and actual engagement. Dialogue is shown to be a particular way of communication among humans *as humans*, so that when dialogue breaks up, human interaction becomes seriously impaired. The second section of the chapter then moves into philosophical reflection on personal human encounter and dialogical thinking, introducing readers to dialogical philosophy (or the so-called philosophy of encounter). The insights gained by proponents of this philosophy are crucial in understanding not only the dynamic of dialogue but why fostering a robust culture of dialogue is most important in a world torn apart by suspicion, hatred, and the looming clash of civilizations. The third section of the chapter, finally, links the insights on dialogical thinking with the pursuit of interreligious dialogue.

Beyond "Holy Wars"

Interpersonal Encounter: The Heart of Dialogue

What is at the heart of dialogue? The plain, simple answer is, of course, the face-to-face encounter of people talking to one another to exchange their views on matters of mutual concern. Thus, dialogue presupposes human community, or, to use the terminology developed previously, dialogue presupposes convivence. This holds also true in an age where social media seem to have lifted space and time restraints, creating the feeling that the world—the entire world, indeed—is at one's own fingertips. However, communication, let's say, on Facebook or Twitter significantly differs from personal encounter face-to-face since it makes everyone using these media be everywhere, but actually nowhere. Sending text messages and posting blogs is virtual personal communication only, with imagined individuals in mind, known and unknown alike. It actually allows—nay, it encourages—hiding behind an alias, a nickname, staying anonymous, or even pretending to be someone else, taking on a network identity. Talking face-to-face in a shared physical space, in contrast, requires corporeal personal presence at one and the same place and time, requires acknowledgment of the actual here and now. This difference is important insofar as it poses specific challenges to the process of communication: In the virtual world no cultural divides seem to exist, everything is reduced to surface information allowing for a multitude of interpretations; whereas, in the actual real world, however, many divides—sensory, intellectual, emotional—come into play and help one to discern what is on the other's mind. Thus, only dialogue can help develop the mental, psychological, and social skills necessary to maintain human community in the face of threats to peaceful convivence. Without dialogue, living togetherness in an increasingly diverse environment is in acute danger of turning into animalistic vitalism, with the survival of the fittest as top priority.

One of the distinctive features of the social life of humans is their communication by language: "It is language which has made man human."[1] Without language human capabilities are slow to develop, if they develop at all. To check on this, the scientifically minded, very rational medieval Emperor Frederic II of Hohenstaufen (1194–1250) conducted—among other dubious experiments—a language deprivation test with young infants, raising them without interaction by word or gesture to find out if these children would develop a natural language on their own. Foster-mothers

---

1. Herder, *Ideen zur Philosophie der Geschichte der Menschheit*, 231 (my translation).

Dialogue, Encounter, and Dialogical Thinking

and nurses were to suckle, bathe, and wash the children, but not to speak with them or show them any affection. As it turned out, the children could not live without these interactions and withered away.[2]

Further, no one can live in complete isolation without losing distinct human capacities over time. This is impressively presented in the Robert Zemeckis movie "Cast Away" first screened in 2000.[3] The main character in this movie, Chuck Noland (played by Tom Hanks), a hectic and time-conscious manager in the business of global logistics, comes to his senses again on a tiny uninhabited island after his cargo plane has crashed into the Pacific Ocean. Finding himself deserted and without any high-tech communication devices that mattered so much in his professional life, Chuck has to learn to survive like a modern Robinson Crusoe. While he does pretty well at this he soon realizes that talking to someone is what he misses most. Thus he paints a face on a washed ashore volleyball from the plane's wreckage and starts conversing and arguing with "Wilson" as he calls it. After a couple of years Chuck succeeds in escaping his solitude on a makeshift raft, taking "Wilson" along to keep him company. Unfortunately though, one day "Wilson" gets lost in the ocean, leaving Chuck overcome by loneliness and determined to die. However, the crew of a freighter passing by pulls his raft aboard and, in the end, returns Chuck to civilization after an overall absence from home of four years.

This movie is instructive insofar as it shows what life looks like when scaled back to its essentials. First of all Chuck must meet some vital basic needs for survival like finding food, making fire, and seeking shelter. But as soon as the basic needs are met, one way or the other in No-land, Chuck longs for communication with other humans. Even though "Wilson" is of Chuck's own making, "Wilson" somehow serves him as a surrogate counterpart helping him stay human. This communication is crucial to Chuck's life—so much so that when "Wilson" falls overboard Chuck desires nothing as much as to quit life and die.

While Chuck and "Wilson" shared a life-preserving interaction, human to human contact is so much richer. When people talk to one another face-to-face, they share much more than just information about something or someone. Certainly, some start talking with a particular goal in mind, perhaps to sell a product or a service, to give instructions on how to operate

---

2. See the *Chronicles* by Franciscan friar Salimbene, at Internet Medieval Sourcebook, http://www.fordham.edu/halsall/source/salimbene1.html.

3. A 20th Century Fox film, starring Tom Hanks, Helen Hunt, and Paul Sanchez.

machinery, or to teach a particular skill. However, most of the time people converse to interact and to disclose what is on their hearts and minds. Even when they are just chatting, humans share joys and sorrows, concerns and reflections, emotions and worries, fears, hope and love. In talking to one another folks not only communicate about how and who they are, but also what to make of challenges faced, how to understand a situation, how to express personal feelings like courtship and tender love. In so doing humans struggle to come to an understanding of what a particular life situation is all about and what they may or should do to engage it rightly. Wherever conflict looms but people are still talking to each other, there is hope for avoiding a clash—maybe only a glimmer of hope, but hope nonetheless. This possibility of hope arises not only in the private sphere of human interrelationships in marriage, family, and with friends, but also in relationships on the social and political planes among peoples of the world. What a sign of hope and relief when news breaks that sides to a bitter conflict have once again returned to the negotiating table, be it in labor disputes or attempts to settle political turmoil.

If, and as long as, talks are going on among those who are suspicious of and hostile to one another, there is hope for strengthening an all too fragile peace, and to maintain peace is of paramount importance for the thriving of life. In the words of Jewish philosopher Martin Buber (1878–1965), "In a genuine dialogue each of the partners, even when he stands in opposition to the other, heeds, affirms, and confirms his opponent as an existing other. Only so can conflict certainly not be eliminated from the world, but be humanely arbitrated and led towards its overcoming."[4]

Wherever people have stopped talking, convinced that there is "no longer anything to say," the situation turns dangerous, because alienation creeps in and anxiety and fear aggravate. Matters then quickly turn from coexistence and convivence to confrontation and scapegoating. When tensions rise, rational sobriety more easily gives way to the pressure of vested interests, and each side looks to shield its own interests by wielding power instead of devoting skills and imagination to solving actual problems. Every time explicit confrontation flares up, nothing but power and craving for military supremacy holds sway. On the political plane, once diplomatic negotiations come to a standstill, war is not far off, as it so happened in

---

4. Buber, "Genuine Dialogue and the Possibilities of Peace," in Buber, *Pointing the Way*, 238.

Dialogue, Encounter, and Dialogical Thinking

the more recent past in the Balkan wars of 1991–2001,[5] the genocides in Rwanda[6] and in the Sudan,[7] to mention only a few.

Given that staying in dialogue is crucial for *humanely* solving or at least arbitrating conflicts, it becomes necessary to describe dialogue more precisely so as to distinguish it clearly from other forms of verbal communication and interaction, because humans carry on conversation with one another in numerous ways. The particular situation and form of the actual verbal communication matter, as is obvious from the difference between casual remarks made among friends and official pronouncements in a public forum. Also, our speaking changes significantly depending on whom we address. Is it a person in authority like a judge, a priest, a lawmaker? Is it our boss, the CEO of our company, a client? Is it a friend, a family member, a peer or a colleague? Communication changes significantly, too, if it is official talk such as that of a political or diplomatic mission or casual conversation or just private chatting. There are many ways in which people speak and stay in conversation with one another. Identifying these and placing them in a table allows breaking down the more generalized concept of verbal communication quickly while at the same time highlighting distinctive features of each.

Table: Forms of being-in-conversation-with-one-another

Description of Meaning	Technical Term
talking to one another about something for the sake of staying in communication	chat; gossip
(Latin: *conversatio*: association with someone); to keep company and be in conversation with someone, to have a talk with someone; (Greek: διάλογος)	conversation; informal talk
talking with or to oneself	monologue; soliloquy
(French: *débat*: lively discussion); argumentation, speaking pro and con; especially detailed consideration and formal discussion of a topic before the legislature	debate; deliberation

5. See Bideleux and Jeffries, *A History of Eastern Europe*; and Allen, *Rape Warfare*.

6. See Melvern, *Conspiracy to Murder*; and Scherrer, *Genocide and Crisis in Central Africa*.

7. See Totten and Markusen, eds., *Genocide in Darfur*; and Straus, "Darfur and the Genocide Debate."

Description of Meaning	Technical Term
(Latin: *disputare, disputatio*, literally: charge) formal rhetorical exercise in which someone proposes and defends a thesis or in which two parties reason in opposition to each other; controversial interchange	disputation
(Greek: διάλογος: conversation); talk, conversational exchange; especially a serious colloquy intended to instruct and come to an understanding	dialogue
(Latin: *discursus*, literally: to run to and fro; then: to hold forth) to speak or write at some length systematically on a subject; methodically organized treatment of a topic; exchange of ideas by a reflective account of the subject matter	discourse
(Latin: *negotiari*: to carry on business); communication by conferences aimed at settling some disputed matter through discussion by agreeing upon a compromise, especially in business or politics	negotiation
semi-official forum for discussion and deliberation by all parties involved in and affected by particular issues for the sake of finding a solution	roundtable talk
technical term referring to the transmission of meaning in human interaction and systematically studied in Dialogue Research and Communications Theory	communication

The above table shows what falls practically within the meaning of dialogue and what makes up its specifics, an understanding quite different from the concerns of the semantically oriented dialogue research and analysis, even though the groups share the term.[8] As can be easily discerned, dialogue is more than just an exchange of information or simply being-in-

---

8. The "International Association of Dialogue Analysis" (IADA) was founded in 1990. For its publications, see Hundsnurscher, *Future Perspectives of Dialogue Analysis*; Weigand and Hauenherm, *Dialogue*; Naumann, *Dialogue Analysis and the Mass Media*.

Dialogue, Encounter, and Dialogical Thinking

conversation. Admittedly, to exchange information is always part of what it means to be in dialogue, but that certainly does not exhaust its meaning. Even less so is dialogue equivalent to negotiation, in which opposing parties try to reconcile conflicting interests and attempt to reach a compromise acceptable for all stakeholders. As mandated representatives, negotiating partners are concerned with the preservation of partisan interests, an attitude that would be quite deadly for dialogue, especially that devoted to religious matters.

Dialogue, understood as genuine conversation among humans, is concerned neither with domination or power, nor with balancing interests. Rather, dialogue has everything to do with gaining adequate insight and proper understanding which simply is not attainable otherwise except by dialoguing. That is why dialogue—unlike waging negotiations, for instance—can never break down or fail. Dialogue can come to a standstill, of course, when participants shun further communication and refrain from any binding commitment.[9] As in every good conversation, moments of creative silence or pauses occur for thought in dialogue, too, but taking a break is different from shunning dialogue altogether. To stifle dialogue out of a perceived sense of threat or fear of potential loss means opting out of communication in face of differences and difficulties instead of working to overcome these. Opting out of dialogue paves the way for going to war, as clearly stated in the 9/11 *Commission Report* when concluding that since "there is no common ground . . . on which to begin a dialogue" with the terrorists, they "can only be destroyed or utterly isolated."[10] Such an attitude, perhaps understandable, is still a highly questionable recommendation if one seeks sustainable peace.

Just as dialogue is not identical with negotiation, it is also not equal to casual conversation. In terms of function, dialogue comes very close to roundtable talks, gatherings which have gradually become a well-established practice in political culture since the beginning of the twentieth century.[11] Roundtable talks, too, aim to resolve common problems by equally

---

9. A very interesting contribution addressing this topic is Dodd's famous "Letter Concerning Some Unavowed Motives in Ecumenical Discussions." See also Margull, "Verwundbarkeit" [*Vulnerability: Remarks on Dialogue*].

10. *The 9/11 Commission Report*, 362.

11. Roundtable talks as a political means for solving issues of national interests played an important role in in the twentieth century, beginning with the Anglo-India roundtable conferences in London, 1930–1932 (see Menon, *Integration of the Indian States*), and the Dutch-Indonesian roundtable conference of 1949 (see Ricklefs, *A History of Modern*

involving every party affected. The ideal of facing one another at the same table, not in a confrontational way but in mutual fellowship concerned with finding ways into a livable future for all—that is why the table is round, not rectangular—has been powerfully captured in the Arthurian legend since the early Middle Ages.[12] Yet, dialogue does not exhaust itself in problem solving, as do roundtable talks. To perceive dialogue as merely a method or tool for mediation of conflicts is to misunderstand it, because such a perception limits it to achieving goals—goals removed from the process of dialogue itself. It is by the interpersonal nature of its process in the encounter with others that dialogue comes into its own and achieves goals which encompass but at the same time also transcend the merely practical.

The Greek root of dialogue means simply: to talk, to speak to one another, to be in conversation with someone. Dialogue, thus, is primarily interpersonal communication with words and the distinctive human way of sharing life. It renounces any intention to use the other, the counterpart, as a means to an end. Instead, getting involved in dialogue implies sharing in human commonness and existential experience by seriously respecting others and honoring their personal integrity. A more refined attempt at definition could describe dialogue as a thematic, content-oriented conversation about contentious questions of existential significance, with which people wrestle in a shared process of honest, authentic deliberation for the sake of maintaining convivence, notwithstanding differences.

However, mere verbal argumentation does not satisfy dialogue either, for such talk can quickly turn into a bluff or a kind of monologic shadow-boxing. Dialogue is something different still, since it also requires commitment to a cognitive process shared with people of different backgrounds holding diverse maxims informed by specific core values and beliefs. The goal of dialoguing is neither to level nor to achieve mish-mash uniformity or conformity of thinking and unanimous opinion. Nor is dialogue concerned with balancing group interests or proselytizing others. Dialogue does not intend or seek to convince or persuade, either. Dialogue, rather, seeks to gain a profound understanding of and insight into apparently irreconcilable tensions through the process of talking to one another—insights not accessible or available any other way. Only from experiences along this way

---

Indonesia). More recently roundtable talks paved the way for a convivial future in post-communist Eastern Europe (see Ash, *The Magic Lantern*; Elster, *The Roundtable*; Bozóki, *The Roundtable Talks of 1989*; Lawson, *Negotiated Revolutions*).

12. As far as historical and literary details of the Arthurian legend and the specifics of the roundtable are concerned, see *The New Arthurian Encyclopedia*.

Dialogue, Encounter, and Dialogical Thinking

does genuine mutual trust build, trust that can accommodate tensions as these arise in any convivential situation. On this basis, human life truly can thrive in all its variety and diversity.

To come to this point is, of course, an achievement not only arduous, but also risky. It expects of all dialogue participants to be willing—if need be—to break away from and put behind them cherished, trusted suppositions (which actually might turn out in the process to be unfounded prejudices) in order to embark on and travel down roads unknown till now, with companions as yet unfamiliar. Would making this journey require a complete and cavalier surrender of one's own insights and proven principles? Certainly not; rather, dialogue calls all participants mutually to examine long held maxims and principles and to re-own them authentically by re-discovering their plausibility and value in face of the actual challenges at hand.

There is no reason—and herein lies the chief evil and pitfall of any fundamentalist refusal of dialogue religious or political—to exempt from dialogue *any* basic principle, insight, or value. However ready for dialogue one may be in terms of attitude, no authentic communication can take place if one shields treasured insights from the broad daylight of competing alternatives. The most that might be achieved this way will be a lukewarm, unconvincing, fraternizing gesture pretending to be hospitable and friendly to strangers. But reservations can never dismantle suspicion and mistrust. Any such kind of talking about differences involves resistance from the outset and, thus, will be very limited in its impact. It keeps strangers at arm's length and does not take their concerns seriously enough. The price of such mock-dialogue is high, for this conversation can never effectively control anxieties and fear of imminent or potential threat, which tend to aggravate the situation more acutely, the less the actual differences are understood. In short, mock- or sham-dialogues don't cultivate genuine trust but spur anxieties instead and thereby undermine convivence and peaceful coexistence.

Dialogue is, of course, not immune from abuse, because speaking and talking back and exchanging views are essentially sequences of speech-acts. The success of dialogue, therefore, critically depends on the way the individual partakers use language, and thus on their actual intentions and personal authenticity in how they avail of language. Dialogue succeeds to that degree in which speakers are able to achieve factual adequacy as well as congruence between what they are actually saying and what they are, in fact, thinking, implying, or intending. One can very well sit at the negotiating table and speak eloquently, all the while aiming to disguise one's actual intention in order to leave the conversation partners in the dark, or to render them compliant by subtle manipulation, because speaking—in and of itself—is not all there is. Much more depends on whether this speaking is authentic and sincere. Mere speaking can be blatantly and entirely monologic; it may even intend to remain so, as long as those speaking do not make a point of coming to an understanding with others, but are, instead, intent on accomplishing something quite different. However, any kind of instrumentalized, inauthentic speech is a subtle form of despotism, such as the cutting remarks and denigrating comments of harassment or the excessive accolades of advertising, which aim to persuade in order to promote certain products and services. Because this misuse of language extends beyond the private and personal realms, it becomes especially harmful when consciously put to use for ideological ends, for instance, in a particular political propaganda.

To illustrate the last remark: In Germany during the time of the Third Reich (1933–1945) the philologist Victor Klemperer (1881–1960), himself as Jew confined to his home at Dresden and banned from access to books or literature of any kind, observed, analyzed, and studied the use of language in Nazi propaganda he randomly ran across. His findings are somewhat—disturbingly—surprising:

> What was the most powerful Hitlerian propaganda tool? Was it the individual speeches of Hitler and Goebbels, their pronouncements on this or that theme, their rabble-rousing against Jews, against Bolshevism? . . . No, the most powerful influence was exerted neither by individual speeches nor by articles, flyers, posters or flags; it was not achieved by things which one had to absorb by conscious thought or conscious emotions.
>
> Instead Nazism permeated the flesh and blood of the people through single words, idioms, and sentence structures which were imposed on them in a million repetitions and taken on board mechanically and unconsciously . . . The Third Reich coined only a very small number of the words in its language, perhaps—indeed probably—none at all. In many cases Nazi language points to foreign influences and appropriates much of the rest from the German language before Hitler. But it changes the values of words and the frequency of their occurrence, it makes common property out of what was previously the preserve of an individual or a tiny group, it commandeers for the party [the NSDAP] that which was previously common property and in the process steeps words and

Dialogue, Encounter, and Dialogical Thinking

groups of words and sentence structures with its poison. Making language the servant of its dreadful system it procures it as its most powerful, most public and most surreptitious means of advertising.[13]

Abuse of language threatens to be fatal for *every* community because it destroys authentic human communication and gives rise to acts of violence. Though this power was once again brought to public attention more recently in the U.S. in the tragic shooting incident in January, 2011, at Tucson, Arizona,[14] it had already been addressed by the ancient Greek philosopher Plato (428/427–347 BCE), who in his various dialogues branded as abusers of language the eloquent, intelligent Sophists who played with words as they pleased, twisting the meaning for the sake of achieving calculated effects on the audience but not really communicating genuine understanding and knowledge, save their own interests.[15] Thus, the Sophists became synonymous with evil, corrupt twisters of wisdom by abusing language and turning it "into an instrument of rape" which "*does* contain violence, albeit in latent form."[16] Several millennia later, Victor Klemperer's observations reconfirmed the violence of language so manipulated, and a younger contemporary of his, philosopher Josef Piper (1904–1997), studying the Platonic dialogues in-depth, came to a quite similar conclusion,

> [T]he abuse of political power is fundamentally connected with the sophistic abuse of the word, indeed, finds in it the fertile soil in which to hide and grow and get ready, so much so that the latent potential of the . . . poison can be ascertained . . . by observing the symptom of the public abuse of language. The degradation,

---

13. Klemperer, *The Language of the Third Reich*, 15–16.

14. In the aftermath of the shooting of Congresswoman Gabrielle Giffords at Tucson, Arizona, Jan. 8, 2011, *Time Magazine* published a special report, Jan. 24, 2011, titled *Guns. Speech. Madness.* One of the articles analyzed the political rhetoric that was identified as one of the causes triggering this horrible act. The gunman shot eighteen others, hitting six of them fatally, a nine-year old girl among them. See "Are we becoming an uncivil society?" in *Time*, 40–41; no author. Another aspect of the matter in question is the discussion about use and abuse of the First Amendment to the Constitution of the U.S.; see Colussi, "Fighting Words?" 28–30.

15. The dialogue *Gorgias* carries the name of one of the most renowned sophists of Plato's times who lived about 483–376 BCE. One of the last *Dialogues* Plato ever wrote goes by the title *Sophists*. Other of his dialogues referring to sophists are *Parmenides* and *Theaetetus*. See also Brann et al., *Plato: Sophist or the Professor of Wisdom*; Plato, *Sophist*; and Jarratt, *Rereading the Sophists*.

16. Piper, *Abuse of Language*, 32; original emphasis.

> too, of man through man, alarmingly evident in the acts of physical violence committed by all tyrannies (concentration camps, torture), has its beginning, certainly much less alarmingly, at that almost imperceptible moment when the word loses its dignity. The dignity of the word ... consists in this: through the word is accomplished what no other means can accomplish, namely, communication based on reality ... [T]he relationship based on mere power, and thus the most miserable decay of human interaction, stands in direct proportion to the most devastating breakdown in orientation toward reality.[17]

Linking the abuse of language with the corruption of human conviviality might appear far-fetched at first sight. However, it is not so. Cultural critic and philosopher Ivan Illich has also observed this critical function and nexus of language, albeit in the context of the alienation of people by industrial processes. Illich speaks of "the industrial corruption of language" and the "materialization of consciousness ... reflected in Western languages."[18] "The operating code of industrial tools encroaches on everyday language and reduces the poetic self-affirmation of men to a barely tolerated and marginal protest. The consequent industrialization of man can be inverted only if the convivial function of language is recuperated, but with a new level of consciousness. Language which is used by people jointly claiming and asserting each person's right to share in the shaping of the community becomes, so to speak, a second-order tool to clarify the relationships of a people to engineered instrumentalities."[19]

Speaking mindfully and telling the truth have been concerns for many religions from early on, as can be seen in Buddhism where the charge to "Right speech" (*samma-vacha*) is one of the elements of the Noble Eightfold Path promising to lead its travelers to salvation.[20] To discourage gossip, which in the long run not only destroys genuine conversation but severs from community and isolates, Judaism teaches the virtue of guarding the tongue (*sh'mira ha-lashon*).[21] Very much along the same line is the exhortation by Jesus in Matt 5:37, "Let your word be 'Yes, yes' or 'No, no'; anything more than this comes from the evil one." Also instructive in this regard is this statement in the letter of James, "Anyone who makes no mistakes in

---

17. Ibid., 32–33.
18. Illich, *Tools for Conviviality*, 89.
19. Ibid., 91.
20. See Bodi, *The Noble Eightfold Path*, 45–64; Conze, *Buddhism*, 43–48.
21. See Pliskin, *Guard your Tongue*; Gluckman, "Gossip and Scandal."

speaking is perfect . . . Does a spring pour forth from the same opening both fresh and brackish water?" (Jas 3:2, 11).

"Harkening to the human voice, where it speaks forth unfalsified, and replying to it, this above all is needed today," said Martin Buber in his acceptance speech upon receiving the Peace Prize of the German Book Trade at Frankfurt in 1953.[22] His remarks centered on the topic of interest here, since Buber entitled his presentation "Genuine Dialogue and the Possibilities of Peace." He saw the crisis of the times—the Cold War marked by escalating verbal and military confrontations between East and West in the middle of the twentieth century—as caused primarily by the corruption of language and the loss of the ability to make proper use of language and dialogue:

> The man in crisis will no longer entrust his cause to conversation because its presupposition—trust—is lacking. This is the reason why the cold war which today goes by the name of peace has been able to overcome mankind. In every earlier period of peace the living word has passed between man and man, time after time drawing the poison from the antagonism of interests and convictions so that these antagonisms have not degenerated into the absurdity of "no-further" into the madness of "must-wage-war." The living word of human dialogue that from time to time makes its flights until the madness smothers it, now seems to have become lifeless in the midst of the non-war.[23]

Buber, who at the time of his speech was nearly seventy-five years old, had lived through World War I and also World War II, the last having brought the Holocaust upon his people, something he expressly referred to in the opening of the address just quoted. Having immigrated to Palestine in 1938 as a convinced Zionist, he thus spoke in 1953 against the background of shattering personal and communal experiences as well as the so-called Cold War (1947–1991) during which the USSR detonated its first nuclear warhead in reaction to which the NATO (North Atlantic Treaty Organization) was founded (1949), while tension between East and West reached its peak in the Korean War of 1950–1953. It was against *this* background that Buber invoked the power of genuine conversation because, "Peoples must engage in talk with one another through their truly human men if the great

---

22. Buber, *Genuine Dialogue*, 234.
23. Ibid., 236–37.

peace is to appear and the devastated life of the earth renew itself."[24] To entrust dialogue with such power, however, was not an idea of Buber's born at the spur of the moment. This, rather, was an insight gained after long years of study and reflection about human interaction and communication by word, making Buber one of the leading representatives of the so-called philosophy of encounter.[25] A more detailed understanding of this kind of thinking will offer valuable insights into the basic structure of dialogue and thereby advance further reflection on our topic, too.

The Philosophy of Encounter

The philosophy of encounter sometimes also goes by the name "philosophy of dialogical personalism" or "dialogical philosophy." It finds its place—alongside phenomenology and existentialism—among developments attempting a fundamental shift and renewal of philosophy after the traumatic experiences of World War I. It emerged in reaction to the devastating events of 1914–1918 in which the bankruptcy and failure of the optimistic idealisms and humanistic philosophies became all too obvious. The experience of a war on a global scale unveiled to those who had eyes to see the intellectual and human misery of the ideologies entertained in those times. The war exposed the chasm within human reasoning, declared good intentions, and actual action. Reason and rationality foundered since they failed in preventing a disaster of such previously unimaginable dimensions, a failure that brought the principles of philosophical idealism and humanistic optimism crashing down. These principles, eagerly and aggressively promoted by intellectuals since the Enlightenment, had centered on and elevated the critically reflecting autonomous individual as the source of knowledge, assumed to be able to achieve the good on its own; but suddenly, this rational I was losing its orientation in a world become chaos. If reason had been any kind of factor in the situation, there should not have been a war at all (still less a second one to follow a mere twenty years later with its ever more efficient mechanisms of destruction and annihilation). No longer could the cognoscenti claim beyond doubt to occupy a place of mindful oversight and concern for the good. Trust in reason was gone and the moral and humanistic optimism lay in shambles.

---

24. Ibid., 235.
25. See Friedman, *Martin Buber*; Avnon, *Martin Buber: The Hidden Dialogue*.

Dialogue, Encounter, and Dialogical Thinking

This disillusionment brought about a rupture that led to a radical break with the past not only in philosophy, but in art[26] as well as in theology[27] and elsewhere. In philosophy Edmund Husserl (1859–1938) presented a new, more radical version of phenomenology,[28] and his student Martin Heidegger (1889–1972) felt urged to rephrase in *Being and Time* the basic philosophical questions of old, a text which became the programmatic source of existentialism.[29] The philosophy of encounter came about as a third distinct kind of philosophical reflection during these post-bellum years, too. It emerged as result of the intensive study and re-reading of religious texts, above all the scriptures of Judaism, putting it in sharp contrast to the often nihilistic character of existentialism, with which it was occasionally confused in its early years.[30] Today, however, hardly anyone outside a small, informed circle is aware that this kind of thinking ever existed.[31] This lacuna results, at least in part, from this philosophy's resistance to systematization of terms and thoughts. In fact, any such endeavor goes straight against its fundamental intentions and insights. Systematization, rather, would contradict the very core of the philosophy of encounter, which is to see the other person as truly another *person*, not as an object. Nor does *the other* fit any idea or concept of the other. *The other* is always a *You* with whom I communicate in the here and now. This turn toward

---

26. The new art-form emerging was called Dadaism, which is not so much concerned with aesthetics as with the bare elements of language (syllables, letters, sounds), painting (color, shape, medium), and sculpture (form, material), music and theater, etc.; see Richter, *Dada*; Jones, ed., *Dada Culture*.

27. The dialectic theology emerged in 1921 with Karl Barth's second edition of his commentary on Romans.

28. A good survey of the *post bellum* development of Husserl's philosophy is found in Smith and Woodruff Smith, ed., *The Cambridge Companion to Husserl*, 45–77. See also Spiegelberg, *The Phenomenological Movement*; and Zaner and Ihde, eds., *Phenomenology and Existentialism*.

29. The first version of *Sein und Zeit* appeared in 1926 and was given as gift to Husserl, to whom Heidegger had dedicated the script. The tenth edition was published in 1963 at Tübingen by Max Niemeyer. An English translation, *Being and Time*, was provided by Macquarrie and Robinson in 1962. For help with the idiosyncratic, difficult style of Heidegger, see Mulhull *Routledge Philosophy Guidebook to Heidegger and "Being and Time."*

30. On existentialism, see Marcel, *The Philosophy of Existentialism*; Cooper, *Existentialism*; Luper, *Existing: An Introduction to Existential Thought*; and Appignanesi, *Introducing Existentialism*.

31. Böckenhoff has given an authoritative and comprehensive survey of this school of thought in his detailed study *Die Begegnungsphilosophie*.

the personal, living You [Thou, *Du*] makes every encounter [*Begegnung*] become a voyage of discovery of someone like, yet very different from, me, and it is in moments of such encounters that life actually happens. It is not the general, abstract ideas which matter in actual life; it is the actual encounter with a *You*. Every encounter with a You is not establishing a subject-object relationship but a subject-subject relationship instead, thereby radically changing the outlook on the world. It is through relationship with other human beings as You that the world around becomes accessible and known; it is through communicating with others that real understanding and comprehension emerges. This approach challenges the Enlightenment predicament to the core, so much so that some hailed the philosophy of encounter as a "Copernican act."[32]

The most famous, most influential, and most articulate representative of this approach has been Martin Buber with his thoroughgoing reflections on the I-Thou relationship.[33] Other representatives besides him were Austrian pedagogue Ferdinand Ebner (1882–1931), a Christian; and the Jewish philosophers Franz Rosenzweig (1886–1929); Hermann Cohen (1842–1918); and, more recently, Emmanuel Lévinas (1906–1995).[34]

I and Thou (1923), Martin Buber's first major work, contains the fundamental and concise statement of the basic assumptions of his thinking. In it Buber first differentiates between the "I-Thou/You" and the "I-It" relationships (always to be read and understood as single lexemes or terms) as the two categorically different approaches to perception of world and reality. Buber holds that the "I-Thou/You" and "I-It" are the two, distinct "basic words" human beings can speak. While the basic word "I-It" (including "I-He" and "I-She") expresses a relation to one's surroundings as things, the "I-You" signifies a personal encounter, namely the encounter between two individuals as persons. "When I confront a human being as my You and

---

32. See Steinbüchel, *Der Umbruch des Denkens*, 75.

33. *The Philosophy of Martin Buber*; Buber, *I and Thou*; Buber, *Between Man and Man*. A critical edition of the works of Martin Buber is currently underway as a joint venture of the Berliner Akademie der Wissenschaften [Academy of Sciences at Berlin, Germany] and the Israel Academy of Sciences and Humanities titled: *Martin Buber Werkausgabe* [*Martin Buber: Edition of Works*] with P. Mendes-Flohr, P. Schäfer, and M. Urban as editors. It began in 2001 and is projected for twenty-one volumes in all. An authoritative and very comprehensive bibliography of the philosopher has been compiled by Martin Buber's long-time secretary Margot Cohn and his son Rafael Buber: *Martin Buber. A Bibliography of His Writings*.

34. See Burggraeve, ed., *The Awakening to the Other*; Hand, *Emmanuel Levinas*; see also Gibbs, *Correlations in Rosenzweig and Levinas*.

speak the basic word I-You to him," Buber says, "then he is no thing among things nor does he consist of things."[35] Not only is the "You . . . more than It," but this I-You encounter represents in fact "the cradle of actual life," life as actually lived.[36] Life happens in the encounter and in the encounter only; outside the encounter there is no real life, that is, life actually appropriated by an individual personal existence, something which has also been discovered within the context of dialogue with Theravada Buddhism in Sri Lanka, for instance.[37]

Buber reflects upon the term encounter, which refers to the two qualitatively different kinds of experience already mentioned. First and foremost, it denotes the encounter between human beings as persons in the I-You relationship; but, secondly, encounter also refers to the instrumental relationship between a person and an object, namely as the I-He, I-She, or I-It. The qualitative difference between the I-It or I-He/I-She over against the I-Thou encounter lies in the personal relational character of the I to a You, because to speak meaningfully of a You requires the personal presence of the one addressed as You. Availing of the personal pronoun You implies the presence of another person, grasped as You in the actual situation only and accessible as You only when directly so addressed. You is always You only in the presence of an I, and, thus, for the Me to become aware of itself as an I requires the You. As Buber describes it, the experience of encounter comes before any other knowledge of being in the world and of being in relation with. This connection occurs either between two individuals relating as "I-You" to an other "I-You" or between one individual relating as "I-You" to somebody else as "I-He/She" or to something else as "I-It." There *is* no world which is related to just an isolated, autonomous I; there is only a world-with, that is, there is only the I—You—We—It—world. World does not exist outside such relationship. This is the fundamental insight of the philosophy of encounter.

Ferdinand Ebner, one other exponent of this philosophy, held that any human being who endeavors to understand the world solipsistically—that is, solely from within an autonomous self, monologically—is indulging in a fictitious, "dream-like vision of spirit" [*Geist*], mind, or rationality. Consequently, anyone who thinks that he or she gains insight by just applying the faculty of a critical mind and the senses to the phenomena of interest

---

35. Buber, *I and Thou*, 59.
36. Ibid., 60.
37. See de Silva, *The Problem of the Self in Buddhism and Christianity*, 5–6.

misjudges where spirit actually is and how mind operates. Mind and spirit are no independent entities which humans use at liberty. Rather, mind and spirit exist only in the verbal self-constituting relationship of I-You when speaking with one another, because it is in words and language where spirit and mind reside, not the physical brain. However, the fact is that humans seek to compensate for the loss of reality in mindless speaking by aesthetic means. Yet, according to Ebner, humans cannot overcome their I-solitariness all by themselves; they cement it only further. "It is the realization of the relationship of the I-You which makes up the genuine life of the intellect and mind of human beings. It is not where one prefers to see it [i.e., mind, spirit]: because in poetry and art, philosophy and mythical religions, however genial, one is having a dream-like vision of spirit [mind]."[38]

The object of knowledge is not, however, solely and exclusively the other person as such in his or her peculiarity. This would leave out recognition of the non-personal world, the world of animated beings and the world of things, the I-It relationships. Rather, the main concern of the philosophy of encounter is adequate comprehension of the mindful, intellectual, and spiritual reality of the world as a whole and in *all* its aspects, for, as Buber put it: "Spirit in its human manifestation is man's response to a You . . . Spirit is word . . . In truth language does not reside in humans, but humans stand in language and speak from within it—so it is with all words, all of spirit and mind. Spirit and mind are not in the I, but between the I and the You."[39]

It is word as spirit and spirit as word, word as speech and actual speaking that constitute mindful communication between human beings. Humans do not just make language serve their needs. Language, rather, is the common ground, the medium, the "in-between" [*Zwischen*] of spirit among humans.[40] Language as the structured web of spirit-filled words and structures forms the basis of human communication, disclosing the

---

38. Ebner, *Das Wort und die geistigen Realitäten*, 86. Some excerpts from this treatise are quoted by Friedman, *The Worlds of Existentialism*, 292–98. See also Schleiermacher, *Das Heil des Menschen und sein Traum vom Geist*.

39. Buber, *I and Thou*, 89.

40. It is worth noting here that the word for "person" in Japanese is *ningen*, a compound of "human" and "between." Speaking of "person"/*ningen*, thus, de-emphasizes personal individuality as it would be in the West over against the in-betweenness of humans and human interpersonality. So it appears that the Japanese term is reflective of a somewhat similar insight to that of the philosophers of encounter. See Kopf, *Beyond Personal Identity*.

Dialogue, Encounter, and Dialogical Thinking

world as world in the presence of those speaking it in talking to one another. In such exchange of words active participation in actual being takes place. Philosophical reflection understood this way, namely as "speech thinking," bids farewell to abstract concepts and turns toward the grammar of the spoken word of the life-world, a grammar which has greater proximity to reality than abstract deductions or philosophical concepts and systems ever could have.

Reflection on the grammar of the spoken word is also a main topic in Franz Rosenzweig's dense major work *The Star of Redemption*.[41] In opposition to the conventional way of doing philosophy by defining logic and constructing highly abstract systems of reasoning Rosenzweig pleads for a philosophical thinking which follows the language actually spoken and used since it is an expression of the essence of actual being of the speaker. Consequently, terms like "moment" (*Augenblick*), "presence" (*Gegenwart*), and "event" (*Ereignis*) figure prominently in Rosenzweig's existential way of thinking, a thinking which is also moored in the presence of God here and now. God is not a topic for metaphysical speculation according to Rosenzweig; God, rather, is experiential reality in the encounter of humans.[42] The explicit reference to the constitutive importance of God for any inter-human encounter was occasioned in part by Rosenzweig's conscious deciding against conversion to Christianity and re-embracing his Jewish tradition in 1913;[43] in part was this the outcome of his studies with his senior by thirty-two years Hermann Cohen in Berlin, who himself had just experienced something quite similar.

Cohen was, besides Paul Natorp (1854–1924), one of the leading figures of Neo-Kantianism at Marburg in Germany. However, after his retirement from university in 1912, Cohen joined the small Institute for the Scientific Study of Judaism [*Institut für die Wissenschaft vom Judentum*] in Berlin, where two crucial events happened: first, it was at Berlin where Cohen gained a new understanding of his Jewish roots, re-discovering and re-embracing these full heartedly; and it was at the Berlin institute, too, where he, second, developed a non-Kantian approach to human existence, a development about which he gives account in his posthumously

---

41. Rosenzweig, *The Star of Redemption*. It is certainly not an unimportant or small detail to know that the first draft of this book was written in the frontline trenches during World War I.

42. See Glatzer, ed., *Franz Rosenzweig: His Life and Thought*.

43. Rosenstock-Huessy, ed., *Judaism despite Christianity*.

published book *Religion of Reason: Out of the Sources of Judaism*.[44] In this book, which is remarkably different from all his previous publications, Cohen perceived the human individual as constituted not by rational capacity as such—that would be the Kantian approach—but by orientation toward and correlation with God. According to Cohen, all knowledge has its final grounding in God, not in human reason, mind, or intellect. In thus regarding the relationship to God as determinative for human life in the world, Cohen seriously reintroduced a dimension into philosophy, which half a century earlier Ludwig Feuerbach had attempted to eliminate by showing that religion is nothing but anthropology gone astray.[45] This prompted Martin Buber to remark, "something formerly unexpressed in philosophy becomes explicit when it [i.e., the philosophy of H. Cohen] says of the reciprocal relationship of man and God, their 'correlation,' that it could 'not enter into completion if it were not preceded by the inclusive correlation of man and man.'"[46]

How did Cohen arrive at this conclusion so contrary to all that he had done before while teaching Kantian philosophy at Marburg? Was he turning back to a simplistic, childlike faith in a senile fashion? Was he a crypto-apologist who wanted to make a case for religion, his in particular? To argue like this would ignore Cohen's solid standing in the Kantian tradition. This foundational insight was not the result of Kant-like abstract systematic logical deduction in the interest of salvaging Judaism; rather, this pivotal turn came about as the unanticipated discovery of his analysis of the structure of encounter. Cohen realized now the existence of a dialectical relationship between God-human and interhuman interaction. For him human to human communication is dependent on the human to God relationship and vice versa. God does not occupy a separate realm outside this world; God becomes present—or absent—in the world in the way that humans interact and communicate. Everything in life reflects this relationship, even on the level of academic pursuits, be it anthropology, sociology, politics, economics, medicine, etc. According to Cohen it is the closing off and turning away from the personal relationship with the Absolute, the ultimate You, which had led to the fictitious idea of man as an autonomous, solitary I entitled to instrumentalize life and espouse a materialistic attitude as representatives of the Enlightenment tradition did. Hailing an abstract

---

44. Cohen, *Religion of Reason*.
45. See especially Feuerbach, *Thoughts about Death and Immortality*.
46. Buber, *Between Man and Man*, 212.

Dialogue, Encounter, and Dialogical Thinking

concept of the human being endowed by nature with an autonomous rational mind is root cause for the distortion of humankind.

Challenging the well-established attitude that the solipsistic, autonomous individual is the truly rational person endowed with the capability to really understand what life and world are all about, Cohen, Rosenzweig, and Buber argue for the need to realize the personalistic dimension of life as it happens in actual encounter between humans. They found a hearing, however, mostly outside the philosophical discourse, among physicians,[47] pedagogues,[48] and theologians, Christian in particular. Notable among the latter are Karl Heim (1874–1958),[49] Friedrich Gogarten (1887–1967),[50] Emil Brunner (1889–1966),[51] Karl Barth (1886–1968),[52] Paul Tillich (1886–1965),[53] and Helmut Thielicke (1908–1986).[54] Attracted by the insights into face-to-face communication in dialogue, many took inspiration from the philosophy of encounter in different ways as they pursued their own independent work—even though one or the other of them felt the sting of some outspoken criticisms by those who had articulated this thinking in the first place. Martin Buber's critique of Karl Barth is one such instructive case in point. Besides being somewhat critical of Barth, Buber's remarks also document a remarkable, genuinely committed form of interreligious dialogue between a Jew and a Christian, which warrant their somewhat extensive quotation here:

> For his presentation of the "basic form of humanity," Barth [in his *Church Dogmatics*], in all the fullness and original power of his theological thinking, claims the specific acquisition of a spiritual movement, the path of which was broken in the eighteenth and nineteenth centuries by a nonchurch but believing idealist [i.e.,

---

47. See Böckenhoff, *Die Begegnungsphilosophie*, 166–82.

48. Ibid., 149–66.

49. For more information on Karl Heim, see Allen, *A Guide to the Thought of Karl Heim*; Holmstrand, *Karl Heim on Philosophy*; Schwarz, "Karl Heim and John Polkinghorne."

50. On Friederich Gogarten, see Kroeger, *Friedrich Gogarten*.

51. On Emil Brunner, see Kegley, ed., *The Theology of Emil Brunner*; Williamson, *Politics and Protestant Theology*.

52. On Karl Barth, see Bromiley, *An introduction to the theology of Karl Barth*; Busch, *Karl Barth*; and Mangina, *Karl Barth*.

53. On Paul Tillich, see Thatcher, *The Ontology of Paul Tillich*; Pauck, *Paul Tillich*.

54. On Helmut Thielicke, see Thielicke, *Notes from a Wayfarer*; Thielicke, *Man in God's World*.

Søren Kierkegaard] and an unbelieving materialist [i.e., Ludwig Feuerbach]. In the twentieth century this movement found, in some measure, an adequate expression through the not unimportant participation of a believing Jew [i.e., Buber]. Not that Barth annexes it for Reformation Protestantism . . . He seeks to do justice to the spirit that blows outside of Christianity, practicing himself, in as difficult a sphere as that of theology, the "freedom of the heart" that he himself teaches. Thus he takes over on the one side, naturally in the manner of genuine independent thinking, our recognition of the fundamental distinction between It and Thou and of the true being of the I in the meeting. But on the other side, he cannot rightly acknowledge that such a concept of humanity could have grown on any other ground than the Christological . . . He asserts, to be sure, that "the theological anthropology . . . comes to expression in statements which are quite similar to those in which humanity had already reached from entirely other sides (for example, by . . . Confucius, by . . . L. Feuerbach, by the Jew M. Buber)." He asks with complete legitimacy: "Shall we, therefore, allow ourselves to hold back from these statements?" . . . Barth is concerned in this connection about "that freedom of the heart between man and man as the root and crown of the concept of humanity"—he finds missing, just as such, in the non-Christians whom he has named . . . What concerns him, therefore, is that man is man insofar as he is willingly human. "Willingly" in the sense that "unwillingly" is out of the question? . . . "Now it does not appear . . . as though this were the case with Confucius, with Feuerbach, with Buber" . . . [The] Protestant world of faith in Barth's understanding of it stands over against the Hasidic in my understanding of it. And there, among the Hasidim—in a world of faith whose teaching is ultimately the commentary on a lived life—the "willingly" of the freedom of the heart is not, indeed, consequence, but certainly the innermost presupposition, the ground of grounds . . . But I would, I could, show Karl Barth here, in Jerusalem, how the Hasidim dance the freedom of the heart to the fellowman.[55]

Buber's remarks are an ideal example of what dialogue means and how it is to be practiced, namely by carefully listening to the other, trying to understand what he or she is saying, and then responding in a way which does not block further communication but invites the other to share life actually lived. And let be it in dancing! That is dialogue properly put to the task.

55. Buber, *Between Man and Man*, 222–24.

DIALOGICAL THINKING AND INTERRELIGIOUS DIALOGUE

One among the various reasons that the philosophy of encounter or dialogical personalism was—and still is—disparaged by many, either through contempt or inattention, is its explicit acknowledgement of religious roots. Especially those who are only willing to accept an irreligious, nihilistic worldview as the sole, definite, and scientifically tenable intellectual stance critique it accordingly. Others find fault with the emphasis on encounter as the fundamental stepping stone to knowledge, charging that this would amount to no more than sheer actualism which holds that everything exists only when and as long as it actually happens and is actually present in the moment of encounter. A further accusation leveled against Buber, Cohen, and colleagues is that of irrationalism. This criticism is based on the fact that because personal encounters escape precise, detailed description in technical terms due to their value-added emotional surplus like personal impression, satisfaction or disappointment and the like, dialogical thinking results in nothing but a vague, opaque mysticism. Therefore, these critics suggest, those who advocate this kind of philosophy should better be called "inspirited mystics" than philosophers.

However, just as the irreligious, even antireligious, standpoint of critics of the philosophy of encounter does not in itself guarantee the appropriateness of the positions they hold, neither does the admitted religiosity of its advocates guarantee the incontestability of their statements. We here confront the fundamental issue of how fraught with uncertainty *every* approach to human knowledge and understanding actually is. The following two illustrations attempt to visualize the significant differences between the enlightened, idealistic monologic principle of an autonomous I perceiving the world and the dialogical approach to world recognition. Though contested by the representatives of the philosophy of encounter, the first model is the dominant one in Western culture and has as such also been at work in many types of attempted dialogue.

Beyond "Holy Wars"

Figure 4.1: Monological-solipsistic perception of the world putting the autonomous I at the center and its resulting model of world recognition and communication

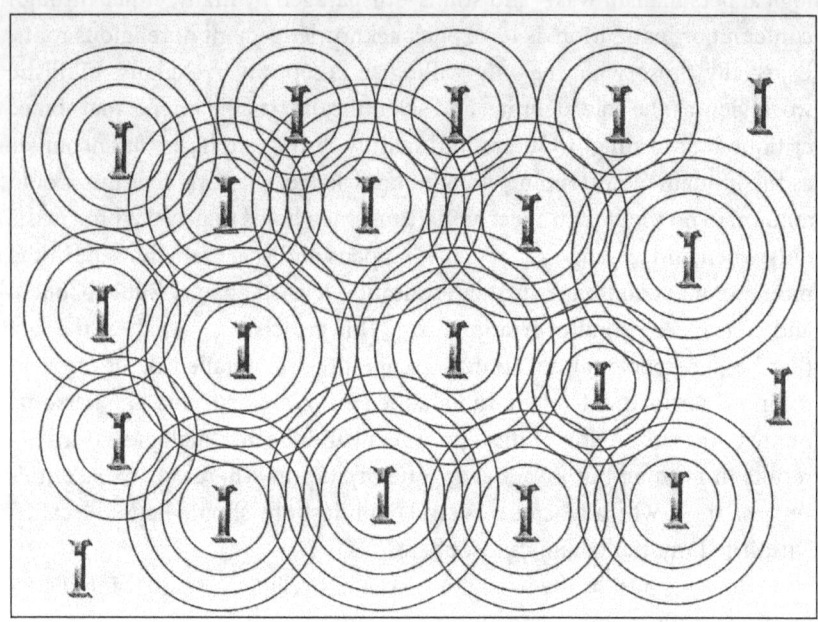

Here, in figure 4.1 the individual I, Descartes's *cogito* or the thinking I, is the decisive and fundamental element which constructs the perception of world around him- or herself. The concentric circles positioned around different individuals illustrate the most common way of thinking; perhaps the diagram seems somewhat reductionist, but it clearly presents the dynamic of solipsism. It reminds one of the first couplet of Edwin Markham's well known *Outwitted*:

> He drew a circle that shut me out—
> Heretic, rebel, a thing to flout.[56]

What catches the eye first is that most I claim their turf and range of action. Some reach out to others; others appear more reluctant, shielding their identity and keeping to themselves; yet others remain completely outside and isolated. Most I demonstrate the potential for a confrontational perception of the other, making it easier to declare the other an enemy instead of striving to come to an understanding of differences and otherness.

56. Markham, *The Shoes of Happiness*, 1.

Dialogue, Encounter, and Dialogical Thinking

The other remains at a distance while the I do not move beyond known territory, a stasis which is deadly for any dialogue. Neither cognitive dependence on one another nor any interdependence of individuals is detectable here. For the autonomous, solipsistic I, the world reaches only as far as the concentric circles extend, a distance which, quite naturally, differs from person to person. There are, partially at least, some overlapping segments shared by several—not by all—individuals. These represent the contents of thought and knowledge held in common and thus the capacity to reach out to someone not I. It is in these intersecting segments that some degree of communication and understanding actually can happen.

Dialogical thinking, in contrast, refuses to instantiate an autonomous I as the all perceiving center of (the) world. In its place appears the speech-bound event of personal communication and encounter between an I and a You, the I-You. This transforms the preceding figure in this way.

Figure 4.2 The basic structure of dialogical thinking and its resultant model of world recognition.

The center of this filigreed sketch is dominated by the I-You interaction. Mutuality and interdependence are apparent immediately. No I is isolated or at the center of world perception, even though every I is at the center of a circle of its own, as is every You. However, no isolated I any longer exist; all relate to a You as the You do to an I, thereby becoming the I-You which opens up further encounters and enables movement beyond what is known so far, a possibility here indicated by the broken lines of the circles. Perception of world is gained by centering on what is outside and beyond the Me in the actual encounter with a particular You. This dynamic relationship implies attentiveness to and openness for the other in all his or her particularity, or, to quote Edwin Markham once more, this dynamic relationship is brought about by "love" and "wit"; Markham continued the couplet cited above with these concluding two lines:

> But love and I had the wit to win:
> We drew a circle that took him in!⁵⁷

Perceiving of human encounter as the encounter between I-You personalities thus requires an appropriate emotional disposition if dialogue is to succeed. This disposition has to be marked by *existential trust*, *mental readiness*, and *intellectual agility* undergirded by *gentle caution*, not just on account of prudence but as the unmediated expression of acknowledging the dialogical structure of reality itself, with far reaching consequences for interreligious dialogue. One of these consequences is the *mutual respect for existing differences*, not as an imposed moral charge but as expression of genuinely understanding the dialogical imprint of reality. Another important insight for dialoguing resulting from the insights gained by the philosophy of encounter is *mutual personal esteem*, regardless of whether one finds the other likeable or not. It is such mutual respect and esteem which resolves the problem of blasphemy, because mutual sensitivity to the existence of serious reservations guards against mockery as it also does against coercion into a forced or artificial exchange of minds. Not paying due attention to these conditions in and of itself would simply vitiate dialogue.

Anyone who thinks dialogically will also take pains *to accord the others*—the particular I-You there are—*the freedom to make their decision voluntarily to enter into dialogue*, even to the point of enduring deferred hopes while patiently waiting upon the others' consent. A dialogue forced on participants will lead to apologetics and arouse deep-seated inner resistance. However well-intended, all efforts for interreligious dialogue that are not genuinely committed to dialogical thinking may become at least the expression of an essentially monological exhibitionism—if not

---

57. Ibid.

instruments of political power or cultural imperialism. Those who peddle their worldview in an exhibitionist manner even at the cost of selling their own religious and cultural tradition at bargain prices cut themselves off from their roots and lose their grounding. However honest and original the gestures toward commitment to an ideologically styled religious pluralism under these circumstances, they can also be seen as systematic enticements to forfeit *any* orientation grounded in religious tradition, an attitude which will gain very little appreciation, if any at all, on the part of those who have really understood what is at stake.

One other aspect still deserves explicit mention here, because it presents an even greater challenge, namely that *those engaging in mutual dialogue must no longer reject absolute claims as inappropriate for the enterprise*. Rather, interreligious dialogue operates under the condition that the specific insights and perceptions of life represented by diverse religious traditions are binding for those raised in that culture. To them their worldview has become undoubted certainty, known as such from earliest times of their upbringing and, as shown in the previous chapter, ingrained in their culture. How to withhold or exempt this identity from dialogue? Genuinely religious people will not fear for their identity in dialogue since they are fully aware that it is not they who have to hold up (their) "religion"; rather, it is the other way round: They are being held by (their) "religion," trusting that what they believe and have faith in will sustain them further and will enable them to face whatever challenge comes their way. Therefore, they will not—since they simply cannot—withhold the essential elements and basics of their belief from dialogue merely out of fear—fear of syncretism, fear of loss and the like. They will, rather, see to it that these essentials are articulated appropriately and that they receive the attention they deserve.

A dialogical attitude of the kind just outlined requires a mature and daring openness willing to take risks, not for the thrill of it but based in trust beyond fear. This stance, of course, renders one vulnerable, because such an attitude has no power to combat the abuse of language, words, and force except its own earnestness and authenticity. Trust in the power of the right and proper word authentically spoken is all that remains, the word that not only unmasks dubious intentions, but that word which also effectively establishes renewed trust and brings about reconciliation. Needless to say, the cultivation of such an attitude is *the* preemptive strategy to harness any craving for "holy wars" and to foster sustainable peace.

5 Overcoming "Holy Wars"
The Christian Contribution

HAVING SCOUTED OUR WAY through the dense thicket of issues surrounding interreligious dialogue we have now come to a clearing which invites us to rest for a moment and catch our breath. We will do so by taking stock of how we have come here and charting the remaining route.

Our expedition took off from the declaration of "Holy War" on the United States by Al Queda terrorists September 11, 2001, and the official response by the U.S. in *The 9/11 Commission Report*. We noticed that the *Report* when addressing the questions "What to do?" and "How to do it?" recommended—besides qualified counterterrorism strategies—only destruction and isolation of the terrorists. Since this strategy did not break the vicious circle of war and revenge, but perpetuated it instead, we felt urged to search for an alternative, being fully aware that any such alternative to counteract religiously motivated terror has, of course, not to play down the seriousness of the threat. It, rather, has to address religious-cultural diversity in light of the threat by getting involved in interreligious dialogue in order to establish mutual trust. However, when pondering this alternative we became immediately aware of difficulties in properly understanding the subject matter regarding attitudes toward religion in Western society based on the global change in the religious landscape everywhere and the average lack of religious literacy in the general population.

Next, we turned to the question "What is religion?" Following an analysis of religion in contemporary consumer society, we went on to see that and how religion is at the core of culture, defining not only the different ways of worship, but also the foods, the overall socio-political life, and in many societies the dress code too. This, consequently, necessitated

Overcoming "Holy Wars"

a critical account of the concepts of religion which exposed us to related philosophical discussions about "religion" past and present. After gaining insight into the discourses on "religion" as pursued in Western intellectual tradition, we spotted the discrepancy between the terminology used to define the phenomena and the actual self-perception by different religious traditions, which never speak of "religion" as such but of *dhārma*, faith, *milla*, denomination, or law instead. Thus noting the incommensurability of all concepts of "religion" with the empirical phenomena they claim to describe, we came to see the true complexity of the issue, which is caused by the reciprocal projection of the terminology employed and the different ideas entertained about the religious traditions actually lived.

Since the established, conventional terminology did not prove to be of help we took a different approach to the issue of interreligious dialogue in chapter three by looking at models and practices of peaceful living togetherness in multicultural environments—tolerance and convivence—realizing that tolerance and convivence are critically dependent on dialogue. Without dialogue, differences can easily mutate into conflicts which have the potential quickly to turn violent. This insight led us to ponder the history of "holy wars" and their various justifications. Doing so clarified the ambiguity of the terminology: "holy war" as an individual challenge for ethical or religious perfection, and "holy war" as military pursuit. This ambiguity made us aware that it is actually impossible to pronounce sweeping statements regarding *jihād* or *crusade*. Neither can we declare any war as "holy," for to do so contradicts the claim in a paradoxical manner, making unacceptable any pursuit of religious-cultural identity and any witnessing for a putative ultimate truth. War does not resolve normative conflicts; *only* dialogue does.

To shield this conclusion against the charge of ideological shortsightedness we had in the next step to explore deeper the canyon of dialogical thinking. We saw that dialogue as interpersonal encounter between humans is decisively a speech-event and as such is critically dependent on the authenticity of verbal exchange among its participants. Distinguishing among several ways humans talk to and converse with one another revealed the specific profile of dialogue as that medium of human communication which is able to establish genuine trust despite differences, a trust which can stand up to conflicts and cope with tensions without breaking up convivence. To understand better how this might work we examined the use and abuse of language by, first, looking at high profile incidents of abusing language for the sake of wielding power—Nazi ideology and Cold War rhetoric—and, secondly, by looking at religious traditions like Buddhism, Judaism, and Christianity, which charge the faithful with the responsibility of honest and mindful speech.

This, then, led us to a brief review of the thinking of the philosophers of encounter, notably Martin Buber, Franz Rosenzweig, and Hermann Cohen who were concerned with analyzing the cause for the blatant failure of idealistic humanism in preventing World War I. Buber, Rosenzweig, and Cohen saw the reason for the inability of humanistic idealism to stop warfare in the distorted view of the human and its mental and moral faculties, a legacy of the Enlightenment era which hailed the enlightened, autonomous rational individual being as the agent of knowledge and wisdom. True world recognition and genuine knowledge, in contrast, come about only by people speaking to one another in actual personal encounter, the philosophers of encounter held. It is the I-You—not the I-It—relationship which opens up the world around, and does so by means of language. Without genuine dialogue no real knowledge of the world is possible; whatever one might claim as such, outside dialogue is nothing but distorted reality.

That is how far we have come. We should now move straight ahead to interreligious dialogue proper without any further delay or detour—yet, without shortcuts leading us astray either. In the following we will, therefore, focus our attention on some principal aspects important for Christians to keep in mind in the actual pursuit of such dialogue. We will first consider some subjects of a more general character before dealing in a second section with the core issue of interreligious encounters, namely the mutually exclusive claims to ultimate authority. The closing part, in which we reach the scenic lookout of our explorations on interreligious dialogue, offers some idea of what it might look like when dialogue has become the signature and hallmark of one's life as a Christian.

Minding Adequacy of Speech

What is the particular contribution Christians can make to overcome the threat of "holy wars" besides fostering convivence and extending hospitality to strangers?[1] How can they meaningfully participate in that kind of dialogue which not only includes but also explicitly addresses and honors the

---

1. See Pohl, *Making Room*; Sutherland, *I Was a Stranger*; Newman, *Untamed Hospitality*; Russell, *Just Hospitality*.

Overcoming "Holy Wars"

beliefs and attitudes of people of diverse cultures and religions? The previous chapters have paved the way to an answer already, because they again and again alerted to the fact that to perceive the problems of interreligious dialogue with sober conscientiousness is one of the basic presuppositions of any genuine dialogue, just as it is of doing Christian theology proper. To think of theology only as pious speculation or reflection about God, the world, and salvation is to fail to comprehend theo*logy* in the essence of the term, replacing it with well-intended mind games and intellectual noncommittal. Christians cannot stay content with such an attitude, however. They always will have to face the reality of the cross with open eyes, that is, to face emerging difficulties, not to deny these.

One of such difficulties is the issue of how to communicate about the ineffable across diverse cultures and in different languages, well knowing that to speak of the Ultimate implies conscious recognition of the general limits of speech. If language actually could capture the Ultimate, the Ultimate would not really be ultimate but penultimate only, over against the comprehending mind able to comprehend it with words. Another issue is how to reconcile conflicting and mutually exclusive claims to ultimate authority, a difficulty which will remain even after the realization of conceptual inadequacies. To get a handle on these difficulties it is necessary to dwell—at least briefly—upon theology and the relationship between faith and reason in a somewhat different perspective than before; otherwise the argument will suffer from merely putative, insubstantial assumptions which might jeopardize the entire venture.

The task of Christian theology is to acknowledge the workings of God in the world today, as of old. For this interpretation to be intelligible— that is, to make sense and remain plausible and comprehensible—calls for utmost soberness. Like any genuine scientific or scholarly argument, theology, too, makes claims to speak the truth (in the sense of appropriate adequacy) about how things are and how they work. Theology, thus, participates in scholarship's nonnegotiable demand for unbiased rationality and soberness, precisely in matters of faith. This claim may come as a surprise, given that faith is usually set in opposition to critical reason. But in fact, faith is not a fallback position to which one resorts at the limits of (present) knowledge.[2] Nor does faith as the subject of study make for less

---

2. On this topic, which can be described as "God of the gaps attitude," see Larmer, "Is There Anything Wrong with 'God of the Gaps' Reasoning?"

than rigorous inquiry and thinking.³ Mental laziness which uses faith in this way will never stand up intellectually or religiously; it certainly does not stand up existentially and, thus, will certainly fail to face the challenge of interreligious dialogue.

Both faith and reason are basic expressions of human life concerned with the successful engagement in and management of personal existence. To hold that faith and reason are mutually exclusive implies on the one hand perceiving faith as an arbitrary knowledge of God, of life, and of world nurtured and informed by long standing specific religious traditions such as Judaism or Christianity, Islam or Buddhism, or just by an irrational emotionally charged feeling of ultimate dependence clouding the mind. On the other hand, the mutually exclusive concept renders critical thinking as such nihilistic and irreligious. However, this poses a mock alternative only, because faith does not simply take up where reason and critical thinking leave off. Rather, faith and reason complement each other in mutually dependent differentiation: faith requires knowledge informed by experience and critical thinking in order not to sink into irrationality or emotionalism, while critical reason at some point is bound to take a particular assumption simply for granted (the hypothetical Archimedean point) without sufficient proof and always requiring corroboration of its findings by life actually lived in order not to turn into solipsistic barrenness or hypocrisy. Medieval philosopher and theologian Anselm of Canterbury (1033/34–1109) aptly captured this relationship in his famous formula *credo ut intelligam*, "I believe, in order to understand [properly]."⁴

The significant differences between faith, science, and critical reason do not lie so much in the diverse methods employed to obtain knowledge, even though these are sometimes considerable.⁵ What accounts for the more distinct profiles of each is their different relative immediacy to existential saturation and fulfillment. While intellectual reflection remains intentionally at arm's length from life actually lived by focusing on general patterns and structures, faith presses toward actual life as lived in the here and now. Faith comes into its own when existential challenges collide with that cultural tradition which has proven reliable for generations in successfully

---

3. Good recent examples of rigorous theological inquiry are Clayton, "Constraint and Freedom in the Movement from Quantum Physics to Theology"; and Tracy, "Creation, Providence and Quantum Chance." See also Russell, *Cosmology from Alpha to Omega*.

4. See Anselm of Canterbury, *Works I*, 93.

5. See Peacocke, *Theology for a Scientific Age*; Barbour, *Religion and Science*.

solving precarious life situations but seems not to do so any longer. This struggle requires resolving obvious discrepancies between time-honored religious claims (with their attending codes of moral conduct) and existential realities (oftentimes conditioned either by unfathomable catastrophes or by new possibilities due to new discoveries or new technologies); thus it necessitates personal authentication and re-owning of that tradition which informs one's worldview and sense of personhood. Yet, faith is not solely concerned with unscrambling existential issues or explaining life and world or with speculating about other possible worlds, such as heaven, paradise, or hell—although such questions have arisen and believers have attempted to answer them in the context of faith over and over again. Rather, the central concern of faith is living a life according to recognized truth in order to accomplish and witness to that which is deemed to be right in life and which is good for life. This requires a permanent critical reaffirmation of truth and initiates a process of ongoing scrutiny of both the criteria for what establishes truth and what the actual challenges of life really are. Thus, to know the truth and discover what is life-furthering in the here and now entails unrelenting intellectual engagement in dialogue, because truth and righteousness are not objectifiable possessions to be protected and defended like ordinary property.[6] Instead, truth and righteousness *are* only inasmuch as they are being searched after and striven for. Only in this process do they become recognizable as such by all who are seriously concerned.

Faith, thus, places considerable intellectual and ethical demands—demands that, especially in today's context, many think are inappropriate and disconcerting to their awareness of autonomy and self-determination. Faith does indeed contest such attitudes and their attendant consciousness because faith holds that life is not a manmade, self-referential artifact but received to be cherished, enjoyed, preserved, and passed on to the next

---

6. This is a reference made to several phenomena such as (a) the English and French kings who were awarded the title *fidei defendor* (Defender of the Faith) by the Pope in the sixteenth century; (b) the Byzantine emperors who were holding this title long before; (c) today's Order of St. Andrew the Apostle—Archons of the Ecumenical Patriarchate in Turkey, which carries "Defenders of the Faith" in its subtitle describing their mission the following way: "Members of the Order of St. Andrew the Apostle understand their core mission to be 'Defenders of the Faith.' Under that rubric they apply their service and resources in three main arenas: education, spirituality, and philanthropy" (see Archons of the Ecumenical Patriarchate, http:// www.archons.org/pdf/Archons_History.pdf; and (d) to the "Defenders-of-the-Christian-Faith" churches found across the U.S., for instance in Bayonne, NJ, or Dorchester, MA (see http://www.faithdefenders.com/home.html.

generation. Faith further holds that the source of life is not an anonymous vital power or merely a macromolecular biological process. Rather, faith holds that life for the human being is at its core personal, self-disclosing will and living context; is word, *logos*; and as such faith is also intelligible and comprehensible—meaning, recognizable in form and structure. In short: Faith maintains—at least according to Jewish, Christian, and Muslim traditions alike—that the living God is the source of all life as its creator and sustainer.

Let us take belief in creation as an example here. The affirmation "God created the world" has obviously little influence on whether tomorrow will be another day—or even exist at all. Nor does this statement make misery and poverty disappear; indeed, it seems poverty and misery can be borne more readily if one does *not* care for a God who is said to have brought life into being and who continues to sustain it here and now. The prevailing injustice and the horrors that occur among people, even people of faith, seem to speak more readily in favor of non-intelligent processes than of the presence of God.[7] Yet, the Jewish, Christian, and Muslim traditions—and not only these[8]—still assert firmly that life has been created. How to make sense out of that claim?

Acknowledging world and life as created and sustained by God is, of course, a statement of faith which, while posed as an assumption beyond rational proof, is not devoid of reason. Those who hearken to it authenticate their belief in creation by living *as if* the statement were true. In fact, to live *as if* is not the rationale just for people of faith, but for everyone else, too, and notably so for scientists, as Thomas S. Kuhn has shown in his pivotal work *The Structure of Scientific Revolutions* of 1962. Scientific thinking throughout the ages, however unconditioned it claimed to be and how untainted by non-rational interests, was always expressed in very definite, unaccounted for models which Kuhn termed "paradigms."[9] This kind of expression applies to the most abstract mathematical axioms as well, which

---

7. This issue was highlighted impressively by the refusal of a Jewish witness who during a Nazi war crime proceeding was asked to take the oath "Under God." According to a newspaper report, this witness "looked at the accused and said 'If God really did exist, *he* wouldn't.'" The witness, then, took the secular oath "in remembrance of" his "murdered family." This incident was reported in the German weekly *Die Zeit*, March 17, 1967.

8. See Eliade, *Essential Sacred Writings from Around the World*, 83–154.

9. Kuhn, *The Structure of Scientific Revolutions*, esp. chapter 5, "The Priority of Paradigms," 43–51.

however arbitrarily formulated are never epistemologically neutral or free of values.[10] In other words, *all* knowledge—scientific or not—hinges on contingent, historically determined assumptions, givens, and premises.

While genuinely religious people are fully aware of the fact that to attain absolute certainty is not the lot of humans, others are determined to prove them wrong by engaging in high-handed, arrogant activity with a reckless and frightening lack of scruples.[11] But not all do. Most that do not join in this chorus just tend to become disengaged from the quest by dismissing it as irrelevant. Such dismissal, however, takes the problem too lightly, because worldviews and attitudes toward life have an enormous impact on how people relate to the world in and around them, how they act, react, and behave. Worldviews are actually decisive for human action, and that is what matters. If one really is concerned about forging sustainable peace, one cannot but call attention to these connections so as to make people aware and help them consciously to cultivate life-furthering, life-sustaining attitudes in order to eliminate life-destructive ones.

A quick look at conducting scientific experiments may illustrate this principle. One can, of course, conduct experiments very well with the sole intention in mind to see what things are about, how they function, and what the results of specific interventions or manipulations will be. At the opening of the modern scientific era English philosopher, statesman, and scientist Francis Bacon (1561–1626) in his *Novum Organum Scientiarum* [*New Instrument of/for Science*] of 1620 proclaimed programmatically that nature has to be vexed and raped, nay "tortured" to make her release her secrets.[12] Nature (whatever one thinks this is)[13] thus became something like raw-material for curious, inquisitive minds. Ignoring restraints when researching, natural scientists are determined only to get access to the powers inherent in nature in order to make these available to serve human interests, desires, and wants. No doubt, this approach has yielded tremendous practical results in nearly every aspect of life. However, nowadays it

---

10. This can easily be seen when studying the history of mathematics and algebra as in Boyer, *A History of Mathematics*; and Grattan-Guinness, ed., *Companion Encyclopedia of the History and Philosophy of the Mathematical Sciences*.

11. This was for instance the case with René Descartes who eagerly searched for a way to overcome death; see Gaukroger, *Descartes*; D. Clarke, *Descartes*. A contemporary attempt of overcoming death can be seen in the public attention that the manipulation of telomeres receives nowadays; see Boia, *Forever Young*; Appleyard, *How to Live Forever*.

12. Pesic, "Wrestling with Proteus."

13. See Whitehead, *The Concept of Nature*; Naddaf, *The Greek Concept of Nature*; Hadot, *The Veil of Isis*.

would be naïve to ignore the consequences of carelessly exploiting "nature" in as unrestricted a manner as done in the past; the side effects of such behavior have become obvious in myriad ecological, economic, and political disasters.

Conversely, when experiments are conducted in the awareness of an overarching context of life, then the materials and objects of research take on somewhat different aspects and appear in a changed perspective, namely as creation yet to be discovered.[14] This leads to a different handling of matter, because in the light of creation even the most short-lived chemical elements—to say nothing of plants, animals, and human beings in particular—speak a different language than they do when considered merely as matter, as reactive material, or as individual autonomous systems.[15] Research pursued in the perspective of creation becomes an encounter, in which everything tells of and points to the source of all life which nurtures and sustains the researchers, too, reminding them at the same time that whatever they do should serve life's purposes.[16] How can we best communicate this understanding across the aisles not just of faith and reason or of religion and science, but also across the manifold cultural and religious divides?

This challenge touches upon yet one other issue, namely the peculiar character of religious—above all, theological—speech, especially when it strives to do its task properly. As with every other human discourse, talking about the Ultimate is and remains human discourse always, availing of contingent words which point to something beyond and above without ever being able to conceptualize this "beyond" satisfactorily. Yet, despite this acknowledged shortcoming, sincere attempts adequately to express the ultimate Beyond have to be made continuously even if these lead only to stammering. Otherwise, any such talking would turn shallow and become

---

14. To cite just one example, the physician Paracelsus (Theophrast Bombast von Hohenheim, 1493–1541), who wrote on philosophical and theological subjects, too, is an impressive representative of this approach to science and still very rewarding and worthwhile to study; see Jacobi, *Paracelsus: Selected Writings*. For an ongoing research project on Paracelsus at the University of Zurich, Switzerland, see http://www.paracelsus.uzh.ch/index.html.

15. A dreadful example of a godless approach toward life and of human subjects in medical trials in particular was staged by the medical establishment under the National Socialist German Workers' Party in Germany (NSDAP) 1933–1945; see Mitscherlich et al., *Doctors of Infamy*.

16. Contemporary examples of research reflecting such an attitude are collected in the volume Shults, Murphy, and Russell, eds., *Philosophy, Science and Divine Action*.

simplistic and superficial, as so often is the—unfortunate—case with professional theologians and religious office bearers. It remains a pressing problem to maintain and keep perceptible the referential character of genuine religious speech.

To be sure, religious speech carefully considered and cautiously used will often result in phrases which outsiders may misperceive as much too vague and paradoxical, often dismissing such phrases quickly as proof of utter ignorance. In fact, some will interpret whatever is said this way as mere guesswork and thereby fail to credit the reverent effort for careful, not casual, speech about matters beyond the ordinary. Nevertheless, to seek an adequate rather than a nonchalant, shortsighted kind of discourse is critical for the success of any interreligious dialogue, insofar as the one really tries to illumine its subject while the other only obscures it and misses the point, thereby leaving dialogue at the mercy of terminological manipulation. Therefore, whoever rejects as senseless the cautious or paradoxical formulas that result from attempting to communicate meaningfully about the ineffable, *ipso facto* demonstrates a grave misunderstanding of the subject matter.

To have a clear sense of the all-surpassing greatness of that to which interreligious dialogue alludes is crucial to its success. Whenever people meet for such dialogue they will concede the embarrassment of the situation but will nevertheless seek adequate expression of that which is of ultimate concern to them. They will, therefore, refrain from dealing a death blow to the ineffable, neither claiming sovereignty for one's personal expression nor refusing any speech in the name of dispassionate neutrality. Genuinely religious persons won't even venture to develop concurrent theories of religion such that "the fundamental fact of religious experience is . . . simply rolled out as thin and flat as to be finally eliminated altogether," as the historian and phenomenologist of religion Rudolf Otto (1869–1937) once pointedly remarked.[17]

However, two quite different attitudes mark groups seeking interreligious dialogue, and just this difference constitutes the decisive distinction between settling for inappropriate concepts of religion and undertaking a project of true inter-*religious* dialogue. The first group works in an intentionally unbiased way, assuming fictitious neutrality for the sake of securing a common basis on which to reconcile conflicting, mutually exclusive claims. Such reconciliation, however, is bogus, for it simply ignores "the

---

17. Otto, *The Idea of the Holy*, 27.

fundamental fact of religious experience" in pretending that these claims are not vital.[18] At best, what results from attitudes like this is theoretical shadowboxing among like-minded elites. However, their efforts will prove insufficient to overcome tensions and, thus, will not be able to go beyond "holy wars," since, to repeat it again, religiously conscientious people will never leave aside their foundational religious insights when engaging in dialogue. They simply cannot do otherwise, and Christians should encourage this conviction in any way possible, even if this aggravates the issue, to which we now turn.

Embracing Others in Their Otherness

In the long history of interreligious dialogue numerous attempts have been made to reconcile competing claims to ultimate validity. One of the most common of these attempts has been to put different religions side by side in order to compare them. However, to do so means to apply a preconceived concept of religion to widely diverse socio-cultural phenomena, a process which fails to grasp the actual differing ways of self-perception of the phenomena so described. To compare religions side by side also fails to critically realize the implications of historical and terminological particularity of the contingent standards of comprehension and understanding applied, and thereby it replicates the typical shortfall of the Enlightenment. Amos Yong in his study *The Cosmic Breath* gives an idea of how this looks with regard to Christianity and Buddhism.

> Christianity and Buddhism are so fundamentally different that any attempt to compare the two can proceed only by ignoring their deep disagreements: kenosis by choice versus kenosis as compulsion; adherence to the Aristotelian logic of noncontradiction versus affirmation of the conjunction of opposites; commitment to revelatory Scripture versus the emphasis on experience and the openendedness of the Dharma; sin versus ignorance as the primordial human problem; other-salvation versus self-salvation;

---

18. This is not just a modern phenomenon, but, rather, a universal one as proven by the following statement from an Arab Muslim of the tenth century: "Moses taught and left the scene, whereupon Christ appeared. Thereafter Mohammed came, who made known the five pillars [of Islam]. Yet, a new faith [certainly] will come [again] later which will replace this one [too]. Thus, [by continuous change of religions] humanity is flogged to death between yesterday and tomorrow [that is: in history]" (quoted according to Kremer, *Über die philosophischen Gedichte des Abul Ala Ma'arry*, 4; my translation).

divine command ethics versus situationist ethics; resurrection versus reincarnation; personal God versus impersonal *shunyata*, and so on.[19]

Moreover, to compare isolated aspects of religions as one might attempt to solve an algebraic equation, fails to carry significant meaning, because, as shown earlier, religions mediate and represent a more or less comprehensive whole which bears the impress of a distinct perception of world and which integrally connects and informs all aspects of life, as succinctly stated by Rabbi de Vries.[20] While curiosity about differences in the way life is actually lived in various "religions" may serve well as a starting point for dialogue, it soon will become obvious that the idiosyncrasies of the different socio-cultural systems called "religions" arise from the overall context of their worldview, which by complex interaction of religious, social, and economic dynamics has set in motion historical and political processes which in turn have formed over time certain distinctive standards accepted as good, valuable, and life-furthering by those who grew up in a place and community where this particular worldview became formative.

Since comparison turns out to be not much of a help in reconciling the basic differences, one must look for an alternative approach in dealing meaningfully with religious diversity, an approach capable of setting one's own religious tradition with its particular claims in relation with those that people of other religions uphold. The specific challenge lies in the willingness to tread lightly and carefully, neither absolutizing one's own claims to ultimate validity nor relativizing others' claims to it, as already demanded by King Ashoka in the third century BCE. What would such an approach look like?

Various concepts have been advanced in trying to reconcile the plurality of religious claims to ultimate authority. I would like to represent these as the set model (1), the cone model (2), and the plot model (3). Diagrams of these models show both their advantages and their limitations for interreligious dialogue.[21]

---

19. Yong, *The Cosmic Breath*, 208.

20. See Vries, *Jewish Rites and Symbols*.

21. Some of the following has been published previously in part by Grundmann, "Living with Religious Plurality." However, all of the figures have been carefully revised and redesigned.

Figure 5.1 The set model, here exemplified with Judaism, Christianity, and Islam

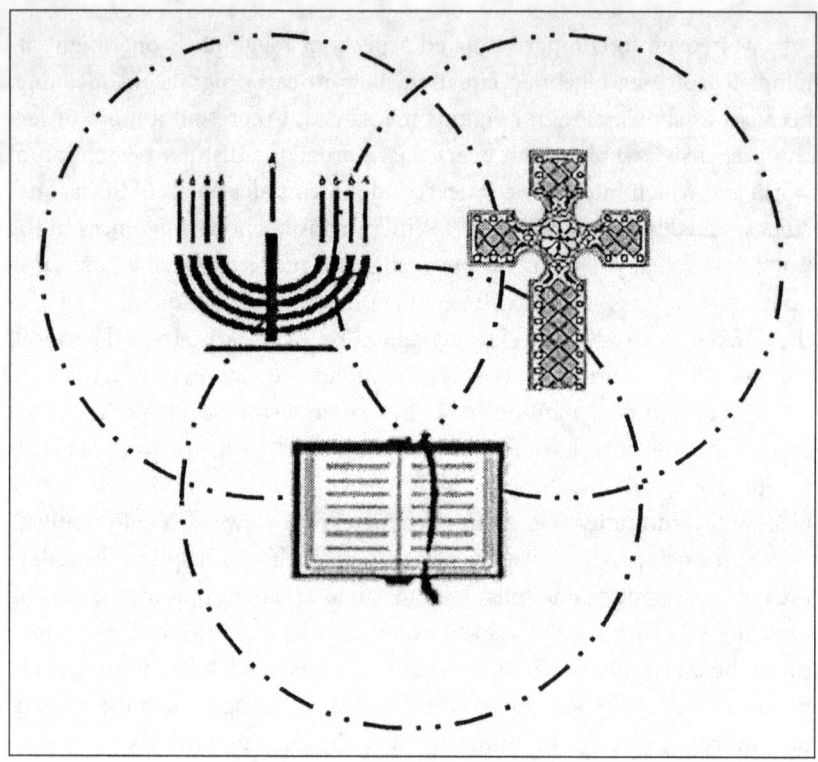

The ideal type of the set model is rendered here with only three identical intersecting circles, recalling Lessing's ring parable quoted above. Though different renderings might highlight more clearly the otherness of the respective religious traditions through varied geometrical figures—triangles, quadrilaterals, or trapezoids—I have opted for circles for the ease of viewing and to indicate the all-comprehensiveness of religious worldviews. Whatever the case, this model quite obviously grants each tradition its integrity. At the same time it illustrates not only distinguishable grades of overlap between different religions, but also a commonly shared central area. This area could delineate, in the parlance of the eighteenth century, "natural religion," but it can also indicate a theoretically assumed "true religion" as common denominator. According to this model the task of interreligious dialogue would be to identify these commonalities, which when identified as such would provide the common ground on which to solve conflicts and tensions.

Overcoming "Holy Wars"

The obvious advantage of the set model is that it rejects judgment. It envisions different religions as equal entities and illustrates both their factual juxtaposition and their mutual interferences/interactions in a globalized world—whether intentional or not. However, the model rests upon a hypothesis which does not do justice to the actual complexity of the real world situation, as it fails to recognize the history and the self-perception of each tradition. The model marshals religions by a particular concept, one that levels out historical and conceptual differences—a decided limitation.

This limitation seems to be taken care of well with the cone model, which in contrast, takes into account historical developments and also recognizes mutual interdependencies of the various religious traditions.

Figure 5.2: The cone model, here culminating in Christianity

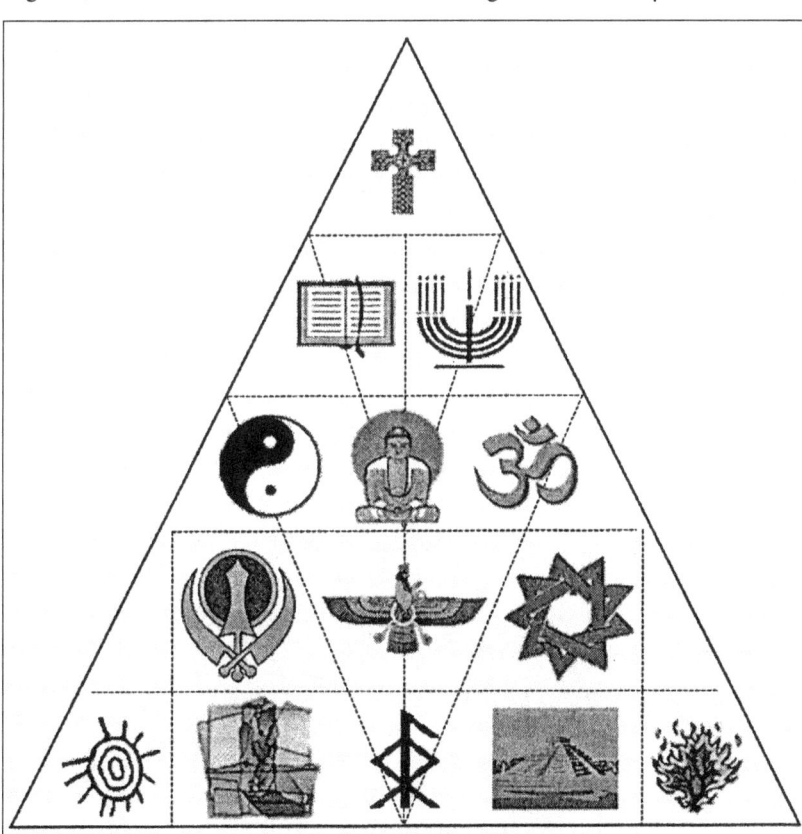

The cone model can, of course, easily be regrouped or arranged according to one's own preferences, as shown in the following figures.

Beyond "Holy Wars"

Figures 5.3–5.5: showing possible rearrangements of the cone

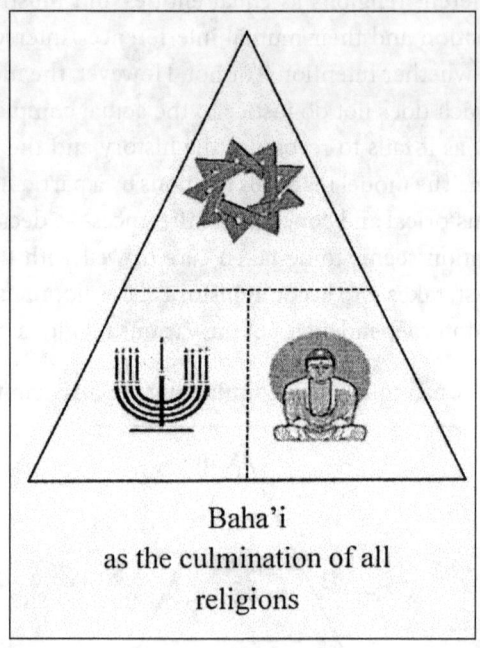

Baha'i
as the culmination of all
religions

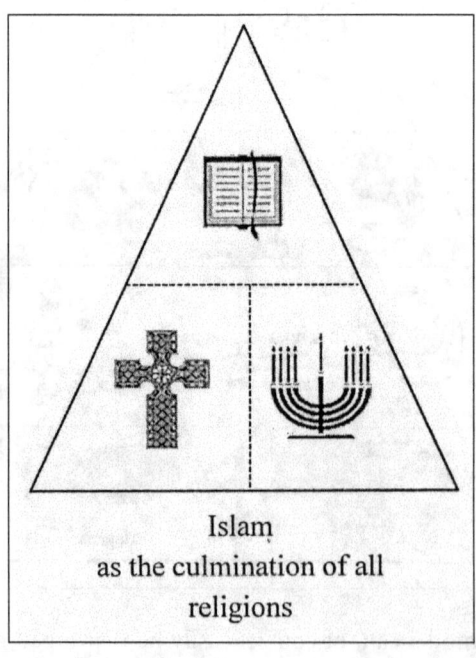

Islam
as the culmination of all
religions

Overcoming "Holy Wars"

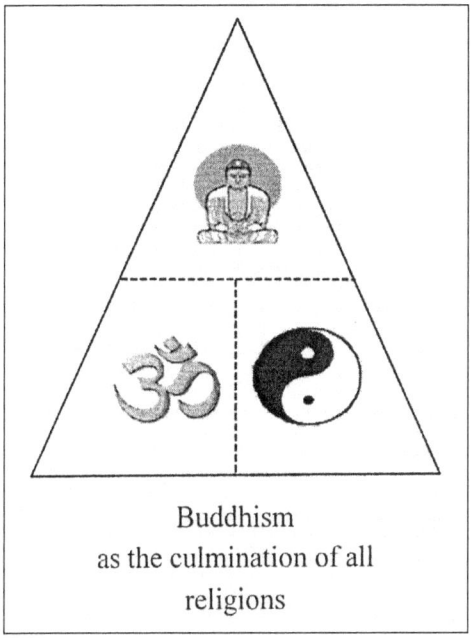

Buddhism
as the culmination of all
religions

This model does not regard other religions disparagingly, for these are integrated as being no less—but also no more—than precursors to the definite, ultimate religion at the top which absorbs all others, elevates and consumes them. This model, in fact, recalls Schleiermacher's definition of Christianity as the "higher power" of all religions, since he held that in Christianity the infinite [God] became manifest in the finite definitively [i.e., in Jesus Christ]. Hegel's characterization of the Christian religion as the "absolute religion" also comes to mind—Christianity perceived as the religion of spirit, of truth, and of freedom. To identify one particular religious tradition as the fulfillment, the crowning culmination, and zenith of all other such traditions expresses, of course, an unshaken self-confidence and certainty, mediating a still unbroken identity, something difficult to maintain any longer in our global age.

Undoubtedly, the strength of the cone model is that it honors the claim to ultimate validity at least of one particular religious tradition. But this goes along with relativizing other such claims. While for this reason people of other traditions might not feel properly understood and accepted, even discriminated against, this model attracts all those who favor

145

an exclusivist or inclusivist theory of religion. In fact, this model invites *both* an exclusivistic and an inclusivistic interpretation. Following a strictly exclusivistic interpretation, the religious longings of all humans will find their fulfillment *only* when they attain to the top of the cone, to the pinnacle belief, which in a more radical interpretation might even deny *any* connection to other religions at all, a stance taken for instance by the Indian Buddhist monk (*bhikkhu*) Vasubandhu who insisted that there is no salvation apart from Buddhism since other religious traditions hold a distorted view of "soul."[22] In contrast, in the inclusivist interpretation, *all* "religions" have some part in salvation—in varying and subtle gradations, of course, but *real* participation, an interpretation favored for instance by the eminent Catholic theologian Karl Rahner who spoke of "anonymous Christians," by which he meant all adherents of non-Christian religions who were upright of heart and earnestly seeking God without prejudice.[23] However, Rahner's inclusivistic approach might not delight those who have consciously decided against conversion to Christianity.[24]

When viewed from above, the cone model reveals a variant depictive as concentric circles as shown in the following figures. Even though the historical and genealogical aspects recede here markedly, the dominant position of the central religious tradition remains obvious.

---

22. See Vasubandhu, *Abhidharmakosa*, 4. The actual dates of Vasubandhu's life are not known. Jehovah's Witnesses for example represent an exclusivistic interpretation of a particular faith as do any fundamentalist groups in any religion.

23. See Karl Rahner, "Church, Churches, and Religions."

24. Yadev has raised an explicit "Protest against the Theology of Anonymous Christianity." However, for a more recent adaption of Rahner's inclusivistic concept, see Ratzinger, *Truth and Tolerance*.

Overcoming "Holy Wars"

Figures 5.6–5.8: The cone model in a bird-eye's view and in three variants

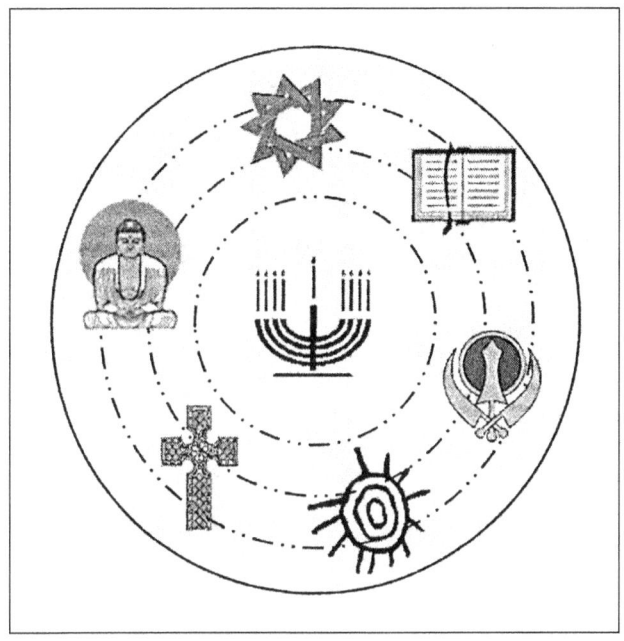

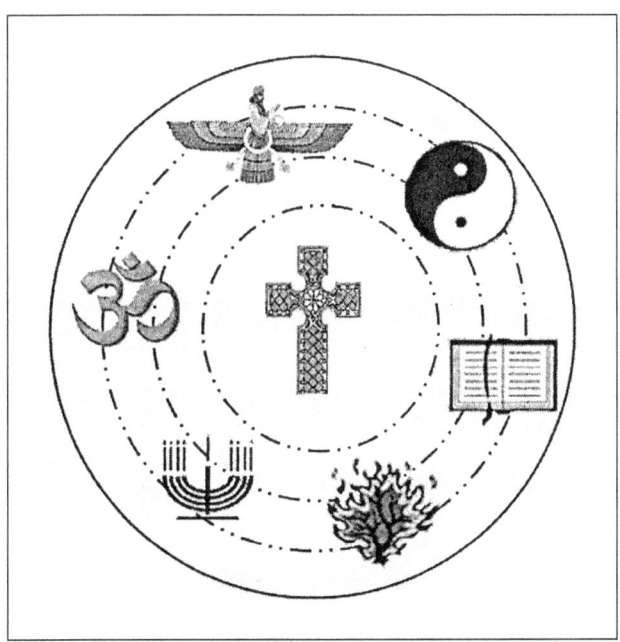

Beyond "Holy Wars"

The third model is the plot model. It represents the prevailing theory of modern religious pluralism which exercises a great influence in the popular media, the political world, and in the academy. This model is free of the limitations of the other types since it merely plots religions side by side evenly, not minding their history, origin, or systematic and cultural developments.

Figure 5.9: The plot model representing the pluralistic theory of religions

Overcoming "Holy Wars"

In the plot model each "religion" holds an equivalent place, neither superior nor inferior to the others. Modern religions come to stand side by side with ancient ones, primal religions are set alongside scripture-based ones with their highly sophisticated traditions of reflection, teaching, and ministries. Thus, this model displays the many-colored diversity of today's religious situation dispassionately and matter-of-factly in a non-hierarchic way as in a kaleidoscope. It discourages any exclusivistic or inclusivistic interpretation; that is its indisputable virtue. Yet, this achievement comes at the cost of denying any religion its claim to ultimate validity. The model thus dissolves religion altogether. Intentionally ignoring the claim to ultimate validity, it forces the various religious traditions into an ideological Procrustean bed suggesting a static co-existence, and thereby distorts the issue significantly. By choosing not to address the root cause of religious diversity this model fails to live up to the challenge to reconcile religiously motivated conflict. To overcome the existential naiveté of this very popular model requires pushing the issue further.

To depict faithfully—at least to some extent—how a decidedly religious way of thinking perceives a multireligious environment, the diagram would look somewhat like the following figures.

Figure 5.10: showing religious perception of other religions in Christian perspective

Beyond "Holy Wars"

Figure 5.11: showing religious perception of other religions in Buddhist perspective

Figure 5.12: showing religious perception of other religions in Muslim perspective

150

Overcoming "Holy Wars"

These illustrations visualize that, from the perspective of a particular religious tradition, its own perception as well as that of the religious neighbors inevitably suffers distortions. While not ignoring the existence of others, it places them into the picture only peripherally and in less sharp focus. One may, of course, now argue that if this is the case, the task of interreligious dialogue would be to address such aberrations in order to correct them. However, even if this process were to succeed, one would merely reiterate the plot model, albeit in enriched detail. Sadly though, the relationship with one's own religious tradition is never as clear and consistent as the above diagrams assume or suggest, because the contours of one's own religious-cultural tradition emerge properly defined at certain points only and hardly ever with respect to the entire tradition as such. Taken by and large, one's own tradition will also always remain somewhat hazy and diffuse for oneself, as the following diagram attempts to illustrate. It makes visible the immense difficulties to be overcome when simply relating to people of other religious traditions, not to speak of wanting to get involved in serious dialogue.

Figure 5.13: Approximation of perceptions of one's own religious tradition within a religiously diverse environment

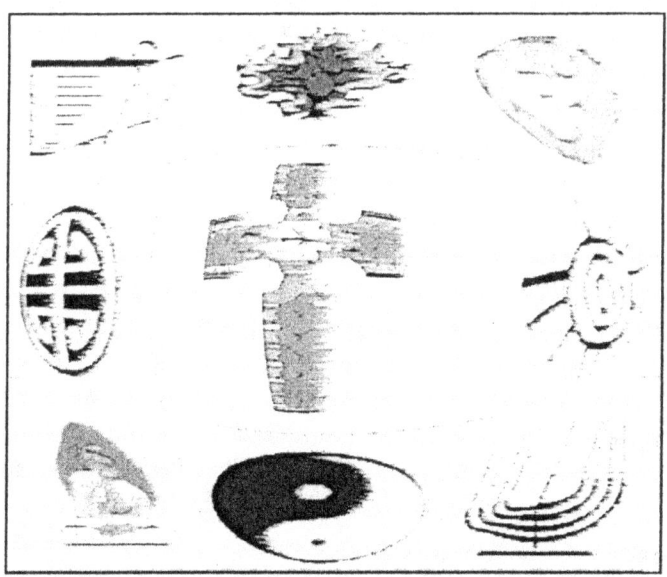

Beyond "Holy Wars"

This somewhat realistic appraisal of how one perceives one's own and the religious traditions of others in a religiously diverse environment visualizes the extreme difficulties interreligious dialogue has to struggle with and—if it were possible at all—to master in order to achieve mutual understanding. The previously shown complexity of the task becomes obvious here again, albeit from a different angle.[25] How could even the most sincere dialogue sufficiently compensate for all the distortions? If the dynamics of each of the different "religions" were also factored in—the continual change and deviation among the believers, the interdependence, interpenetration, and overlapping of challenges in a globalized world—then it would become fully evident that any such systematization of interreligious encounter is doomed to fail, a very disturbing insight indeed.

The most important result to put on record here is that all efforts toward a handy theory of interreligious dialogue, all attempts toward constructing tidy models, have to be regarded as inadequate for the task, even as outright failures. It suggests that all models with their resulting paradigms should be dispensed with. Yet—and here may be the saving grace—this insight aligns well with that of the philosophy of encounter which, as pointed out above, maintains that one can never have an accurate perception of the other, the You, as she or he really is. One can never fix determinatively the otherness of others in a neat, convenient concept; one ought not even attempt such defining, because this will always lead to misconceptions.[26] Any idea of the other unavoidably represents already an abstraction. One comes to know the other only as the other one, the You in his or her otherness in the embrace of actual encounter.[27] It is in these encounters too, that one will discover God as the totally Other altogether. Consciously to do so is the precise task of interreligious dialogue proper.

A theologically responsible and politically prudent examination of interreligious dialogue, therefore, involves systematically deconstructing all models of dialogue.[28] In this way, and *only* in this way, will one succeed in

---

25. See above figure 2.2.

26. Perhaps the biblical prohibition of images as pronounced in Exod 20:4 and repeated in Deut 5:8: "You shall not make for yourself an idol, whether in the form of anything that is in heaven above, or that is on the earth beneath, or that is in the water under the earth!" is actually meant to require the most unprejudiced encounter between humans, as well as between humans and God.

27. See Levinas, *Otherwise Than Being*.

28. Yong, too, noted from his engagement in the Christian-Buddhist dialogue recently, "that each of the three major approaches of exclusivism, inclusivism, or pluralism faces

clearing the way to genuine encounter between humans with their distinctive otherness as well as with the truly Ultimate. Deconstruction for the sake of dialogue has to be the watchword. This maxim may seem too neatly stated, but it is decisive. The success of the entire venture vitally depends upon it because any dialogue in which one is only eager to uphold theories or concepts, in which one looks for the corroboration of ideas—any such dialogue is doomed to founder from the outset since it is not really open. Instead, it abides by a hidden agenda and serves vested interests. The requisite openness and matter-of-fact quality of genuine dialogue, in contrast, depends on dispensing with the security of given concepts and models. This implies, of course, to take risks, since the outcome of the dialogue is never certain and cannot be guaranteed.

A report by Hans Jochen Margull (1925–1982) about an interreligious dialogue held at Colombo, Sri Lanka, in 1974, is highly instructive in this regard. It shows how religious people coped with unexpected difficulties which arose in the process of their dialoguing. Buddhists, Hindus, Muslims, Jews, and Christians were gathered to dialogue on the topic "Toward World Community—Basics and Requirements for Coexistence," a topic of burning interest today more than ever before. Margull noticed with great surprise that the participants in the dialogue could not find *one* single element in common among them, not even "spirituality," which previously everyone had taken simply for granted. Actually, those assembled at Colombo that time felt it even highly "questionable" that there was *any* common ground at all to be found among the various religions. And so the dialogue on "this point" led "to silence," albeit a "commonly shared silence."[29]

Observations like these clearly point the way which people have to take if they are really concerned that peace may prevail on earth. People in dialogue have to resist the temptation to evade significant difficulties and to level out differences. Christians cannot practice conflict avoidance by downplaying or ignoring issues which surface in the encounter with people of other faiths. Instead, they will note these attentively, probe their significance, and will in this way make such issues accessible for the discourse by all so that convivence—and thus lasting peace—will have a better chance to succeed.

---

major methodological hurdles that sometimes impede authentic dialogue" (*The Cosmic Breath*, 13–14).

29. Margull, "Verwundbarkeit," 419. Margull, "Der Dialog von Colombo," 525–34 (my translation). Samartha edited the official documents of this dialogue as *Towards World Community*.

To engage in dialogue may therefore appropriately be likened to making a journey on which the participants set out with their eyes wide open, knowing only the general direction but neither the exact route to take nor the definite destination, nor even how long their journey will last. Yet, in the course of time everyone will somehow become enriched and will change to some extent in this conviventual enterprise, and, should the occasion arise, part with familiar images, cherished and longstanding, if these prove no longer sufficiently plausible. Recognizing delusions, prejudices, and deceptions as what they are—as one certainly will sooner or later—one cannot but leave these behind; even though sometimes painful, this divesting should not be regarded as loss but as liberation. Any such journey which does not bring about a heightened awareness and a change of mind has not really been undertaken, as philosopher Ernst Bloch has noted in his metaphor of serious inquiry and going on a hike:

> When a person goes for a walk, he takes himself along. Yet at the same time he so gets away from himself that the meadow, the wood, the mountain he happens to pass enrich him. He also learns, literally, to know again what it is to go astray and what the way is; and the house which welcomes him back, finally, does not by any means affect him as something taken for granted, but as something he has now attained and arrived at . . . To be bad at going for a walk means to remain unaffected as a human being by that process. This kind of person only changes location, not himself, while on the move through it.[30]

From this insight, finally, it follows that a genuinely religious position that is also theologically responsible and sound cannot content itself with just noticing and documenting the differences among religions and raising curious questions. Christian theology will have to make clear that interreligious dialogue is always happening as an encounter between human individuals—women and men—who belong to different religious-cultural traditions and who worship differently. This assertion is not as trivial as it might appear at first reading, for it challenges the conventional way of talking about the subject matter. The World Council of Churches, for instance, when first launching such a program, took much care to speak always about dialogue as a "dialogue between women and men of different faiths" or of "interfaith dialogue" for short.[31] Unfortunately though, the misleading

---

30. Bloch, "Reiseform des Wissens," 201; my translation.
31. Until 1992 the "Dialogue Desk" at the World Council of Churches (WCC) at

term "interreligious dialogue," suggesting that different "religions" are in dialogue—as if they ever could be—was established too firmly already as a technical term and prevailed.

In practical terms, however, the question remains: What one individual is able to speak authoritatively for an entire religious tradition as such? Even the recognized authorities of the Church, the *Sangha*, the *Ummah*, or the *Synagogue* can no longer count on the general, unequivocal consent of the members of their own traditions in whose name they claim to speak when participating in such events. Such dissolving solidarity, for instance, became apparent at the (first) Interreligious Day of Prayer for Peace at Assisi in October, 1986. Not only did orthodox Buddhists (*Theravadins*) as well as Shiite Muslims stay away from the occasion on account of religiously informed reasons, so did the person invited to speak on behalf of Confucianism decline the invitation, arguing that Confucianism is a distinctive "cultural form" not a "religion." Pope John Paul II (1920–2005), the principal host of the event, also had to face outspoken reproach from within the Roman Catholic Church since some church members perceived the meeting he arranged as nothing but a "syncretistic marketplace."[32]

True, the Prayers for Peace at Assisi—the one in 1986 and also the subsequent one on January 24, 2002, which was occasioned by the attacks of 9/11—were not events for the purpose of pursuing interreligious dialogue. Yet, the criticisms they received made it very clear that no one can even pretend any more that representational dialogue will work these days as it had in previous centuries. When genuinely religious people meet for interreligious dialogue today, they do so neither because they have been ordered by their authorities nor out of mere curiosity. Rather, they do so as persons who are existentially troubled—for them no less than the entire world has been set tottering—and it is *this* experience which makes them seek dialogue. Driven by the quest for a truly reliable grounding in all the uproar occasioned by globalization, they recognize dialogue as their destiny. Theoretical answers will not satisfy them any longer; only genuine dialogue will do, that is, dialogue existentially verified and personally authenticated. Anglican bishop Kenneth Cragg (1913–2012), who spent his entire life in Palestine, gathered the stories of Christians and Muslims

---

Geneva, Switzerland, was called "Dialogue with People of Other Faiths and Ideologies"; see Samartha, *Between Two Cultures*; and also Francis, ed., *New Approaches to Inter-faith Dialogue*.

32. See Genthe and Grothe, "Von Assisi bis Kyoto," 116. As far as Islam is concerned, see Esposito and Mogahed, *Who Speaks for Islam?*

engaged in interfaith dialogue in the Middle East of his time and published these stories in a book with the telling title *Troubled by Truth*.[33] Likewise, French missionary Jean Faure who was passionately engaged in lifelong dialogue with his Muslim neighbors in Togo, West Africa, summed up his commitment to the task with an allusion to Anselm of Canterbury, "*interfides quaerens intellectum*—crushed between different faiths: the faith searches for understanding."[34] For Jean Faure dialogue was never a methodology or technique, dialogue was his lifelong existential pursuit.

The truly engaged will never see dialogue as a special task, because dialogue has become their fate. They cannot but embrace others in their distinctive otherness in dialogue. That action implies risks, of course, but they have no other way to go. However, trusting in the strength of an unmediated certainty nourished by faith, Christians eagerly expect in every encounter with people of other faiths the self-disclosure and self-revelation of the living God reconfirming acknowledged truth anew. If such revitalizing of the Ultimate does really happen—and that is indeed what the Christian faith dares to hold to with its insistence on the resurrection of Christ—today's experience of religious plurality would not question the Ultimate at all. Rather, the experience of religious plurality and variety would question only whether the established continuum of speech about the Ultimate is still appropriate. Indeed, the present situation, to an extent unknown before and unparalleled in the radical nature of its expression, only intensifies the quest for the living God as the truly Ultimate; it only deepens the need to find more adequate ways to communicate about that which really makes sense—ultimately—not just for a few privileged but for everyone.

As powerful as this insight may be, to communicate it to the general public today requires meeting the challenge of an increased religious illiteracy and inarticulateness. In a time when definite answers have lost their convincing plausibility people tend to dismiss the question "What is truth?" altogether. However, such dismissal is precisely *not* a solution. It is only a suspension of that all important question which, if not given the attention it deserves, motivates religious fanatics to force ignorant contemporaries to listen to *their* version of truth by taking to arms. Therefore, the irrefutable task to avoid such an outcome is to cultivate and foster the attitude of staying-in-dialogue-together on *all* matters of ultimate concern, especially in times of radical relativism.

33. Cragg, *Troubled by Truth*.
34. Schoen, *Jean Faure*, 10; my translation.

Living a Dialogical Existence

The Christian perception of God holds that the living God *as the living God* is always before and beyond all knowledge and awareness of God. Christians do not entertain an idea of God as conceived by idealistic philosophy Kantian style, according to which God is the highest instance of knowledge and the absolute moral principle, necessary to prop up the entire system of thought.[35] The Christian perception of God is not beholden to any abstract idea. Rather, it arises from acknowledging the history of divine self-disclosure beginning with the creation, finding expression in the covenants with Noah (Gen 8:21–22), Abraham (Gen 12:3), and Moses (Exod 19–20), and also in the words of the prophets—in their stern admonitions, their announcements of judgment, and their words of comfort and promise. In Jesus Christ this history of divine self-disclosure attained a new quality by taking on universal dimensions, because in him God became fully human—not an avatar, that is, a god disguised as a human person—but truly a human like other humans, suffering pain,[36] dying, and being buried. Yet, the Christian faith dares to believe, on account of the witness and testimony by those who were with him, that he did not remain in the grave but was "raised from death."[37] Confidently trusting this message, women and men throughout the centuries did find the way to life—and are still finding it—by becoming his disciples.[38]

Against this background, the specifically Christian motivation for engaging in open, unreserved, and unconditional dialogue with people of other faiths results from their trust in the revelation of the presence of the risen Lord, who has promised to be with his disciples "always, to the end of the age."[39] Christians also confidently trust that it is the Spirit of truth "who will guide" them "into all the truth" for the glorification of Christ (John 16:13–14). So, in every encounter the faithful expect that Christ will reveal

---

35. See especially Kant's writings *A New Exposition of the First Principles of Metaphysical Knowledge* (in *Kant's Latin Writings*, 57–109); besides *The One Possible Basis for a Demonstration of the Existence of God*. See also England, *Kant's Conception of God*.

36. See Heb 5:7–8: "In the days of his flesh, Jesus offered up prayers and supplications, with loud cries and tears, to the one who was able to save him from death . . . although he was son, he learned obedience through what he suffered."

37. See Mark 16:6; Matt 27:64; Luke 24:34, 46; John 21:14.

38. See especially Acts 2:1–47.

39. See Matt 28:20.

his presence today, as he did before at Emmaus[40] and on the shore at the Sea of Tiberias.[41] Not instantly recognizable for who he is, the risen Christ surprises his disciples as the one unknown, even as one who is a stranger.[42] However, he does not remain so for long: As soon as he calls disciples by their names they promptly recognize him. But he keeps surprising his disciples again, because he withdraws and disappears once he has become recognized as who he really is. Thus, he keeps his sovereignty and makes it impossible to tie him down. God's self-revelation so remains a vivid and dynamic encounter which oscillates between disclosure and retraction, recognition and concealment. This certainly is very disconcerting, but it actually is not alien to biblical tradition at all.

Early in the tradition, Moses had to recognize the paradoxical character of God's revelation. When he asked for the proper name of the one who spoke to him in the burning bush so that by the means of a name he could relate the strange phenomenon with the world of ordinary human experience and make it known to others, he received as an answer, "I will be who I will be!" (Exod 3:14). This answer can also be read as, "I will prove to be who I will prove to be"; that is, God always will reveal God self as the living God, never to be fixed in stereotypes but always to be realized anew by humans as the living God in actual encounter. The first disciples, too, had to revise their ideas about their Lord and Master over and over again. As the ones who had thrown in their lot with Jesus of Nazareth by leaving their families and homes to follow him around from Galilee to Jerusalem supposing that he "was the one to redeem Israel" (Luke 24:21), the disciples saw their expectations crashing when they witnessed Jesus' fate and dishonorable death on a cross. Hiding after his execution out of fear and shame, they grew anxious while the realities of the hour induced them to become apathetic. But then, all of a sudden, they experienced the surprising presence of Jesus Christ as their Lord right among them—surprising in that it was a totally new, totally unexpected self-disclosure of the living God—and so, as they gradually came to understand who he really was, they realized their calling.

---

40. Luke 24:13–32.

41. John 21:1–14.

42. Even Mary Magdalene's longstanding cordial familiarity with Jesus did not save her from mistaking the Risen Christ for the gardener. Only when called by her name she came to realize (John 20:11–18).

> When it was evening on that day, the first day of the week, and the doors of the house where the disciples had met were locked for fear of the Jews, Jesus came and stood among them and said "Peace be with you." After he said this, he showed them his hands and his side. Then the disciples rejoiced when they saw the Lord. Jesus said to them again "Peace be with you. As the Father has sent me, so I send you."[43]

Sent by the risen Christ, the disciples were mandated to proclaim the Gospel to all the world.[44] Heeding this charge, they soon realized, however, that their mission entailed a constant overstepping of well-established religious, ethnic, cultural, and social boundaries, a practice which occasioned severe conflict already early on, threatening to dash the incipient Church to pieces. For example, Paul ignited a debate over whether accepting the Gospel required abiding by the ritual laws of the Jews—the position favored by Peter and others from Jerusalem—or not, so that Gentiles free of these laws need not submit to circumcision, for instance, but could become Christians without, which was the position of Paul.[45] (It speaks for the reliability of the biblical account that this conflict was not put under the rug or brushed aside but recorded and thus brought into the open for beneficial consideration by all.)

A different account in Acts tells the story of Peter who in a vision sees ritually unclean animals which he is asked to feast on. But as a faithful Jewish Christian he refuses to do so, arguing that he had "never eaten anything . . . profane or unclean." He then is told by the angel who showed him all this, "What God has made clean, you must not call profane." Not only did this incident momentarily make Peter become aware of his exclusivistic shortsightedness, it also empowered him to accept the invitation to Caesarea into the house of a god-fearing Gentile, the Roman Centurion Cornelius, where he then spent several days preaching and baptizing, something he was afraid of doing before.[46] The insight to be gained from this story is that genuine Christian discipleship has to be acted out in unconditional openness to encounters with the people around, neither shunning them on account of their cultural or religious backgrounds nor judging them

---

43. John 20:19–21.
44. See Matt 28:16–20 and Mark 16:15.
45. See Acts 15:1–41; Gal 2:1–10.
46. See Acts 10:1–48.

prematurely but, instead, always being prepared to notice and expect the presence of the risen Christ in the encounters.

When Christians live by and from confident trust in God's self-revelation in the world, their existence becomes thoroughly dialogical; so, too, does their faith. Christians do not "have" or "own" faith in the sense of a personal habit, belonging, or virtue; they only "have" faith inasmuch as they actualize it by living it out over against the challenges of the times by bringing the living God into dialogue with the world and the world into dialogue with the living God. Their faith forms and stays alive in word and deed as they continuously relate faith and world—their calling to discipleship and the great and small challenges of their surroundings. Christians thereby shape history, imprinting it with the presence of the living God, and in this way they bear witness for the still ongoing history of salvation.

Further, Christians are commissioned to keep the legacy of Christ's mission alive: "As the Father has sent me so I send you!" (John 20:21). Unfortunately though, this directive—being sent, as Christ was—has often been gravely distorted in the course of the history of Christianity, notably by those who understood and understand this "great commission" to mean partisan propaganda for churches, sects, or particular denominations whereas this commission is a mandate to live an unreserved dialogical existence, just as Jesus did. Looking at him for orientation—that is, of course, the Jesus as known to us through the Gospel narratives and the writings of Paul and other apostolic authors—it is instructive to notice that Jesus' life was dialogical to its core. In numerous parables and similes Jesus made nature speak.[47] He also engaged in explicit dialogue with his contemporaries—friends and adversaries,[48] with the twelve, and with the general public.[49] Jesus also dialogued with God in prayers, notably so during the dark night in Gethsemane[50] and on the cross.[51] What also emerges from studying the accounts of the New Testament is an image of Jesus as someone who actually never did insist doggedly on his own preconceived views.

---

47. See for instance Mark 4:26–29 (parable of the seed growing); Matt 13:24–30 (parable of the tares); 13:31–32; Mark 4:30–32; Luke 13:18–19 (parable of the mustard seed) etc.

48. See Matt 12:1–8; Mark 2:23–28; Luke 6:1–5 (plucking grain on the Sabbath); John 3:1–21 (discourse with Nicodemus); Luke 5:33–39; Mark 2:18–22 (issue about fasting).

49. See Matt 5–7 (Sermon on the Mount); Luke 8:9–10 (reason for speaking in parables); Matt 18:21–22 (on reconciliation).

50. See Matt 26:36–46; Mark 14:32–42; Luke 22:39–46. But see also John 17:1–26.

51. Matt 27:46.

Rather, he allowed himself to have his mind changed, especially when confronted with unconditional openness and honest trust. An example of this is his encounter with the Canaanite woman pleading for the healing of her daughter[52]; others include the Centurion of Capernaum who interceded on behalf of his sick servant, the band of ten lepers at Samaria ousted from their community, and the Gadarene demoniacs, to mention only a few.[53]

However, as dialogical existence becomes tangible in Jesus of Nazareth, to an outside observer, such a posture appears in at least one respect to founder at its base, because Jesus became the object of mockery, scorn, and jest. When he asserted during the trial, "For this I was born . . . to testify to the truth," Pilate pointedly replied, "What is truth?"[54] The etymology of the Greek term for truth used here is *alētheia* (ἀλήθεια). This expression originally described an attitude or posture more than a substantive content or an abstract concept of "truth." The attitude described means "concealing nothing," "not withholding," or "not holding back" anything; etymologically *alētheia* (ἀλήθεια) is made up by the negating prefix ἀ-, meaning "non/not" and ληθεια, meaning "withholding."[55] And indeed, according to the Gospels Jesus did not conceal anything out of fear for his life nor did he shun critical confrontation in order to please. Instead, the Gospels show him as the one mocked, punished, and crucified, which is surely not an attractive role model for a life. Jesus suffered an ending which took the Church several centuries to become reconciled with. Only when the Roman authorities, notably the Emperors Constantine (270–337) and Theodosius I (347–395) recognized and appropriated the cross for their interests did the cross become the dominant Christian emblem.[56] While the cross as a domesticated symbol thus lost its embarrassment—the longer it was evoked, the more—the New Testament has kept a clear awareness of its scandal—always, however, in light of the resurrection.[57]

Jesus did testify to the truth and did abide by the truth, and he did so in a radical way. That he foretold his passion several times[58] indicates that

---

52. Matt 15:21–28.
53. See Matt 8:5–13; Luke 17:11–19; Matt 8:28–34.
54. John 18:37–38.
55. "Etymologically ἀλήθεια has the meaning of nonconcealment" (Bultmann, ἀλήθεια, in *Theological Dictionary of the New Testament*, 1:238).
56. See Elsner, *Imperial Rome and Christian Triumph*; and Spier, *Picturing the Bible*.
57. See 1 Cor 1:18–24.
58. See Mark 8:31–33; 9:30–32; 10:32–34; Matt 16:21–23; 17:22–23; 20:17–19; Luke 9:22, 43–45; 18:31–34.

he was fully aware that his unreserved dialogical openness implied ultimate existential risk, a strong and most powerful reminder of the vulnerability of dialogical existence. And Jesus also drew the attention of the disciples to that risk. He did not want them to entertain wishful thinking, telling them that "those who love their life will lose it"[59] while "those who lose their life ... will find it," that is, those who throw in their life for the sake of witnessing to the truth.[60] Jesus wanted to be clear about what discipleship in his name meant. Commitment to this task is all demanding, and Jesus clearly set the conditions. He gave himself *completely* and completely gave *himself* on the cross; that is authenticity perfectly realized. There is no shortcut in Christian discipleship.

Christians, too, are called to witness to the truth, trusting that God's Spirit will lead them into all the truth for the glorification of Jesus Christ: "Christians should not be hesistant about testing their beliefs in a pluralistic world and this testing happens in authentic dialogue with those in other faiths."[61] Beyond simply stating or claiming it, they are to testify to the truth, not just by argument, but by their entire way of life and being. Their mandate is to live an authentic dialogical existence and to encourage others to do likewise. *That* is their mission and their great calling. Trusting that Christ will reveal himself anew and in new ways in encounters and dialogues with people of every kind—scientists, scholars, atheists, nihilists, secularists, people of other faiths—Christians will dispute over the truth and actively engage in the discourse for the sake of finding the truth, because as long as truth is not recognized as such, it remains ambiguous and contested. To further the recognition of truth Christians will not conceal or withhold anything from others in such dialogues, nor will they keep quiet about their values. On the contrary, Christians will have to engage these in the pursuit of finding the truth. How to do it they can learn, at least in part, from the Apostle Paul, who was once challenged by Christians from Corinth regarding his claim of authority and the content of his message. Speaking of himself and his coworkers Paul replied,

> We have renounced the shameful things that one hides; we refuse to practice cunning or to falsify God's word; but by the open statement of the truth we commend ourselves to the conscience of everyone in the sight of God ... For we do not proclaim ourselves;

59. See John 12:25.
60. Matt 10:39.
61. Yong, *The Cosmic Breath*, 240–41.

we proclaim Jesus Christ as Lord . . . For it is the God who said, "Let light shine out of darkness," who has shone in our hearts to give the light of the knowledge of the glory of God in the face of Jesus Christ.[62]

Christians will not hide the core of their faith; they simply cannot.[63] Unpopular though it is, Christians thereby take upon themselves the risk of causing conflict in the encounter wherever actual dialogue takes them. This they do not for the sake of proving themselves right, but because they cannot stay content and satisfied with the mere penultimate. So they push further, confidently trusting that ultimately the risen Christ will become known as the one he really is—to them as well as to others. In their radical openness they create an entirely new sense of communal striving for the good of all and past all existing differences. Just so, in honestly seeking and cultivating this kind of critical, robust dialogue Christians move the entire community beyond lurking threats of "holy wars" and, thus, forge genuine, sustainable peace.

---

62. 2 Cor 4:2–6. Jensen has given an impressive example on how this might look in a dialogue with Buddhists in his *In the Company of Others*.

63. See Matt 12:34; Acts 4:20.

Bibliography

Albright, Madeleine. *The Mighty and the Almighty: Reflections on America, God, and World Affairs*. New York: HarperCollins, 2006.
Allen, Beverly. *Rape Warfare: The Hidden Genocide in Bosnia-Herzegovina and Croatia*. Minneapolis: University of Minnesota Press, 1996.
Allen, Edgar Leonhard. *A Guide to the Thought of Karl Heim: Jesus Our Leader*. London: Hodder & Stoughton, 1950.
al-Mawardi, Abu al-Hasan. *Al-Ahkam al-Sultaniyya w'al-Wilayat al-Diniyya* [The Ordinances of Governance]. Translated by Wafaa H. Wahba. London: Garnet, Al-Ahkam al-Sultaniyya, 1996.
American Backlash: Terrorists bring war home in more ways than one. A special report by SAALT (South Asian American Leaders of Tomorrow). Washington DC, 2001.
An-Na'im, Abdullahi A. *Inter-religious Marriages among Muslims: Negotiating Religious and Social Identity in Family and Community*. New Delhi: Global Media, 2005.
Anselm of Canterbury. *Works I*. Edited and translated by Jasper Hopkins and Herbert Richardson. Toronto: Mellen, 1974.
Appignanesi, Richard. *Introducing Existentialism*. 3rd ed. Cambridge: Icon, 2002.
Appleyard, Brian. *How to Live Forever or Die Trying: On the New Immortality*. London: Simon & Schuster, 2007.
Aquinas, Thomas. *Summa contra gentiles*. 4 vols. in 5. Translated by A. C. Pegis et al. Notre Dame, IN: University of Notre Dame Press, 1955–1975.
"Are We Becoming an Uncivil Society? The Debate about Charged Political Rhetoric Preceded the Tragedy in Tucson—and Then Was Revived by It." *Time Magazine*, Jan. 24, 2011, 40–41.
Arrian. *Anabasis of Alexander, Books I–IV*. Translated and edited by P. A. Brunt. 2 vols. LCL 236, 269. Harvard: Harvard University Press, 1976, 1983.
Ash, Timothy Garton. *The Magic Lantern: The Revolution of '89 Witnessed in Warsaw, Budapest, Berlin, and Prague*. New York: Random House, 1993.
Athamina, Kahlil, and Roger Heacock, eds. *The Frankish Wars and their Influence on Palestine: Selected papers presented at Birzeit University's International Academic Conference held in Jerusalem, March 13–15, 1992*. Birzeit, Palestine: Birzeit University Press, 1994.
Augustine. *The City of God against the Pagans*. Edited and translated by Robert W. Dyson. Cambridge: Cambridge University Press, 1998.
———. *Confessions*. Translated by Veron J. Bourke. Washington, DC: Catholic University of America Press, 1953.
AVESTA Zoroastrian Archive. Online: http://www.avesta.org/.

Bibliography

Avnon, Dan. *Martin Buber: The Hidden Dialogue*. Lanham, MD: Rowman & Littlefield, 1998.

Balslev, Anindita Niyogi, and Jitendranath N. Mohanty, eds. *Religion and Time*. Studies in the History of Religions 54. Leiden: Brill 1993.

Barbour, Ian G. *Religion and Science: Historical and Contemporary Issues*. San Francisco: HarperCollins, 1997.

Barre, Elisheva. *Torah for Gentiles: The Messianic and Political Implications of the Bnei Noah Laws*. Jerusalem: Pomeranz, 2008.

Baum, Wilhelm, and Dietmar W. Winkler. *The Church of the East: A Concise History*. London: Routledge, 2010.

Beck, Lewis White. *A Commentary on Kant's Critique of Practical Reason*. Chicago: Chicago University Press, 1996.

Becker, Dieter, and Andreas Feldtkeller, eds. *Mit dem Fremden leben: Perspektiven einer Theologie der Konvivenz: Theo Sundermeier zum 65. Geburtstag* [Living Together with the Stranger: Perspectives on a Theology of Convivence]. 2 vols. Erlangen: Erlanger Verlag für Mission und Ökumene, 2000.

Begon, Rabbi Dov. We Are Waging a *Milkhemet Mitzwah*. Israelnationalnews.com. Online: http://www.israelnationalnews.com/Articles/Article.aspx/6412.

Belasco, Amy. *The Cost of Iraq, Afghanistan, and Other Global War on Terror Operations Since 9/11*. Congressional Research Service, March 29, 2011, 7–5700 RL33110.

Berger, David. *The Jewish-Christian Debate in the High Middle Ages*. Philadelphia: Jewish Publication Society, 1979.

Berger, Peter L. *The Heretical Imperative: Contemporary Possibilities of Religious Affirmation*. Garden City, NY: Anchor, 1979.

Berkhout, Carl T., and Russell, Jeffrey B. *Medieval Heresies: A Bibliography 1960–1979*. Subsidia Mediaevalia 11. Toronto: Pontifical Institute of Medieval Studies, 1981.

Bernard, Saint. *On Consideration*. Translated by George Lewis. Oxford: Clarendon, 1908.

Bideleux, Robert, and Jeffries, Ian. *A History of Eastern Europe: Crisis and Change*. 2nd ed. London: Routledge, 2007.

Biechler, James E., and H. Lawrence Bond, eds. [Nicholas of Cusa] *On Interreligious Harmony: Text, Concordance and Translation of* De pace fidei. Texts and Studies in Religion 55. Lewiston, NY: Mellen, 1991.

Bloch, Ernst. *Atheism in Christianity: The Religion of the Exodus and the Kingdom*. Translated by J. T. Swann. New York: Herder & Herder, 1972.

———. "Reiseform des Wissens" [Journeying, the Form of Knowledge]. *Merkur* 16 (1962) 201–10.

Böckenhoff, Joseph. *Die Begegnungsphilosophie: Ihre Geschichte, ihre Aspekte* [Philosophy of Encounter: Its History, Its Aspects]. Freiburg: Alber, 1970.

Bodi, Bhikkhu. *The Noble Eightfold Path: The Way to the End of Suffering*. 2nd rev. ed. Kandy, Sri Lanka: Buddhist Publication Society, 1994.

Boia, Lucian. *Forever Young: A Cultural History of Longevity*. London: Reaktion, 2004.

Bonney, Richard. *Jihād: From Qur'ān to bin Laden*. Basingstoke, UK: Palgrave Macmillan, 2004.

Boyce, Mary. *Textual Sources for the Study of Zoroastrianism*. Chicago: University of Chicago Press, 1984.

Boyer, Carl B. *A History of Mathematics*. 2nd ed. Revised by Uta C. Merzbach. New York: Wiley & Sons, 1989.

Bibliography

Bozóki, Andreás. *The Roundtable Talks of 1989: The Genesis of Hungarian Democracy—Analysis and Documents*. Budapest: Central European University Press, 2002.

Brann, Eva, Peter Kalkavage, and Eric Salem. *Plato: Sophist or The Professor of Wisdom*. Newburyport: Focus, 1996.

Britannica Book of the Year 2013. Chicago: Encyclopedia Britannica, 2013.

Bromiley, Geoffrey W. *An Introduction to the Theology of Karl Barth*. Grand Rapids: Eerdmans, 1979.

Bromley, David G., and J. Gordon Melton, eds. *Cults, Religion, and Violence*. Cambridge: Cambridge University Press, 2002.

Brown, Jonathan. *The Canonization of al-Bukhari and Muslim: The Formation and Function of the Sunni Hadith Canon*. Leiden: Brill, 2007.

Brunner, Rainer, and Werner Ende. *The Twelver Shia in Modern Times: Religious Culture and Political History*. Social, Economic, and Political Studies of the Middle East and Asia 72. Leiden: Brill, 2001.

Buber, Martin. *Between Man and Man*. Translated by Ronald Gregor-Smith; with an introduction by Maurice Friedman. London: Routledge, 2002.

———. "Genuine Dialogue and the Possibilities of Peace." In *Pointing the Way: Collected Essays*, translated and edited by Maurice Friedman, 232–39. New York: Harper & Brothers, 1957.

———. *I and Thou*. Translated by Walter Kaufmann. New York: Scribner's Sons, 1970.

———. *The Philosophy of Martin Buber*. Edited by Paul Arthur Schilpp and Maurice Friedman. Library of Living Philosophers 12. Lasalle, IL: Open Court, 1967.

Buber, Martin, and Franz Rosenzweig. *Scripture and Translation*. Edited and translated by Lawrence Rosenwald and Everett Fox. Indiana Studies in Biblical Literature. Bloomington: Indiana University Press, 1994.

Bultmann, Rudolf. ἀλήθεια, ἀληθής, ἀληθινός, ἀληθεύω. In *Theological Dictionary of the New Testament*, edited by Gerhard Kittel and Gerhard Friedrich and translated by Geoffrey W. Bromiley, 1:238–51. Grand Rapids: Eerdmans, 1964.

Bundespräsidialamt [Office of the President of the Federal Republic of Germany, formerly Bonn, now Berlin]. "Speech by Roman Herzog, President of the Federal Republic of Germany, prior to the lectures on the topic Towards a Universal Civilization at the Institute of Islamic Understanding (IKIM), Kuala Lumpur, April 3, 1997." Script.

Burggraeve, Roger, ed. *The Awakening to the Other: A Provocative Dialogue with Emmanuel Levinas*. Leuven: Peeters, 2008.

Burleigh, John H. S., ed. *Augustine: Earlier Writings*. London: SCM, 1953.

Busch, Eberhard. *Karl Barth: His Life from Letters and Autobiographical Texts*. Translated by John Bowden. Minneapolis: Fortress, 1976.

Bynum, Carolyn Walker. *Holy Feast and Holy Fast: The Religious Significance of Food to Medieval Women*. Berkeley: University of California Press, 1987.

Calvin, John. *Institutes of the Christian Religion*. Translated by Henry Beveridge. Grand Rapids: Eerdmans, 1957.

Capps, Walter H. *Religious Studies: The Making of a Discipline*. Minneapolis: Fortress, 1995.

Caputo, N. *Nahmanides in Medieval Catalonia: History, Community, and Messianism*. South Bend, IN: University of Notre Dame Press, 2008.

Carroll, James. "The Bush Crusade." *The Nation* 279 (2004) 14–22.

———. *Crusade: Chronicles of an Unjust War*. New York: Metropolitan, 2004.

Bibliography

Cassirer, Ernst, Paul Oskar Kristeller, and John Herman Randall Jr. *The Renaissance Philosophy of Man*. Chicago: University of Chicago Press, 1948.

Castro, Américo. *España en su historica: cristianos, moros y judios*. Buenos Aires: Losada, 1949.

———. *The Spainards: An Introduction to their History*. Translated by Willard F. King and Selma Margaretten. Berkeley: University of California Press, 1971.

Cavanaugh, William T. *The Myth of Religious Violence: Secular Ideology and the Roots of Modern Conflict*. Oxford: Oxford University Press, 2009.

Chamberlin, William Henry. *America's Second Crusade*. Colorado Springs: Myles, 1962.

Chazan, Robert L. *Barcelona and Beyond: The Disputation of 1263 and Its Aftermath*. Berkeley: University of California Press, 1992.

———. *Daggers of Faith: Thirteenth-Century Christian Missionizing and the Jewish Response*. Berkeley: University of California Press, 1989.

———. *European Jewry and the First Crusade*. Berkeley: University of California Press, 1987.

Christian Arabic Apologetics during the Abbasid Period (750–1258). Edited by Samir Khalil Samir and Jørgen S. Nielsen. Studies in the History of Religions 63. Leiden: Brill Academic, 1994.

Christiansen, Eric. *The Northern Crusades*. 2nd ed. London: Penguin, 1997.

Clarke, Desmond M. *Descartes: A Biography*. Cambridge: Cambridge University Press, 2006.

Clarke, Richard A. *Against All Enemies: Inside America's War on Terrorism*. New York: Simon & Schuster, 2004.

Clayton, Philip. "Constraint and Freedom in the Movement from Quantum Physics to Theology." In *Philosophy, Science and Divine Action*, edited by F. Leron Shults, Nancey Murphy, and Robert John Russell, 191–226. Philosophical Studies in Science and Religion 1. Leiden: Brill, 2009.

Cohen, Hermann. *Religion of Reason: Out of the Sources of Judaism*. Translated by Simon Kaplan, with introductions by Leo Strauss et al. New York: Ungar, 1972.

Cohen, Jeremy. *Sanctifying The Name of God: Jewish Martyrs and Jewish Memories of the First Crusade*. Philadelphia: University of Pennsylvania Press, 2004.

———. "Scholarship and Intolerance in the Medieval Academy: The Study and Evaluation of Judaism in European Christendom." *American Historical Review* 91 (1986) 592–613.

Cohn, Margot, and Rafael Buber. *Martin Buber. A Bibliography of His Writings. 1897–1978*. Jerusalem: Magnes, 1980.

Colussi, Frank J. "Fighting Words?—Free Speech and the Westboro Baptist Church." *The Cresset* 74 (2011) 3, 28–30.

Conze, Edward. *Buddhism: Its Essence and Development*. 1951. Reprint, Birmingham, UK: Windhorse Publications, 2001.

Cook, David. *Understanding Jihad*. Berkeley: University of California Press, 2005.

Cooper, David E. *Existentialism: A Reconstruction*. Oxford: Blackwell, 1999.

Cooperson, Michael. *Al-Ma'mun*. London: Oneworld, 2005.

Corrigan, Kathleen. *Visual Polemics in the Ninth-Century Byzantine Psalters: Iconophile Imagery in Three Ninth-Century Byzantine Psalters*. Cambridge: Cambridge University Press, 1992.

Cox, Harvey. *Many Mansions: A Christian's Encounter with Other Faiths*. Boston: Beacon, 1988.

Bibliography

Cragg, Kenneth. *Troubled by Truth: Biographies in the Presence of Mystery*. Eugene, OR: Wipf & Stock, 2009.
Cragg, Kenneth, and R. Marston Speight. *The House of Islam*. 3rd ed. Belmont, CA: Wadsworth, 1988.
Crouzet, Denis. *Les Guerriers de Dieu. La violence au temps des troubles de religion vers 1525–vers 1610*. [Warriors of God: Violence in Times of Religious Unrest 1525–1610]. 2 vols. Seyssel, France: Champ Vallon, 1990.
Cuffel, Alexandra. *Gendering Disgust in Medieval Religious Polemics*. Notre Dame: Notre Dame University Press, 2007.
Dallen, Michael Ellias. *The Rainbow Covenant: Torah and the Seven Universal Laws*. Springdale, AR: Lightcatcher, 2003.
Dawson, Lorne L. *Comprehending Cults: The Sociology of New Religious Movements*. 2nd ed. New York: Oxford University Press, 2006.
Davidson, Herbert A. *Moses Maimonides: The Man and His Works*. Oxford: Oxford University Press, 2005.
DeLong-Bas, Natana J. *Wahhabi Islam: From Revival and Reform to Global Jihad*. Oxford: Oxford University Press, 2004.
Demacopoulos, George E. *Archons of the Ecumenical Patriarchate: Defenders of the Faith*, no date. Online: www.archons.org/pdf/Archons_History.pdf.
De Silva, Lynn A. *The Problem of the Self in Buddhism and Christianity*. New York: Harper & Row, 1979.
DeYoung, Ursula. *The Homeric Gods and Xenophanes' Opposing theory of the Divine*. Classic Technology Center, Harvard University, 2000. Online: http://ablemedia.com/ctcweb/showcase/deyoung4.html.
Diccionario enciclopédico Espasa. Madrid: Espasa-Calpe, 1985.
Dodd, Charles Harold. "Letter Concerning Some Unavowed Motives in Ecumenical Discussions." *The Ecumenical Review* 2 (1949) 52–56.
Ebner, Ferdinand. *Das Wort und die geistigen Realitäten. Pneumatologische Fragmente*. [The Word and Spiritual Realities: Pneumatological Fragments]. Vol. 1 of *Schriften* [Writings], edited by Franz Seyr. Munich: Kösel, 1963.
Edict of Milan. Quoted in *De Mort. Pers.*, by Lactantius, in *Translations and Reprints from the Original Sources of European History*, translated by the University of Pennsylvania, Department of History, 4/1:28–30. Philadelphia: University of Pennsylvania Press, [1897?–1907?]. Internet Medieval Sourcebook, Fordham University, 1996. Online: http://www.fordham.edu/halsall/source/edict-milan.html.
Eicher, Joanne B., ed. *Dress and Ethnicity: Change across Space and Time*. Oxford: Berg, 1995.
Eisenhower, Dwight David. *Crusade in Europe*. Garden City, NY: Doubleday, 1948.
El Guindi, Fadwa. *Veil: Modesty, Privacy and Religion*. Oxford: Berg, 1999.
Eliade, Mircea. *Essential Sacred Writings from Around the World*. New York: HarperCollins, 1977.
Elsner, Jas. *Imperial Rome and Christian Triumph: The Art of the Roman Empire 100–450 AD*. Oxford: Oxford University Press, 1998.
Elster, John, ed. *The Roundtable Talks and the Breakdown of Communism, Constitutionalism in Eastern Europe*. Chicago: University of Chicago Press, 1996.
The Encyclopaedia of Islam. 12 vols. Leiden: Brill, 1960–2004.
Encyclopaedia Judaica. 26 vols. New York: Macmillan, 1971–1996.

Bibliography

The Encyclopedia of Judaism. 3 vols. Edited by Jacob Neusner, Alan J. Avery-Peck, and William Scott Green. Leiden: Brill, 1999.

Encyclopaedia of the Qur'an. 6 vols. Edited by Jane Dammen McAuliffe. Leiden: Brill, 2001–2006.

Encyclopedia of New Religious Movements. Edited by Peter B. Clarke. New York: Routledge, 2006.

The Encyclopedia of Religion. 16 vols. Edited by Mircea Eliade. New York: Macmillan, 1987.

Encyclopedia of Religion. 2nd ed. 15 vols. Edited by Lindsay Jones. Detroit: Thomson Gale, 2005.

Encyclopedia of Religion and War. Edited by Gabriel Palmer-Fernandez. New York: Routledge 2004.

Encyclopedia of Terrorism. Edited by Harvey W. Kushner. Thousand Oaks, CA: Sage, 2003.

England, F. E. *Kant's Conception of God*. 2nd ed. New York: Humanities, 1968.

Eposito, John L. *Unholy War: Terror in the Name of Islam*. Oxford: Oxford University Press, 2002.

Esposito, John L., and Dalia Mogahed. *Who Speaks for Islam? What a Billion Muslims Really Think*. New York: Gallup, 2007.

Faithdefenders.com. Online: http://www.faithdefenders.com/home.html.

Feil, Ernst. "The Problem of Defining and Demarcating *Religion*." In *On the Concept of Religion*, edited by Ernst Feil, 1–35. Translated by Brian McNeil. Atlanta: Scholars, 1999.

Fernandes, Edna. *Holy Warriors: A Journey into the Heart of Indian Fundamentalism*. Granta, UK: Portobello, 2009.

Feuerbach, Ludwig. *The Fiery Book: Selected Writings of Ludwig Feuerbach*. Translation with an introduction by Zawar Hanfi. Garden City, NY: Anchor, 1972.

———. *Thoughts about Death and Immortality*. Translated and with an introduction by James A. Massey. Berkeley: University of California Press, 1981.

Firestone, Reuven. "Holy War in Modern Judaism? 'Mitzvah War' and the Problem of the 'Three Vows.'" *Journal of the American Academy of Religion* 74 (2006) 954–82.

———. "Judaism: Medieval Period." In *Encyclopedia of Religion and War*, edited by Gabriel Palmer-Fernandez, 244–47. New York: Routledge, 2004.

———. "This War is about Religion and Cannot Be Won Without It: Our Own House Needs Order." *Sh'ma A Journal of Jewish Responsibility*, Dec. 1, 2001. Online: http://www.shma.com/2001/12/this-war-is-about-religion-and-cannot-be-won-without-it-our-own-house-needs-order/.

Flahiff, George B. "Deus Non Vult: A Critic of the Third Crusade." *Mediaeval Studies* 9 (1947) 162–88.

Foltz, Richard C. *Religions of the Silk Road. Overland Trade and Cultural Exchange from Antiquity to the Fifteenth Century*. New York: St. Martin's Griffins, 1999.

Forey, Alan J. *The Military Orders: From the Twelfth to the Early Fourteenth Centuries*. New Studies in Medieval History. Burlington, VT: Ashgate, 1992.

Forst, Rainer. *Toleration in Conflict: Past and Present*. Translated by Ciaran Cronin. Ideas in Context. Cambridge: Cambridge University Press, 2013.

Foss, Michael. *People of the First Crusade*. London: Arcade, 1997.

Francis, T. Dayanandan, ed. *New Approaches to Inter-faith Dialogue*. Uppsala: Church of Sweden Mission, 1980.

Freire, Paulo. *Education for Critical Consciousness*. New York: Seabury, 1973.

―――. *Pedagogy of the Oppressed*. Translated by Myra Bergman Ramos, with an introduction by Donaldo Macedo. New York: Continuum, 1970.
Freud, Sigmund. *The Future of an Illusion*. Translated by W. D. Robson-Scott. New York: Liveright & Institute of Psychoanalysis, 1928.
―――. *Moses and Monotheism*. Translated by Katherine Jones. New York: Vintage, 1967.
―――. *Totem and Taboo*. Translated and edited by James Strachey. New York: Norton, 1990.
Friars and Jews in the Middle Ages and Renaissance. Edited by Steven J. McMichael and Susan E. Myers. The Medieval Franciscans 2. Leiden: Brill, 2004.
Friedman, Maurice S. *Martin Buber. The Life of Dialogue*. New York: Routledge, 1955.
―――, ed. *The Worlds of Existentialism: A Critical Reader*. Chicago: University of Chicago Press, 1964.
Friedman, Yohanan. *Prophecy Continuous: Aspects of Ahmadi Religious Thought and Its Medieval Background*. Oxford: Oxford University Press, 2003.
Frisch, Max. *Sketchbook 1946–1949*. Translated by Geoffrey Skelton. New York: Harcourt B. Jovanovich, 1977.
―――. *Sketchbook 1966–1971*. Translated by Geoffrey Skelton. New York: Harcourt Brace Jovanovich, 1983.
Fronsdal, Gil, trans. *The Dhammapada: A New Translation of the Buddhist Classic with Annotations*. Foreword by Jack Kornfield. Boston: Shambala, 2005.
Gabrieli, Francesco. *Arab Historians of the Crusades: Selected and Translated from the Arabic Sources*. Translated by E. J. Costello. Islamic World Series. London: Routledge, 1969.
Gandhi, Mohandas Karamchand. *Gandhi—An Autobiography: The Story of My Experiments With Truth*. Boston: Beacon, 1993.
Garfield, Jay L., trans. *The Fundamental Wisdom of the Middle Way—Nāgārjunās Mūlamadhyamakakārikā*. Oxford: Oxford University Press, 1995.
Gaukroger, Stephen. *Descartes: An Intellectual Biography*. Oxford: Oxford University Press, 1995.
Genthe, Hans, and Heiner Grothe. "Von Assisi bis Kyoto" [From Assisi to Kyoto]. In *Materialdienst des Konfessionskundlichen Instituts Bensheim* [Materials and Documents] 37/6 (1986) 116.
Gervers, Michael, ed. *The Second Crusade and the Cistercians*. New York: St. Martin's, 1992.
Gibbs, Robert. *Correlations in Rosenzweig and Levinas*. Princeton, NJ: Princeton University Press, 1992.
Girard, René. *Violence and the Sacred*. Translated by Patrick Gregory. Baltimore: Johns Hopkins University Press, 1977.
Given, James B. *Inquisition and Medieval Society: Power, Discipline, and Resistance in Languedoc*. Ithaca, NY: Cornell University Press, 1997.
Goethe, Johann Wolfgang von. *Faust*. Original German and new translation by Walter Kaufmann. New York: Random House, 1961.
Glatzer, Nahum Norbert, ed. *Franz Rosenzweig: His Life and Thought*. New York: Schocken, 1961.
Global Ethic Foundation. Online: http://www.weltethos.org.
Gluckman, Max. "Gossip and Scandal." *Current Anthropology* 4 (1963) 307–16.
Goldberg, Edwin C. *Swords and Plowshares: Jewish Views of War and Peace*. New York: URJ, 2006.

Bibliography

Gottwald, Norman K. "Two Models for the Origin of Ancient Israel: Social Revolution or Frontier Development." In *The Quest for the Kingdom of God: Studies in Honor of George E. Mendenhall*, edited by H. B. Huffmon, F. A. Spina, and A. R. W. Green, 5–24. Winona Lake, IN: Eisenbrauns, 1983.

Graham-Leigh, Elaine. *The Southern French Nobility and the Albigensian Crusade*. Rochester, NY: Boydell & Brewer, 2005.

Grattan-Guinness, Ivor, ed. *Companion Encyclopedia of the History and Philosophy of the Mathematical Sciences*. 2 vols. London: Routledge, 1994.

Green, Peter. *Alexander of Macedon, 356–23 BC: A Historical Biography*. Berkeley, CA: University of California Press, 1991.

Greenberg, Judith, ed. *Trauma at Home: After 9/11*. Lincoln: University of Nebraska Press, Bison, 2003.

Gregory, Brad S. *The Unintended Reformation: How a Religious Revolution Secularized Society*. Cambridge, MA: Belknap, 2012.

Griffis, Margaret, ed. "Casualties in Iraq: The Cost of Occupation." Antiwar.com, 2009. Online: http://antiwar.com/casualties/.

Grimm, Jacob, and Wilhelm Grimm. *Deutsches Wörterbuch*. 32 vols. Münich: Deutscher Taschenbuch Verlag, 1984.

Grundmann, Christoffer. *In Wahrheit und Wahrhaftigkeit: Für einen kritischen Dialog der Religionen* [In Truth and Truthfulness: For a Critical Dialogue of Rreligions]. Hanover: Lutherisches Verlagshaus, 1999.

Guardian. "Full Text: bin Laden's Letter to America." *Guardian*, Observer Worldview, November 24, 2002. Online: http://www.theguardian.com/world/2002/nov/24/theobserver.

Hadot, Pierre. *The Veil of Isis: An Essay of the History of the Idea of Nature*. Cambridge, MA: Belknap, 2008.

Hand, Seán. *Emmanuel Levinas*. London: Routledge, 2009.

Handke, Peter. *C. G. Jung: Selbstsuche—Selbstfindung—Selbstwerdung* [Searching the Self—Finding the Self—Becoming the Self]. Gaggenau, Germany: Scientia Nova Verlag Neue Wissenschaft, 2002.

Hanly, Michael, ed. and trans. *Medieval Muslims, Christians, and Jews in Dialogue: The Apparicion Maistre Jehan de Meun of Honorat Bovet*. Tempe, AZ: Arizona Center for Medieval and Renaissance Studies, 2005.

Hartman, Rabbi Donniel. "Rabbinic Limitations on War: Deuteronomy 20 permits wars of aggression, but the talmudic rabbis made it difficult to declare one." My Jewish Learning.com. Online: http://www.myjewishlearning.com/beliefs/Issues/War_and_Peace/Peace_and_Nonviolence/Limitations_on_War.shtml.

Hegel, Georg Wilhelm Friedrich, *Lectures on the Philosophy of Religion*. Edited by Peter C. Hodgson. Berkeley: University of California Press, 1984.

Heidegger, Martin. *Being and Time*. Translated by John Macquarrie and Edward Robinson. London: SCM, 1962.

Heimert, Alan, and Delblanco, Andrew, eds. *The Puritans in America: A Narrative Anthology*. Cambridge: Harvard University Press, 1985.

Herder, Johann Gottfried. *Against Pure Reason: Writings on Religion, Language, and History*. Translated, edited, and with an introduction by Marcia Bunge. Minneapolis: Fortress, 1993.

———. *Ideen zur Philosophie der Geschichte der Menschheit* [Outlines of a Philosophy of the History of Man]. Wiesbaden, Germany: Fourier, 1966.

Bibliography

Herzog, Chaim, and Mordechai Gichon. *Battles of the Bible*. London: Greenhill, 1978.
Herzog, Roman. *Preventing the Clash of Civilizations: A Peace Strategy for the Twnety-First Century*. Edited by Henrik Schmieglow. Basingstoke, UK: Palgrave Macmillan, 1999.
Hexham, Irving, and Karla Poewe. *New Religions as Global Cultures*. Boulder, CO: Westview, 1997.
Hick, John. "Religious Pluralism." In *The Encyclopedia of Religion*, edited by Mircea Eliade, 12:331–33. New York: Macmillan, 1987.
Hill, Charles Leander, trans. *The Loci Communes of Philip Melanchthon; with a Critical Introduction by the Translator*. 1944. Reprinted, Eugene, OR: Wipf & Stock, 2007.
Hillenbrand, Carole. *The Crusades: Islamic Perspectives*. Edinburgh: Edinburgh University Press, 1999.
Hinnells, John R. *The Zoroastrian Diaspora: Religion and Migration*. Oxford: Oxford University Press, 2005.
Hobbes, Thomas. *Leviathan*. Edited by Richard Tuck. Cambridge: Cambridge University Press, 1991.
Hodgson, Peter C. *Hegel and Christian Theology: A Reading of the Lectures on the Philosophy of Religion*. Oxford: Oxford University Press, 2005.
Hofstadter, Richard, *Antiintellectualism in American Life*. New York: Vintage, 1962.
Holbach, Paul Henri, Baron d'. *Superstition in All Ages*. Translated by A. Knoop. New York: Eckler, 1920.
Holmstrand, Ingemar. *Karl Heim on Philosophy, Science and the Transcendence of God*. Uppsala: Almqvist & Wiksell, 1980.
Holt, Mack P. *The French Wars of Religion 1562–1626*. Cambridge: Cambridge University Press, 1995.
Holt, Peter Malcolm. *The Mahdist State in Sudan, 1881–1898*. Oxford: Clarendon, 1958.
Holzhey, Helmut. *Cohen und Natorp*. Basel: Schwabe, 1986,
Horton, Myles, and Paulo Freire. *We Make the Road by Walking: Conversations on Education and Social Change*. Edited by Brenda Bell, John Gaventa, and John Peters. Philadelphia: Temple University Press, 1990.
Hume, David. *Dialogues Concerning Natural Religion*. 2nd ed. London: n.p., 1779.
———. *Principal Writings on Religion, Including Dialogues Concerning Natural Religion and The Natural History of Religion*. Edited by J. C. A. Gaskin. Oxford: Oxford University Press, 1993.
Hultkrantz, Åke. *Shamanistic Healing and Ritual Drama*. New York: Crossroad, 1997.
Hundsnurscher, Franz, ed. *Future Perspectives of Dialogue Analysis*. Beiträge zur Dialogforschung 8. Tübingen: Niemeyer, 1995.
Huntington, Samuel P. "The Clash of Civilizations?" *Foreign Affairs* 72 (1993) 22–28.
———. *The Clash of Civilizations and the Remaking of World Order*. New York: Simon & Schuster, 1996.
Hutcheson, Harold R., ed. and trans. *Lord Herbert of Cherbury's De religione laici*. New Haven: Yale University Press, 1944.
Huyse, Philip. "Kerdir and the First Sasanians." In *Proceedings of the Third European Conference of Iranian Studies*, edited by Nicholas Sims-Williams, vol. 1:1109–20. Wiesbaden: Reichert, 1998.
Idliby, Ranya, Suzanne Oliver, and Priscilla Warner. *The Faith Club: A Muslim, a Christian, a Jew—Three Women Search for Understanding*. New York: Free Press, 2006.
Illich, Ivan. *Tools for Conviviality*. New York: Harper & Row, 1978.

Bibliography

Inbar, Efraim. "War in Jewish Tradition." *The Jerusalem Journal of International Relations* 9 (1987) 83–99.

InterAction Council. Online: http://www.interactioncouncil.org.

Iraq Coalition Casualty Count. Online: http://icasualties.org.

Jackson, Peter, trans. *The Mission of Friar William of Rubruck: His Journey to the Court of the Great Khan Möngke, 1253–1255*. London: Hakluyt Society, 1990.

Jarratt, Susan C. *Rereading the Sophists: Classical Rhetoric Refigured*. Carbondale: Southern Illinois University Press, 1991.

Jensen, David H. *In the Company of Others: A Dialogical Christology*. Cleveland, OH: Pilgrim, 2001.

Johnston, Mark D. "Ramon Llull and the Compulsory Evangelization of Jews and Muslims." In *Iberia and the Mediterranean World of the Middle Ages: Studies in Honor of Robert I. Burns S.J.*, edited by Larry J. Simon, 3–37. Leiden: Brill, 1995.

Jones, Dafydd, ed. *Dada Culture: Critical Texts on the Avant-Garde*. Amsterdam: Rodopi, 2006.

Kammen, Michael. *Mystic Chords of Memory: The Transformation of Tradition in American Culture*. New York: Vintage, 1993.

Kassis, Hanna E. *A Concordance of the Qur'an*. Foreword by Fazlur Rahman. Berkeley: University of California Press, 1983.

Kant, Immanuel. *Critique of Practical Reason*. Translated by L. W. Beck. 3rd ed. New York: Macmillan, 1993.

———. *Kant's Latin Writings: Translations, Commentaries and Notes*. Edited by Lewis White Beck in collaboration with Mary J. Gregor, Ralf Meerbote, John A. Reuscher. New York: Lang, 1986.

———. *The One Possible Basis for a Demonstration of the Existence of God*. Translated by Gordon Treash. Lincoln: University of Nebraska Press, 1994.

———. *Religion within the Boundaries of Mere Reason and other writings*. Edited by Allan Wood and George di Giovanni. Cambridge Texts in the History of Philosophy. Cambridge: Cambridge University Press, 1999.

Kegley, Charles W., ed. *The Theology of Emil Brunner*. New York: Macmillan, 1962.

Kenney, Jeffrey T. *Muslim Rebels: Kharijites and the Politics of Extremism in Egypt*. Oxford: Oxford University Press, 2006.

Kerber, Walter. *Der Begriff der Religion*. Munich: Kindt, 1993.

Khadduri, Majid. *War and Peace in the Law of Islam*. Baltimore: Johns Hopkins Press, 1955.

Kim, Ho-dong. *Holy War in China: The Muslim Rebellion and State in Chinese Central Asia, 1864–1877*. Stanford, CA: Stanford University Press, 2004.

Klemperer, Viktor. *The Language of the Third Reich: Lti—Lingua Tertii Imperii: A Philologist's Notebook*. London: Athlone, 2002.

Knitter, Paul F. "Theocentric Christology." *Theology Today* 40 (1983) 130–49.

Kopf, Gereon. *Beyond Personal Identity: Dogen, Nishida, and a Phenomenology of No-Self*. Richmond, UK: Curzon, 2001.

Kraemer, Joel L. *Maimonides: The Life and World of One of Civilization's Greatest Minds*. New York: Doubleday, 2008.

Kraybill, Donald B., ed. *The Amish and the State*. Baltimore: Johns Hopkins University Press, 2003.

———. *On the Backroad to Heaven: Old Order Hutterites, Mennonites, Amish, and Brethren*. Baltimore: John Hopkins University Press, 2001.

Bibliography

Kremer, Alfred von. *Geschichte der herrschenden Ideen des Islam.* [History of the Governing Concepts of Islam]. 1868. Reprint, Hildesheim: Olms 1984.

———. *Über die philosophischen Gedichte des Abul Ala Ma'arry, Eine culturge-schichtliche Studie* [On the Philosophical Poems of Abul Ala Ma'arry—A Treatise in Cultural History]. Vienna: Tempsky, 1888.

Kristeller, Paul Oskar. *Eight Philosophers of the Italian Renaissance.* Stanford, CA: Stanford University Press, 1964.

———. "The Platonic Academy of Florence." *Renaissance News* 14 (1961) 147–59.

Kroeger, Matthias. *Friedrich Gogarten. Leben und Wirken in zeitgeschichtlicher Perspektive* [Friedrich Gogarten: Life and Work in Historical Perspective]. Stuttgart: Kohlhammer, 1997.

Kuhn, Thomas S. *The Structure of Scientific Revolutions.* Chicago: University of Chicago Press, 1962.

Küng, Hans. "Christianity and World Religions: Dialogue with Islam." In *Toward a Universal Theology of Religion*, edited by Leonard Swidler, 192–209. Faith Meets Faith Series. Maryknoll, NY: Orbis, 1987.

———. *Global Responsibility: In Search of a New World Ethic.* Translated by John Bowden. New York: Continuum, 1993.

———. *Yes to a Global Ethic.* New York: Continuum 1996.

Küng, Hans, and Helmut Schmidt, eds. *Global Ethic and Global Responsibilities: Two Declarations.* London: SCM, 1998.

Lactantius, Caecilius Firmianus. *Divinae Institutiones.* In *Corpus Scriptorum Ecclesiasticorum Latinorum*, edited by Samuel Brandt, 19/1:274–397. Vienna: Tempsky, 1890.

Lally, P., et al. "How Are Habits Formed: Modeling Habit Formation in the Real World." *European Journal of Social Psychology* 40 (2010) 998–1109. Online: doi:10.1002/ejsp.674.

Lantzer, Jason S. *"Prohibition Is Here to Stay": The Reverend Edward S. Shumaker and the Dry Crusade in America.* South Bend, IN: University of Notre Dame Press, 2010.

Larmer, Robert. "Is There Anything Wrong with 'God of the Gaps' Reasoning?" *International Journal for Philosophy of Religion* 52 (2002) 129–42.

Lawson, George. *Negotiated Revolutions: The Czech Republic, South Africa, and Chile.* Burlington, VT: Ashgate, 2005.

Lessing, Gottfried Ephraim. *Nathan the Wise, Minna von Barnhelm and Other Plays.* Edited by Peter Demetz. Foreword by Hannah Arendt. German Library 12. New York: Continuum, 1991.

Levinas, Emmanuel. *Otherwise Than Being or Beyond Essence.* Translated by Alphonso Lingis. Martinus Nijhoff Philosophy Texts 3. Dordrecht: Kluwer Academic, 1991.

Library of Congress. "Bibles and Scripture Passages Used by Presidents in Taking the Oath of Office." Online: http://lcweb2.loc.gov/ammem/pihtml/pibible.html.

The Limits of Social Cohesion: Conflict and Mediation in Pluralist Societies: A Report of the Bertelsmann Foundation to the Club of Rome. Edited by Peter L. Berger. Boulder, CO: Westview, 1998.

Lincoln, Bruce. *Holy Terrors: Thinking about Religion after September 11.* Chicago: University of Chicago Press, 2003.

Living Islam. "Documentation of 'Greater Jihad' Hadith." Online: http://www.livingislam.org/n/dgjh_e.html.

Livius.org. Articles on Ancient History. Ashoka's Rock Edicts. Online: http://www.livius.org/sh-si/shahbazgarhi/shahbazgarhi2.htm.

Bibliography

Locke, John. *A Letter Concerning Toleration*. Edited by James H. Tully. Indianapolis: Hackett, 1983.

Luhmann, Niklas. *Observations on Modernity*. Stanford, CA: Stanford University Press, 1998.

Lull, Ramon [Raymond]. *The Book of the Gentile and the Three Wise Men*. In *Doctor Illuminatus: A Ramon Lull Reader*. Edited and translated by Anthony Bonner. Princeton: Princeton University Press, 1993, 73–172.

Luper, Steven. *Existing: An Introduction to Existential Thought*. New York: McGraw-Hill, 2000.

Luther, Martin. *Luther's Works*. Edited by Jaroslav Pelikan and Helmut T. Lehmann. 55 vols. St. Louis: Concordia, 1955–1986.

Maccoby, Hyam, ed. and trans. *Judaism on Trial: Jewish-Christian Disputations in the Middle Ages*. East Brunswick, NJ: Associated University Presses, 1982.

MacMullen, Ramsey. *Christianizing the Roman Empire: A.D. 100–400*. New Haven: Yale University Press, 1984.

Make a World of Difference: Hearing Each Other, Healing the Earth. Parliament of the World's Religions, 3–9 December 2009, Melbourne, Australia, General Program.

Maalouf, Amin. *The Crusades through Arab Eyes*. New York: Schocken, 1984.

Mangina, Joseph L. *Karl Barth: Theologian of Christian Witness*. Louisville: Westminster John Knox, 2004.

Maimonides, Moses. *The Commandments: Sefer Ha-Mitzvoth of Maimonides*. Translated by Charles B. Chavel based on J. Kapach's translation of the original Arabic Text, *Kitab al-faraid*. 2 vols. in one. London: Soncino, 1967.

———. *The Guide for the Perplexed*. Translated by Michael Friedländer. 2nd ed. New York: Dover, 2000.

Mandal, Dhaneshwar. *Ayodhya: Archeology After Demolition*. Rev. ed. New Delhi: Orient Longman, 2003.

Marcel, Gabriel. *The Philosophy of Existentialism*. New York: Citadel, 1968.

Marenbon, John, and Giovanni Orlandi, eds. and trans. *Peter Abelard: Collations* [Dialogue between a Philosopher, a Jew, and a Christian]. Oxford: Oxford University Press, 2001.

Margull, Hans-Jochen. "Der Dialog von Colombo: Ein weiteres Kolloquium zwischen Hindus, Buddhisten, Juden, Christen und Muslimen" [Dialogue at Colombo]. *Ökumenische Rundschau* 23 (1974) 525–34.

———. "Verwundbarkeit—Bemerkungen zum Dialog" [Vulnerability: Remarks on Dialogue]. *Evangelische Theologie* 34 (1974) 410–20.

Markham, Edwin. *The Shoes of Happiness and Other Poems*. New York: Doubleday, 1915.

Markowski, Michael. "Crucisignatus: Its Original and Early Usage." *Journal of Medieval History* 10 (1984) 157–65.

Martini, Raymond. *Pugio Fidei, . . . adversus Mauros, et Iudaeos; nunc primùm in lucem*. Paris: Henault, 1651; Reprint, Farnborough, UK: Gregg, 1967.

Marx, Karl. *Critique of Hegel's "Philosophy of Right."* Translated by Annette Jolin and Joseph O'Malley. Cambridge: Cambridge University Press, 1970.

Masani, Rustom. *Zoroastrianism: The Religion of the Good Life*. London: Macmillan, 1968.

McGilvray, James Clifford. *The Quest for Health and Wholeness*. Tübingen: German Institute for Medical Missions, 1981.

Meir-kahne.anglefire.com. *Parashat Ki Tetzei: Holiness in Times of War* Online: http://meir-kahane.angelfire.com/kitetzei.html.

Bibliography

Melvern, Linda. *Conspiracy to Murder: The Rwandan Genocide.* Rev. ed. London: Verso, 2006.
Menon, V. P. *Integration of the Indian States.* London: Orient Longman, 1995.
Miller, Perry, and Thomas H. Johnson, eds. *The Puritans.* 2nd ed. 2 vols. New York: Harper & Row, 1963.
Mirabaud, M. De [alias d'Holbach]. *The System of Nature: or, The Laws of the Moral and Physical World.* Project Gutenberg. Online: http://www.gutenberg.org/ebooks/8909.
Mishneh Torah. Sefer Shoftim, Melachim uMilchamot. Translated by Eliyahu Touger. Chabad. org. Online: http://www.chabad.org/library/article_cdo/aid/682956/jewish/Mishneh-Torah.htm.
Mitscherlich, Alexander. *Gesammelte Schriften* [Collected Works]. Vol. 5, edited by Helga Haase. Frankfurt: Suhrkamp, 1983.
———. *Toleranz—Überprüfung eines Begriffes* [Tolerance—Rechecking a Concept]. Frankfurt: Suhrkamp, 1974.
———. "Wie ich mir—so ich dir: Zur Psychologie der Toleranz" [I Do unto You as I Do unto Myself—The Psychology of Tolerance]. *Psyche* 5 (1951) 1–15.
Mitscherlich, Alexander, and Fred Mielke. *Doctors of Infamy: The Story of the Nazi Medical Crimes.* Translated by Heinz Norden. 1949. Reprint, Whitefish, MT: Kessinger, 2007.
Moazami, M. "Millennialism, Eschatology, and Messianic figures in Iranian Tradition." *Journal of Millennial Studies* 2/2 (2000). Online: http://www.bu.edu/mille/publications/winter2000/winter2000.html.
Momen, Moojan. *An Introduction to Shi`i Islam: The History and Doctrines of Twelver Shi'ism.* New Haven: Yale University Press, 1985.
Monecal, Maria Rosa. *The Ornament of the World: How Muslims, Jews, and Christians Created a Culture of Tolerance in Medieval Spain.* Boston: Little, Brown, 2002.
Monier-Williams, M. *Sanskrit—English Dictionary.* New Delhi: Motilal Barsanidass, 1971.
Monsutti, Alessandro. *War and Migration: Social Networks and Economic Strategies of the Hazaras of Afghanistan.* Translated by P. Camiller. New York: Routledge, 2005.
More, Thomas. *Utopia.* Translated and edited by Robert M. Adams. New York: Norton, 1992.
Mulhull, Stephen. *Routledge Philosophy Guidebook to Heidegger and "Being and Time."* 2nd ed. London: Routledge, 2005.
Murphy, Thomas Patrick, ed. *The Holy War.* Columbus: Ohio State University Press, 1976.
Murray, Allan V., ed. *The Crusades: An Encyclopedia.* 4 vols. Santa Barbara, CA: ABC-CLIO, 2006.
Musa, Aisha Y. *Hadith as Scripture: Discussions on the Authority of Prophetic Traditions in Islam.* New York: Palgrave, 2008.
Naddaf, Gerard. *The Greek Concept of Nature.* Albany: State University of New York Press, 2005.
Natanson, Maurice. *Edmund Husserl: Philosopher of Infinite Tasks.* Evanston, IL: Northwestern University Press, 1973.
National Commission on Terrorist Attacks Upon the United States. "Public Statement—Release of 9/11 Commission Report—The Hon. Thomas H. Kean and the Hon. Lee H. Hamilton, July 22, 2004." Online: http://govinfo.library.unt.edu/911/report.
Naumann, Bernd, ed. *Dialogue Analysis and the Mass Media: Proceedings of the International Conference, Erlangen, April 2—3, 1998.* Tübingen: Niemeyer, 1999.
The New Arthurian Encyclopedia. Edited by Norris J. Lacy. Updated ed. New York: Garland, 1996.

Bibliography

Newman, Elizabeth. *Untamed Hospitality: Welcoming God and Other Strangers*. Grand Rapids: Brazos, 2007.

Niditch, Susan. *War in the Hebrew Bible: A Study in the Ethics of Violence*. New York: Oxford University Press, 1993.

Nietzsche, Friedrich. *The Gay Science—With a Prelude in Rhymes and an Appendix of Songs*. Translated with commentary by Walter Kaufmann. New York: Random House, 1974.

———. *The Portable Nietzsche*. Translated by Walter Kaufmann. New York: Viking, 1954.

———. *Thus Spake Zarathustra*. Translated by Thomas Common. New York: Dover, 1999.

———. *The Will to Power: An Attempted Transvaluation of All Values*. Translated by Antony M. Ludovici. New York: Russell & Russell, 1964.

Niewöhner, Friedrich. *Veritas sive Varietas—Lessings Toleranzparabel und das Buch von den drei Betrügern* [Truth or/as Variety—Lessing's Parable of Tolerance and the Book of the Three Cheaters]. Heidelberg: Schneider, 1988.

Nikhilananda, Swami, and William E. Hocking. *The Bhagavad Gita*. Whitefish, MT: Kessinger, 2006.

The 9/11 Commission Report: Final Report of the National Commission on Terrorist Attacks Upon the United States. Authorized ed. New York: Norton, 2004.

Nolan, Cathal J. *The Age of Wars of Religion, 1000–1650: An Encyclopedia of Global Warfare and Civilization*. 2 vols. Westport, CT: Greenwood, 2006.

Noth, Albrecht. *Heiliger Krieg und Heiliger Kampf in Islam und Christentum* [Holy War and Holy Fight in Islam and Christendom]. Bonner Historische Forschungen 28. Bonn: Rohrscheid, 1966.

Nukariya, Kaiten. *Zen Buddhism: The Religion of the Samurai*. St. Petersburg, FL: Red and Black, 2008.

O'Brien, John Maxwell. *Alexander the Great: The Invisible Enemy*. New York: Routledge, 1992.

O'Callaghan, Joseph F. *Reconquest and Crusade in Medieval Spain*. Philadelphia: University of Pennsylvania Press, 2004.

Office of Faith-based and Neighborhood Partnerships. "The President's Interfaith and Community Service Campus Challenge." Online: http://www.whitehouse.gov/administration/eop/ofbnp/interfaithservice.

Osama Bin Laden. *Declaration of War Against the Americans Occupying the Land of the Two Holy Places*. Online: http://www.terrorismfiles.org/individuals/declaration_of_jihad1.html.

Osterhammel, Jürgen, and Niels P. Petersson. *Globalization: A Short History*. Translated by Dona Geyer. Princeton: Princeton University Press, 2005.

Otto, Rudolf. *The Idea of the Holy*. Translated by John W. Harvey. London: Oxford University Press, 1950.

Oxford English Dictionary. 13 vols. Edited by James A. H. Murray. Oxford: Oxford University Press, 1971.

Palmer, John A. "Xenophanes' Ouranian God in the Fourth Century." *Oxford Studies in Ancient Philosophy* 16 (1998) 1–34.

Paracelsus (Theophrast Bombast von Hohenheim). *Paracelsus: Selected Writings*. Edited with an introduction by Jolande Jacobi. Translated by Norbert Guterman. Princeton: Princeton University Press, 1995.

Park, Young-Sik. *Konvivenz der Religionen* [Convivence of Religions]. Frankfurt: Lang, 2006.

Bibliography

Pauck, Wilhelm, and Marion Pauck. *Paul Tillich: His Life & Thought*. New York: HarperCollins, 1989.
Peacocke, Arthur. *Theology for a Scientific Age: Being and Becoming—Natural, Human, and Divine*. Enlarged ed. Minneapolis: Fortress, 1993.
Pesic, Peter. "Wrestling with Proteus: Francis Bacon and the 'Torture' of Nature." *ISIS* 90 (1999) 81–94.
Peters, Rudolph. *Islam and Colonialism: The Doctrine of Jihad in Modern History*. The Hague: Mouton, 1979.
The Pew Forum on Religion and Public Life. Online: http://religions.pewforum.org/pdf/affiliations-all-traditions.pdf.
Phillips, Jonathan and Martin Hoch, eds. *The Second Crusade: Scope and Consequences*. Manchester: Manchester University Press, 2001.
Pieper, Joseph. *Abuse of Language—Abuse of Power*. San Francisco: Ignatius, 1992.
Pinkerton, James. "Century In, Century Out—It's Crusade Time." *Newsday*, Dec. 4, 2003. Online: http://newamerica.net/node/6322.
Plato. *Sophist*. Translated, with introduction and notes by Nicholas P. White. Indianapolis: Hackett, 1993.
Pliskin, Zelig *Guard Your Tongue: A Practical Guide to the Laws of Loshon Hora Based on Chofetz* [Hebrew: *Netzor Loshoncha May-ra*]. New York: Weissman, 1975.
Pohl, Christine D. *Making Room: Recovering Hospitality as a Christian Tradition*. Grand Rapids: Eerdmans, 1999.
Pointing: Where Language, Culture and Cognition Meet. Edited by Sotaro Kita. Mahwah, NJ: Erlbaum, 2003.
Popper, Karl. *The Open Society and Its Enemies*. 5th ed. 2 vols. Princeton: Princeton University Press, 1971.
The Press Association. *A Moment in Time: The Millennium Celebrated Around the Globe*. London: HarperCollins UK, 2000.
Prothero, Stephen. *Religious Literacy: What Every American Needs to Know—and Doesn't*. New York: HarperCollins, 2007.
Public Law 107–306—Nov. 27, 2002, Title VI, Sect. 602, Purposes, paragraphs 4 & 5, 116 Stat. 6408. Online: http://www.archives.gov/legislative/research/9-11/public-law-107-306.pdf.
The Qur'an. Edited by M. A. S. Abdel Haleem. New York: Oxford University Press, 2008.
Thesanhedrin.org. Historical Overview. Online: http://www.thesanhedrin.org/en/index.php/Historical_Overview
Rad, Gerhard von. *Holy War in Ancient Israel*. Translated by Marva J. Dawn. Grand Rapids: Eerdmans, 1991.
Rahner, Karl. "Church, Churches, and Religions." In *Theological Investigations*, translated by David Bourke, 10:30–49. London: Darton, Longman, & Todd, 1973.
Rajagopalachari, C[hakravarti]. *Mahābhārata*. Mumbai: Bharatiya Vidya Bhavan, 1994.
Rathaus Hamburg. Epiramm. Online: http://en.wikipedia.org/wiki/File:Hamburger_Wahlspruch_%28Rathausinschrift%29.jpg.
Ratzinger, Joseph Cardinal. *Truth and Tolerance: Christian Belief and World Religions*. Translated by Henry Taylor. San Francisco: Ignatius, 2004.
"Rechtsstreit: Einigung in Sicht—Überschuhe für Heizungsableser—Türkische Familie verwehrte Zutritt" ["Lawsuit: Settlement Possible—Overshoes for Meter-reader—Turkish Family Refused Entry"]. *Schwäbisches Tagblatt*, February 26, 1998.

Bibliography

"Religion and Food [Thematic Issue]." *Journal of the American Academy of Religion* 63/3 (1995) 429–582.

Repgen, Konrad. "Negotiating the Peace of Westphalia: A Survey with an Examination of the Major Problems." In *1648 War and Peace in Europe*, edited by Klaus Bussmann and Heinz Schilling, 1:355–72. Münster: Veranstaltungsgesellschaft 350 Jahre Westfälischer Friede, 1998.

Richards, E. G. *Mapping Time: The Calendar and Its History.* Oxford: Oxford University Press, 1998.

Richards, John F. *The Mughal Empire.* New Cambridge History of India 1/5. Cambridge: Cambridge University Press, 1993.

Ricoeur, Paul. *Husserl: An Analysis of His Phenomenology.* Evanston, IL: Northwestern University Press, 1967.

Richter, Hans. *Dada: Art and Anti-art.* 1965. Reprint, Oxford: Oxford University Press, 1997.

Ricklefs, M. C. *A History of Modern Indonesia since c.1200.* 4th ed. New York: Palgrave Macmillan, 2008.

Riley-Smith, Jonathan. *The First Crusade and the Idea of Crusading.* Philadelphia: University of Pennsylvania Press, 1986.

Rilke, Rainer Maria. *Ausgewählte Werke: Buch der Bilder* [Selected Works: Book of Images]. Edited by Rilke Archiv Weimar. Vol. 1. Leipzig: Insel, 1938.

Robinson, Ian S. "Gregory VII and the Soldiers of Christ." *History* 58 (1973) 169–92.

Rosen, Steven S. *Essential Hinduism.* Foreword by Graham M. Schweig. Westport, CT: Praeger, 2006.

Rosenbaum, Mary Helene, and Stanley Ned Rosenbaum. *Celebrating Our Differences: Living Two Faiths in One Marriage.* New York: Ragged Edge, 1998.

Rosenstock-Huessy, Eugen, ed. *Judaism Despite Christianity: The 1916 Wartime Correspondence between Eugen Rosenstock-Huessy and Franz Rosenzweig.* Chicago: University of Chicago Press, 2011.

Rosenwald, Lawrence. "On the Reception of Buber and Rosenzweig's Bible." *Prooftexts* 14 (1994) 141–65.

Rosenzweig, Franz. *The Star of Redemption.* Translated by William W. Hallo. Notre Dame, IN: Notre Dame University Press, 1985.

Roth, Norman. *Conversos, Inquisition, and the Expulsion of the Jews from Spain.* Madison: University of Wisconsin Press, 2002.

Rousseau, Jean-Jaques. *The Social Contract or: Principles of Political Right.* Translated by Maurice Cranston. London: Penguin Classics, 1968.

Rubruck, William. *The Journey of William of Rubruck to the Eastern Parts of the World, 1253–55, as Narrated by Himself, with Two Accounts of the Earlier Journey of John of Pian de Carpine.* Translated and edited by William Woodville Rockhill. London: Hakluyt Society, 1900.

Russell, Frederick H. *The Just War in the Middle Ages.* Cambridge Studies in Medieval Life and Thought 3/8. Cambridge: Cambridge University Press, 1975.

Russell, Letty M. *Just Hospitality: God's Welcome in a World of Difference.* Louisville: Westminster John Knox, 2009.

Russell, Robert John. *Cosmology from Alpha to Omega: Theology and Science in Creative Mutual Interaction.* Philadelphia: Fortress, 2008.

Sack, Daniel. *Whitebread Protestants: Food and Religion in American Culture.* New York: St. Martin's, 2000.

Bibliography

Salimbene: On Frederick II, 13th Century. Internet Medieval Sourcebook, Fordham University, 1996. Online: http://www.fordham.edu/halsall/source/salimbene1.html.

Samartha, Stanley John, ed. *Between Two Cultures: Ecumenical Ministry in a Pluralist World*. Geneva: World Council of Churches, 1996.

———. *Towards World Community: The Colombo Papers*. Geneva: World Council of Churches, 1974.

Schoen, Ulrich. *Jean Faure: Missionar und Theologe in Afrika und im Islam* [Jean Faure: Missionary and Theologian in Africa and among Muslims]. Göttingen: Vandenhoeck & Ruprecht, 1984.

Scherrer, Christian P. *Genocide and Crisis in Central Africa: Conflict Roots, Mass Violence, and Regional War*. Foreword by Robert Melson. Westport, CN: Praeger, 2002.

Schiffman, Lawrence, H., and Joel B. Wolowelsky, eds. *War and Peace in the Jewish Tradition*. New York: Yeshiva University Press, 2007.

Schimmel, Annemarie. *Mystical Dimensions of Islam*. Chapel Hill: University of Carolina Press, 1975.

Schleiermacher, Friedrich Daniel Ernst. *The Christian Faith*. Edited by H. R. Mackintosh and J. S. Stewart. 2nd ed. Edinburgh: T. & T. Clark, 1956.

———. *On Religion: Speeches to its cultured despisers*. Translated by Richard Crouter. Cambridge: Cambridge University Press, 1988.

Schleiermacher, Theodor. *Das Heil des Menschen und sein Traum vom Geist: Ferdinand Ebner, ein Denker in der Kategorie der Begegnung* [Man's Salvation and His Dream of Spirit: Ferdinand Ebner, Thinker in the Category of Encounter]. Berlin: Töpelmann, 1962.

Schmidt, Helmut. "Zeit, von Pflichten zu sprechen! Ein gewaltsamer Zusammenprall der Kulturen kann vermieden" [Time to Address the Duties! A Clash of Civilizations Can Be Avoided]. *Die Zeit*, October 3, 1997, 17–18.

Schmidt-Leukel, Perry. *Gott ohne Grenzen: Eine christliche und pluralistische Theologie der Religionen* [God without Confines: A Christian and Pluralistic Theology of Religons]. Gütersloh: Gütersloher, 2005.

———. "Was sind Religionen?" In *Fremde Nachbarn: Religionen in der Stadt* ["What Are Religions?" In *Strange Neighbors: Religion in the City*], 13–33. Hamburg: Rissen, 1997.

———. "Zur Klassifikation religionstheologischer Modelle" [On Classification of Theological Models of Religions]. *Catholica* 47 (1993) 163–83.

Schulze, Gerhard. *Die Erlebnisgesellschaft: Kultursoziologie der Gegenwart* [Event Society: Sociology of Present-Day Culture]. 2nd enlarged ed. Frankfurt: Campus, 2005.

Schütz, Alfred, and Thomas Luckmann. *The Structures of the Life-World*. Translated by R. M. Zaner and H. Tr. Engelhardt, Jr. Northwestern University Studies in Phenomenology & Existential Philosophy. Evanston, IL: Northwestern University Press, 1973.

Schwarz, Hans. "Karl Heim and John Polkinghorne: Theology and Natural Sciences in Dialogue." *Journal of Interdisciplinary Studies* 9 (1997) 105–20.

Seager, Richard Hughes, ed. *Buddhism in America*. Columbia Contemporary American Religion Series. New York: Columbia University Press, 1999.

———. *The Dawn of Religious Pluralism: Voices from the World's Parliament of Religions, 1893*. La Salle, IL: Open Court, 1993.

Sen, Amulyachandra. *Ashoka's Edicts*. With a preface by Suniti Kumar Chatterji. Calcutta: Bani Munshi, 1956.

Bibliography

The Siege and Capture of Jerusalem 1099; Collected Accounts. Internet Medieval Sourcebook, Fordham University, 1997. Online: http://www.fordham.edu/halsall/source/cde-jlem.html.

Shannon, Albert C. *The Medieval Inquisition.* Washington, DC: Augustinian College Press, 1983.

Shapiro, Marc B. *Studies in Maimonides and His Interpreters.* Scranton, PA: University of Scranton Press, 2008.

Shults, F. LeRon, Nancey Murphy, and Robert John Russell, eds. *Philosophy, Science and Divine Action.* Philosophical Studies in Science and Religion 1. Leiden: Brill, 2009.

Silkroad Experiences—Roads of Dialogue. 2010. Online: http://www.silkroadexperiences.org.

Simpson, John, ed. *The Concise Oxford Dictionary of Proverbs.* Oxford: Oxford University Press, 1985.

Slossen, Preston William. *The Great Crusade and After: 1914–1928.* New York: MacMillan, 1937.

Smith, Barry, and David Woodruff Smith, eds. *The Cambridge Companion to Husserl.* Cambridge Companions to Philosophy. Cambridge: Cambridge University Press, 1995.

Smith, William G. *The Oxford Dictionary of English Proverbs.* London: Claredon, 1935.

Spiegelberg, Herbert. *The Phenomenological Movement: A Historical Introduction.* 3rd. ed. The Hague: Nijhoff, 1984.

Spier, Jeffrey. *Picturing the Bible: The Earliest Christian Art.* New Haven: Yale University Press, 2009.

Spinoza, Baruch. *Complete Works.* Translations by Samuel Shirley. Indianapolis: Hackett, 2002.

Stall, Frits. *Agni: The Vedic Ritual of the Fire Altar.* 2 vols. Berkeley, CA: Asian Humanities, 1983.

Stein, Murray. "Individuation." In *The Handbook of Jungian Psychology: Theory, Practice and Applications,* by Renos K. Papadopoulos, 194–214. London: Routledge, 2006.

Steinbüchel, Theodor. *Der Umbruch des Denkens: Die Frage nach der christlichen Existenz erläutert an Ferdinand Ebners Menschdeutung* [The Turn in Thinking: The Quest for a Christian Existence Explained according to Ferdinand Ebner's Interpretation of Man]. 1936. Reprinted, Darmstadt: Wissenschaftliche Buchgesellschaft, 1966.

Straus, Scott. "Darfur and the Genocide Debate." *Foreign Affairs* 84 (2005) 123–33.

Strayer, Joseph R. *The Albigensian Crusades.* Ann Arbor, MI: University of Michigan Press, 1992.

Study Bible. New Revised Standard Version. Edited by the Society of Biblical Literature. London: Harper Collins, 1989.

Suermann, Harald. "Orientalische Christen und der Islam: Christliche Texte aus der Zeit von 632–750" [Oriental Christians and Islam—Christian texts from 632–750]. *Zeitschrift für Missionswissenschaft und Religionswissenschaft* 52 (1983) 120–36.

Sundermeier, Theo. "Convivence: The Concept and Origin." *Scriptura* 10 (1992) 68–80.

———. "Konvivenz als Grundstruktur ökumenischer Existenz heute" [Convivência: A principal pattern for ecumenical coexistence today]. In *Ökumenische Existenz heute,* 1:49–100. Munich: Kaiser, 1986.

Sutherland, Arthur. *I Was A Stranger: A Christian Theology of Hospitality.* Nashville: Abingdon, 2006.

Bibliography

Swidler, Leonard, et al., eds. *Death or Dialogue. From the Age of Monologue to the Age of Dialogue*. Philadelphia: Trinity, 1990.
Talmage, Frank E., ed. *Disputation and Dialogue: Readings in the Jewish-Christian Encounter*. New York: Ktav, 1975.
Taraporevala, Sooni. *Zoroastrians of India. Parsis: A Photographic Journey*. Bombay: Good Books, 2000.
Thatcher, Adrian. *The Ontology of Paul Tillich*. Oxford Theological Monographs. Oxford: Oxford University Press, 1978.
Theological Dictionary of the New Testament. Edited by Gerhard Kittel and Gerhard Friedrich. Translated by Geoffrey W. Bromiley. 10 vols. Grand Rapids: Eerdmans, 1964–1976.
Thielicke, Helmut. *Man in God's World: The Faith and Courage to Live and Die*. Translated by John W. Doberstein. Cambridge: Lutterworth, 1987.
———. *Notes from a Wayfarer: The Autobiography of Helmut Thielicke*. Translated by David R. Law. St. Paul, MN: Paragon House, 1998.
Throop, Palmer Allan. *Criticism of the Crusade: A Study of Public Opinion and Crusade Propaganda*. Amsterdam: Swets & Zeitlinger, 1940.
Time Magazine. Guns. Speech. Madness.—Where We Go from Arizona. Thematic issue Jan. 24, 2011.
Totten, Samuel, and Eric Markusen, eds. *Genocide in Darfur: Investigating the Atrocities in the Sudan*. London: Routledge, 2006.
Tracy, Thomas F. "Creation, Providence and Quantum Chance." In *Philosophy, Science and Divine Action*, edited by F. Leron Shults, Nancey Murphy, Robert John Russell, 227–61. Philosophical Studies in Science and Religion 1. Leiden: Brill, 2009.
Tramontin, Mary, and James Halpern. "The Psychological Aftermath of Terrorism: The 2001 World Trade Center Attacks." In *Trauma Psychology: Issues in Violence, Disaster, Health, and Illness*, edited by Elizabeth K. Caroll, 1:1–32. Praeger Perspectives. Westport, CT: Praeger, 2007.
Tyerman, Christopher. *God's War: A New History of the Crusades*. Cambridge, MA: Belknap, 2006.
United Nations. *Universal Declaration of Human Rights*. Online: http://www.un.org/Overview/rights.html.
Universal Declaration of Human Rights. Edited by Eleanore Roosevelt et al., 1948. Reprinted, Bedford, MA: Applewood, 2000.
University of Florida. Online: http://grove.ufl.edu/~silkroad/constitution.html.
University of Zurich. Paracelsus Project. Online: http://www.paracelsus.uzh.ch/index.html.
U.S. Department of Defense. Online: http://www.defense.gov/news/casualty.pdf.
U.S. Department of State, Office of International Information Programs. "The 9/11 Commission Report: Final Report of the National Commission on Terrorist Attacks Upon the United States, Washington DC, 2004. A list of the 77 countries whose citizens died as a result of the attacks on September 11, 2001." Online: http://www.interpol.int/public/ICPO/speeches/10020911List77countries.asp.
van Buitenen, J. A. B. *The Bhagavadgita in the Mahabharata: Text and Translation*. Chicago: University of Chicago Press, 1981.
VanRuymbeke, Bertrand, and Randy J. Sparks, eds. *Memory and Identity: The Huguenots in France and the Atlantic Diaspora*. The Carolina Lowcountry and the Atlantic World. Columbia: University of South Carolina Press, 2003.

Bibliography

Vasubandhu. *Abhidharmakosa*. Translated into French by Louis de la Vallée Poussin. Translated by Leo M. Pruden. 4 vols. Berkely, CA: Asian Humanities, 1988–1991.

Voltaire's Philosophical Dictionary. New York: Carlton House, 1901. Project Gutenberg. Online: http://www.gutenberg.org/ebooks/18569.

Vries, Simon Philip de. *Jüdische Riten und Symbole*. [Jewish Rites and Symbols]. Wiesbaden: Fourier, 1982.

Waldman, Marilyn Robinson. "The Fulani Jihad: A Reassessment." *Journal of African History* 6 (1965) 333–55.

Walker, Carolee. *Five Year 9/11 Remembrance Honors Victims from 90 Countries*. Online: http://www.america.gov/st/washfileEnglish/2006/September/20060911~.html.

Walshe, Maurice. *The Long Discourses of the Buddha: A translation of the Digha Nikāya*. Boston: Wisdom, 1995.

Wasson, R. Gordon. *Soma: Divine Mushroom of Immortality*. Ethno-mycological Studies 1. New York: Harcourt Brace Jovanovich, 1971.

Watt, William Montgomery, and Pierre Cachia. *A History of Islamic Spain*. Edinburgh: University Press of Edinburgh, 1996.

Webster, Jonathan J. *Continuing Discourse on Language: A Functional Perspective*. Edited by Ruqaia Hasan, Christian Matthiesen, and Jonathan Webster. 2 vols. London: Equinox, 2008.

Weigand, Edda, and Eckhard Hauenherm, eds. *Dialogue Analysis: Units, Relations, and Strategies beyond the Sentence: Contributions in Honour of Sorin Stati's 65th Birthday*. Beiträge zur Dialogforschung 13. Tübingen: Niemeyer, 1997.

White, Deborah. "Iraq War Facts, Results & Statistics at January 31, 2012." Online: http://usliberals.about.com/od/homelandsecurit1/a/IraqNumbers.htm/.

White House, The: Office of the Press Secretary. "President George W. Bush September 16, 2001." Online: http://georgewbush-whitehouse.archives.gov/news/releases/2001/09/20010916-2.html.

Whitehead, Alfred North. *The Concept of Nature*. Cambridge: Cambridge University Press, 1920.

Williamson, Rene de Visme. *Politics and Protestant Theology: An Interpretation of Tillich, Barth, Bonhoeffer, and Brunner*. Baton Rouge: Louisiana State University Press, 1976.

Willi-Plein, Ina, and Thomas Willi. *Glaubensdolch und Messiasbeweis: Die Begegnung von Judentum, Christentum und Islam im 13. Jahrhundert in Spanien* [The Dagger of Faith and Messianic Proof—The Encounter of Judaism, Christianity, and Islam in 13th Century Spain]. Neukirchen-Vluyn: Neukirchner, 1980.

Wilson, Dick. *When Tigers Fight: The Story of the Sino-Japanese War, 1937–1945*. New York: Viking, 1982.

Windelband, Wilhelm, and Heinz Heimsoeth. *Lehrbuch der Geschichte der Philosophie* [Textbook for the History of Philosophy]. 15th ed. Tübingen: Mohr/Siebeck, 1957.

Wolohojian, Albert Mugrdich, trans. *The Romance of Alexander the Great*. New York: Columbia University Press, 1969.

Yacoobi, Sakena. "Women Educating Women in the Afghan Diaspora: Why and How." In *Religious Fundamentalisms and the Human Rights of Women*, edited by Cortney W. Howland, 229–35. Basingstoke, UK: Palgrave MacMillan, 2001.

Yadev Bibhuti S. "Protest against the Theology of Anonymous Christianity." *Religion and Society* 24, no. 4 (1977) 69–81.

Yong, Amos. *The Cosmic Breath: Spirit and Nature in the Christianity-Buddhism-Science Trialogue*. Philosophical Studies in Science and Religion 4. Leiden: Brill, 2012.

Bibliography

Zagorin, Perez. *How the Idea of Religious Toleration Came to the West*. Princeton: Princeton University Press, 2005.

Zahid, H. Bukhari, et al., eds. *Muslims' Place in the American Public Square: Hopes, Fears, and Aspirations*. Walnut Creek, CA: AltaMira, 2004.

Zaner, Richard M., and Don Ihde, eds. *Phenomenology and Existentialism*. New York: Putnam, 1973.

Zarathushtrian Assembly at Buena Park, California. Online: http://www.zoroastrian.org/articles/The_Good_Religion_and_Zoroastrianism.htm.

Zepezauer, Frank. *The Feminist Crusades: Making Myths and Building Bureaucracies*. Bloomington, IN: AuthorHouse, 2007.

Index of Names

Abelard, Peter (*medieval scholastic philosopher, theologian*), 42
Abraham (*biblical patriarch*), 99, 157
Ahura Mazda (*The uncreated spirit, highest entity in Zoroastrianism*), 87, 99
Al Mahdi, Muhammad Ahmed (*19th cent. religious leader in Sudan*), 91n96
Albert the Great (Albertus Magnus) (*medieval theologian*), 42
Albright, Madeleine (*U.S. Secretary of State 1997–2001*), 9
Alexander the Great (*4th cent. BCE Macedonian Emperor*), 16
Al-Mawardi (*10th/11th century Arab Muslim Jurist*), 91n95
Angra Mainyu (*The destructive spirit in Zoroastrianism*), 87
Anselm of Canterbury (*11th cent. founder of medieval scholasticism*), 134, 156
Aquinas, Thomas. See Thomas Aquinas
Arjuna (*leader of the Pandavas, hero in the Mahabharata and Gita*), 85, 101n135
Ashoka the Great (*3rd cent. BCE Emperor of India*), 61, 141
Augustin (Augustinus, Aurelius) (*4th/5th cent. Latin church father*), 31n, 41, 92, 93
Aurangzeb (*Indian Mughal Emperor during the 17th/18th century*), 91n96

Bacon, Francis (*16th/17th cent. English philosopher and politician*), 137
Barth, Karl (*20th century eminent Swiss Protestant theologian*), 117n27, 123
Beg, Yaqub (*19th century King of Kashgar, China*), 91n96
Berger, Peter (*contemporary American sociologist of religion*), 30, 82, 83
Bin Laden, Osama (Bin Ladin) (*founder of Al-Queda*), 2, 5
Bloch, Ernst (*20th century German-Jewish philosopher*), 52, 154
Brundage, James A., 96
Brunner, Emil (*20th century German Protestant theologian*), 123
Buber, Martin (*20th century Jewish Philosopher*), 81, 106, 115, 118–20, 122–25, 132
Bush, George W. (*43rd President of the U.S.*), 2, 3

Calvin, John (*eminent 16th century Swiss Protestant reformer*), 43, 44
Castro, Americo (*20th century Spanish cultural historian*), 71
Cherbury, Herbert of (*17th cent. diplomat and religious philosopher*), 44, 45
Cicero (*1st cent. BCE Roman philosopher and orator*), 40, 53, 93

Index of Names

Clairvaux, Bernard of (*medieval reformer of the Cistercian Order*), 95
Cohen, Hermann (*19th/20th cent. German-Jewish philosopher*), 118, 121–23, 132
Constantine (*the Great; 4th cent. Roman Emperor*), 62, 161
Cox, Harvey (*contemporary American theologian*), 12
Cragg, Kenneth (*20th century Anglican Bishop of Jerusalem*), 155
Cusa, Nicholas of (*15th cent. Cardinal, humanist philosopher*), 43

Dalai Lama (*Head of the yellow Hat Tibetan Buddhists*), 8, 15
Descartes, René (*17th century French philosopher*), 126, 137n11
Diocletian (*3rd/4th cent. Roman Emperor*), 62
Dirre, Paul Dietrich of (*alias: d'Holbach, Paul Thiry; French Enlightenment philosopher*), 45

Ebner, Ferdinand (*19th/20th cent. Austrian teacher and philosopher*), 118, 119
Effendi, Essad (*19th century Sheik-Ul-Islam*), 91n97
Eisenhower, Dwight D. (*34th President of the U.S.*), 2n8
Eposito, John L. (*contemporary American scholar of Islamic Studies*), 14
Eschenbach, Wolfram von (*medieval German knight and poet*), 41
Eugene III (*Pope, 1145–1153*), 95

Faure, Jean (*20th century French missionary in Togo*), 156
Feuerbach, Ludwig (*19th century German philosopher*), 45, 48, 49, 122, 124
Fodio, Usman dan (*18th/19th cent. founder of the Sokoto Caliphate in Nigeria*), 91n97
Forst, Rainer (*contemporary German sociologist*), 67n22
Frederic II of Hohenstaufen (*medieval Emperor of the Holy Roman Empire*), 104
Freire, Paulo (*20th cent. Brazilian educator and philosopher*), 71
Freud, Sigmund (*19th/20th cent. Austrian founder of psychoanalysis*), 52
Frisch, Max (*20th cent. Swiss novelist*), 33

Gandhi, Mohandas K., Mahatma (*leader of Indian independence*), 8
Giffords, Gabrielle (*U.S. Representative 2006–2012*) 113n14
Girondi, Moses ben Nahman (Nahmanides or Romban) (*Spanish medieval Jewish scholar, physician and Sephardic Rabbi*), 99
Goethe, Johann Wolfgang von (*18th/19th century German poet*), 78
Gogarten, Friedrich (*20th century German theologian*), 123
Gregory VII (*Pope, 1073–1085*), 93

Hamilton, Lee H. (*U.S. Senator*), 6
Hanks, Tom (*contemporary American actor*), 105

Index of Names

Hegel, Georg Friedrich W. (*18th/19th cent. German philosopher*), 48, 145
Heidegger, Martin (*20th cent. German philosopher, existentialist*), 117
Heim, Karl (*19th/20th cent. German Protestant systematic theologian*), 123
Herder, Gottfried (*18th cent. German philosopher, theologian, poet*), 46
Herzog, Roman (*President of Germany 1994–1999*), 11n47
Hick, John H. (*20th cent. British philosopher of religion*), 35
Hieronymus (i.e., Jerome; *4th/5th cent. Translator of the Bible into Latin*), 80
Hobbes, Thomas (*17th cent. English political philosopher*), 44
Hume, David (*18th cent. Scottish Enlightenment philosopher*), 45
Huntington, Samuel P. (*20th/21st cent. American political scientist*), 10
Husserl, Edmund (*19th/20th cent. German philosopher*), 19n, 117

Illich, Ivan (*20th cent. Austrian priest, philosopher, and social critic*), 71, 114
Isaac (*biblical patriarch*) 99

Jacob (*biblical patriarch*) 99
Jesus Christ (Jesus of Nazareth), 20, 22, 160, 162
John Paul II (*Pope, 1978–2005*), 155
Justin Martyr (*Christian apologist of the 2nd century*), 79n53
Juvenal (*1st/2nd cent. Roman poet and satirist*), 28

Kahn, Abdur Rahman (*19th cent. Emir of Afghanistan*), 91n96
Kant, Immanuel (*18th/19th cent. German philosopher; critical reasoning*), 46, 47, 157n35
Kean, Thomas H. (*U.S. Senator*), 6
Kennedy, John F. (*35th President of the U.S.*), 6
Kepler, Johannes (*16th/17th cent. German astronomer and mathematician*), 44n38
Kierkegaard, Søren (*19th cent. Danish philosopher; existentialist*), 124
Klemperer, Victor (*20th cent. German-Jewish philologist*), 112, 113
Knitter, Paul (*contemporary American Roman Catholic theologian*), 36
Komnenos, Alexios I (*medieval Byzantine Patriarch*), 93
Krishna (*Avatar of Lord Vishnu in Hinduism*), 85, 101n135
Kuhn, Thomas S. (*20th century American philosopher of science*), 136
Küng, Hans (*contemporary Roman Catholic German theologian*), 12

Lactantius (*3rd/4th century Christian author*), 40, 52
Leibnitz, Gottfried Wilhelm (*18th cent. German philosopher*), 46
Lessing, Gotthold Ephraim (*18th cent. German philosopher and novelist*), 64–66, 142
Lévinas, Emmanuel (*20th cent. French-Jewish philosopher*), 118
Locke, John (*17th/18th cent. English Enlightenment philosopher*), 64, 65

Index of Names

Luhmann, Niklas (*20th cent. German sociologist*), 85
Lull, Raymond (*medieval Spanish theologian*), 42
Luther, Martin (*15th/16th cent. eminent German Protestant reformer*), 43, 76, 81

Maimon, Moses ben (Maimonides or Rambam) (*12th cent. Sephardic philosopher, physician, and Rabbi*), 97, 98, 100n135
Margull, Hans Jochen (*20th cent. German missiologist*), 153
Markham, Edwin (*19th/20th American poet*), 126, 128
Martini, Raymond (*13th cent. Catalan theologian and polemicist*), 80
Marx, Karl (*19th cent. philosopher; co-founder of Communism*), 49, 53
Medici, Marsilio Ficino (*15th cent. Italian humanist philosopher*), 42
Melanchthon, Philip (*eminent 16th cent. German Protestant theologian*), 43
Mitscherlich, Alexander (*20th century German psychoanalyst*), 67
Mohammed II, Sultan (*15th century Sultan of the Ottoman Empire*), 43
Möngke, Great Kahn (*medieval 4th Great Kahn of the Mongol empire*), 79
More, Thomas (*15th/16th cent. English humanist philosopher and statesman*), 64
Moses (*receiver of the Ten Commandments, main biblical prophet*), 157, 158

Muhammad (Mohammad) (*receiver of the Qur'an, principal prophet in Islam*), 73, 90

Natorp, Paul (*19th/20th cent. German philosopher; neo-Kantianism*), 121
Newton, Isaac (*17th/18th cent. English mathematician and physicist*), 44n38
Nietzsche, Friedrich (*19th cent. German philosopher*), 50, 51
Noah (*biblical patriarch*), 157

Otto, Rudolf (*19th/20th cent. German Protestant theologian and scholar of comparative religion*), 139

Paracelsus (*alias: Theophrast Bombast von Hohenheim; 16th cent. Swiss physician and alchemist*), 138n14
Paul (*Apostle*), 70, 159, 160, 162
Peter (*Apostle*), 159
Pieper, Josef (*20th cent. German philosopher*), 77, 113
Plato (*5th/4th cent. BCE Greek philosopher*) 113
Popper, Karl (*20th cent. British philosopher*), 26

Rahner, Karl (*20th cent. Roman Catholic systematic theologian*), 146
Rilke, Rainer Maria (*19th/20th cent. Bohemian-Austrian German poet*), 77, 78
Rosenzweig, Franz (*19th/20th cent. German-Jewish philosopher*), 81, 118, 121, 123, 132
Rousseau, Jean-Jaques (*18th cent. French Enlightenment philosopher*), 26, 45

Index of Names

Rubruck, Willem (*13th cent. Flemish Franciscan missionary*), 79

Saladin (*12th cent. Sultan of Egypt and Syria*), 65, 66, 97
Schiller, Friedrich (*18th/19th cent. German novelist and poet*), 66n21
Schleiermacher, Friedrich Daniel Ernst (*eminent 19th cent. Protestant theologian*), 38, 47, 48, 49, 145
Schmidt, Helmut (*Chancellor of West Germany 1974-1982*), 11n49
Schulze, Gerhard (*contemporary German sociologist*), 31, 32
Spinoza, Baruch (*17th cent. Dutch Jewish philosopher*), 64
Sundermeier, Theo (*contemporary German missiologist*), 71, 72

Theodosius (the Great) (*4th cent. Roman Emperor*), 161
Thielicke, Helmut (*20th cent. German Protestant theologian*), 123
Thomas Aquinas (*eminent medieval scholastic theologian*), 42, 93n105
Tillich, Paul (*20th cent. German Protestant systematic theologian*), 123

Urban II (*Pope 1042-1099*), 93

Vasubandhu (*4th cent. Indian Buddhist monk*), 146
Vishnu (*The principal deity of Indian religions, Hinduism*), 85
Voltaire (*18th cent. French Enlightenment philosopher*), 45
Vries, Simon Philip de, Rabbi (*19th/20th cent. Dutch Rabbi*), 38, 141

Watt, W. Montgomery (*20th cent. Scottish scholar of Islamic studies*), 89
Wolff, Christian (*17th/18th cent. German Enlightenment philosopher*), 46

Xenophanes (*ancient Greek philosopher and religious critic*), 49

Yacoobi, Sakena (*contemporary Afghani women's activist*), 89

Zemecki, Robert (*contemporary American film director*), 105
Zoroaster (Zarathustra) (*7th/6th cent. BCE founder of Zoroastrianism*), 86

Index of Scripture

Old Testament

Genesis

1:3	78
1:14	78
1:24	78
8:21–22	157
12:3	157

Exodus

3:14	53, 158
19–20	157
20:4	152n26

Deuteronomy

3:6	96n118
5:8	152n26
7:1–2	96n118
20:3	100n135
20:8	100n135
20:16–18	96n118
25:19	96n118

Joshua

6:17	96n118
10:28–40	96n118

1 Samuel

8:20	98
15:1–3	96n118
25:28–29	101n135

1 Chronicles

4:42–43	96n118

Psalms

1:1	70
148:5	78

Jeremiah

48:10	100n135

New Testament

Matthew

5–7	160n49
5:37	114
6:21	34n14
8:28–34	161n53
10:39	162
12:1–8	160n48
12:34	34n14, 163n63
13:24–30	160n47
13:31–31	160n47
16:21–23	162n58
17:22–23	162n58
18:21–22	160n49

Index of Scripture

Matthew (*cont.*)

20:17–19	162n58
26:36–46	160n50
27:46	160n51
27:64	157n37
28:16–20	159n44
28:20	157n39

Mark

2:18–22	160n48
2:23–28	160n48
4:26–29	160n47
4:30–32	160n47
8:31–33	162n58
9:30–32	162n58
10:32–34	162n58
14:32–42	160n50
16:6	157n37
16:15	159n44

Luke

5:33–39	160n48
8:9–10	160n49
9:22	162n58
9:43–45	162n58
13:18–19	160n47
17:11–19	161n53
18:31–34	162n58
22:39–46	160n50
24:13–32	158n40
24:21	158
24:34	157n37
24:46	157n37

John

1:1–4	78
3:1–21	160n48
12:25	162n59
16:13–14	157
17:1–26	160n50
18:37–38	161
20:11–18	158n42
20:19–21	159
20:21	160
21:1–14	158n41
21:14	157n37

Acts

2:1–47	157n38
4:20	163n63
10:1–48	159n46
15:1–41	159n45

Romans

13:12	88
13:14	88

1 Corinthians

1:18–24	161n57

2 Corinthians

4:2–6	163
6:14–16	70

Galatians

2:1–10	159n45

Ephesians

6:10–17	88

Philippians

1:30	88n82

Colossians

2:1	88n82

1 Thessalonians

2:2	88n82

1 Timothy

6:12	88n82

2 Timothy

4:5	88n82

Hebrews

5:7–8	157n36
12:1	xi, 88n82

James

3:2	115
3:11	115

1 Peter

5:8–9	88

Index of Subjects and Places

9/11/2001 (9/11) attacks, 1, 4, 11, 27, 130, 155
The 9/11 Commission Report, 1n2, 4–6, 8, 12, 109, 130

absolute claims, 129
abuse of language (*see also* misuse of language), 129, 131
adhārma, 86
advertising, 28
Afghanistan, 1, 61
Africa, 10, 91
aggression, 8, 69, 101
Ahmadiyya, 92
al Qaeda (al Queda; Al Queda), 5, 8, 12, 13, 84, 130
Amalekites, 97, 99
America, 5
American Revolution, 65
Amish, 9
Anglo-Indian roundtable conferences (1930–1932), 109n11
"anonymous Christians," 146
Arabia, 91
Arabic, 75
Aramaic (i.e. language), 75
Arthurian legend, 110
asha, 87
Asia, 91
Aum sect, 84
Australia, 10
autonomy (i.e., of individuals), 135
avatar, 85, 157

Babri Masjid Mosque, 3n16
Baghdad, 69
Baha'i, 144
Balkan wars (1991–2001), 107
Bangladesh, 61
belief (beliefs, believing), 23, 34, 41, 42, 110
b^{e}rith, 56, 57, 142
Berlin, 121
Bertelsmann Foundation, 82
Bhagavad-Gita, 3n16, 85–86, 101n135
Bible (i.e., Christian Bible), 40, 75
biblical religion, 53
blasphemer(s), 70
blasphemy, 27, 68, 69, 128
bodhisattva Avalokiteshwara, 8
Book of Joshua, 3
"both-and" approach, 74
Buddha (Thatagatha), 55
Buddhism, 4, 14, 15, 20, 26, 32, 40, 54, 55, 75, 114, 119, 132, 134, 140, 144, 146
Buddhist(s), 17, 36, 56, 61, 73, 90, 150, 153, 155
Bundahishn, 87n81
burkha, 17

calendar(s), 73–74
Canaanites, 97, 99
Catholicism (Roman Catholicism), 25
certainty (absolute certainty), 37, 68, 78, 129, 137

Index of Subjects and Places

chador, 17
China, 3, 8, 9, 24, 80
Christ (*see also* Jesus Christ), 35, 41, 43, 73, 80, 92, 93, 156, 158, 160
Christendom (*see also* Christianity), 52, 93
Christian (Christians), 15, 20–22, 41, 42, 51, 62, 66, 70, 71, 73, 79, 80, 83, 90, 92, 96, 123, 132, 133, 136, 140, 149, 153, 155, 156, 157–63
Christian discipleship, 162
Christian military orders, 94
Christianity, 10, 20, 32, 35, 43, 47, 48, 50, 52, 54, 55, 62, 64, 121, 124, 132, 134, 140, 142, 143, 145, 146
Christology, 36
Church (i.e., Christian Church; church), 16, 41, 49, 65, 73, 84, 92, 94, 96, 155, 159, 161
"clash of civilizations," 10–13, 103
"clash of cultures," 10
Club of Rome, 82
coexistence, 106
Cold War (1947–1991), 115, 132
Colombo, 153
communication (to communicate), 101, 103, 104, 107, 109–11, 113, 114, 116, 120, 123, 127, 131, 133, 138, 156
comparative religion, 54
complexity, 29
conflict(s) (violent conflicts, normative conflicts), 21, 60, 83, 107, 131, 149
conflict avoidance, 153
Confucian-Chinese civilization, 10
Confucianism, 54, 75, 155
consumer society, 24
conventions, 30
conversation(s), 109

convivence (*Convivência*), 21, 60, 71, 74, 83, 103, 104, 106, 110, 131, 132
conviviality, 60, 71, 114
Council of Claremont (1095), 93
County of Edessa (1098), 94n109
County of Tripoli (1109–1289), 94n109
creation, 136, 138
critical rationalism (*see also* rationality, reason), 26
cross (i.e., of Jesus of Nazareth), 22, 36, 133, 160, 161, 162
crusade (Crusade, Crusades), 2, 3, 65, 92–96, 99, 131
crusader(s), 65
crusader states, 94
culture, 54, 81, 129
cultus, 41, 42
"*cuius regio eius religio*," 9n38
cyberspace, 28

Dadaism, 117n26
Daoism (Taoism), 3, 14, 25, 54, 75
dar al-Islam (*see also* Ummah), 35, 90
Dastar, 17
De pace fidei (by N. of Cusa), 43
death of God, 50, 53
dedication, 24
democracy, 26, 83
Department of State (U.S.), 10
devotion, 44
dhamma, 55, 57, 61, 99
dharma (Dharma), 3, 27, 55, 57, 85–86, 99, 131, 140
dialectic theology, 117n27
dialogical existence, 157–63
dialogical philosophy, 103, 116
dialogical thinking, 21, 125, 127, 131
dialogue (*see also* interreligious dialogue), 5, 18, 19, 23, 39, 54, 68, 69, 82, 84, 101–4, 106,

Index of Subjects and Places

107, 109, 110, 115, 119, 123, 127, 128, 135, 139, 141, 153, 157, 160, 163
Dialogues concerning Natural Religion (by D. Hume), 45
din, 55–57
diplomacy, 102
Dissenters (i.e., English), 63
doctrina, 41
Dresden, 112
Dungan Revolt (1618–1707), 91n96
Dutch-Indonesian roundtable conference (1949), 109n11

Edict of Milan (313), 62
Edict of Nantes (1598), 63n7
Edict of Saint-Germain (1562), 63n7
edicts of toleration, 63
Egypt, 8, 97
Egyptian Islamic Jihad, 92
empirical religion, 24
encounter (i.e., personal encounter), 118, 119, 121–25, 127, 128, 138, 153, 154, 163
Enlightenment (i.e., European Enlightenment; post-Enlightenment), 13, 26, 35, 42, 53, 116, 118, 122, 132, 140
Epistola De Tolerantia (by J. Locke), 65n15
The Essence of Christianity (by L. Feuerbach), 49
Europe, 9, 10, 42, 43, 53, 55, 62
event society, 31
exclusivism (exclusivist), 21, 146, 149, 159
existentialism, 116, 117

faith, 23, 34, 62, 131, 133–36, 138, 160
Faith Clubs, 40
fanatics, 1, 156
fides, 41–43

Five Pecks of Rice Rebellion, 3n15
France, 63, 91n97
Frankfurt School of sociology, 67n22
freedom (i.e., as political virtue), 29, 64, 68, 83, 84
freedom (i.e., freedom of choice), 25–28, 31, 63
freedom of conscience (i.e., of mind, of heart), 63, 124, 128
French Revolution, 65
Fulani Jihad, 91n
fundamentalist(s), 11, 12, 84, 111
Fuqaha, 89

Germany, 83, 112, 121
ghazi (*ghazawāt*), 90, 91
Global Ethic Foundation, 12n50
global politics, 10, 13
global strategy, 5
globalization, 5, 14, 155
God, 20, 27, 48, 49, 51, 53, 54, 65, 78, 80, 121, 122, 133, 134, 136, 141, 146, 152, 156, 157, 160
goodwill (good intentions), 69, 116
Gospel(s), 75, 159, 161
gossip, 114
Great Britain (United Kingdom, Britain), 17, 91n97
Greece, 24
Greek (i.e., language), 75
guarding the tongue (*sh'mira ha-lashon*), 114

habit(s), 29, 30
Hadith, 90
halakha, 98
Hamburg, 83
Hasidim (Hasidic), 124
hatred, 101, 103
healing of memories, 7
Hebrew (i.e., language), 75, 79, 80, 81

199

Index of Subjects and Places

heretic(s), 84
"Hermeneutic of the Stranger," 72n36
hierocracy, 8, 26
hijab, 17
Hijra, 73
Hindu(s), 15, 17, 56, 90, 153
Hinduism (Indian religions), 3, 20, 40, 54, 55
history of religions, 54
Holocaust, 115
Holy Land, 94
Holy scripture (Holy Scriptures), 2, 15, 75, 99
"holy War" ("holy Wars"), 3, 11–13, 21, 27, 60, 85, 88, 92, 96, 97, 99, 100, 101, 129, 130–32, 140, 163
"holy warriors," 90, 100
hope, 53, 106
hostility, 69
Huguenots, 62, 63n5
human(-ly), 101, 103, 107, 116
human rights, 63
Humanism (i.e., European Humanism), 42–44
Hutterites, 9

I and Thou (by M. Buber), 118
inclusivism (inclusivistic), 21, 146, 149
independence, 25
India, 3, 24, 61, 74, 86, 91, 92
Inquisition(s), 84, 85n67, 96n116
Institute for Islamic Understanding (IKIM), Kuala Lumpur, Malaysia, 11
InterAction Council, 11
intercultural communication, 6
interfaith dialogue (interreligious dialogue), 154
International Association for Dialogue analysis (IADA), 108n8

internet, 14
Interreligious Day of Prayer (Assisi 1986), 155
interreligious dialogue (see also: dialogue, interfaith dialogue), 6, 8, 13, 18, 19, 21, 23, 38, 39, 56, 59, 69, 70, 79, 123, 128–30, 132, 134, 139, 142, 151, 152, 154, 155
interreligious marriages, 74
intolerance, 5, 60, 67, 68, 101
Iran (Persia), 86
Iraq, 1
Islam, 5, 14, 20, 26, 32, 40, 43, 54, 55, 62, 75, 89–91, 134, 142, 144
Islamic civilization, 10
Islamist, 1, 5, 6
Israel, 8, 56, 97–99

Japan, 4, 8, 40
Japanese civilization, 10
Jehovah's Witnesses, 146n22
Jerusalem, 65, 93, 94, 124, 158, 159
Jesus Christ, 36, 46, 48, 158
Jew (Jews, Jewish), 16, 17, 21, 36, 42, 62, 65, 66, 70, 71, 73, 79, 80, 90, 99, 112, 121, 123, 124, 136, 153
Jihād (jihad), 2, 3, 89–92, 97, 99, 131
Judaism, 15, 20, 32, 38, 40, 43, 47, 54, 55, 56, 62, 75, 99, 114, 122, 132, 134, 142
"just war," 93

Karakorum, 79
Kharijites, 92
Kingdom of Jerusalem (1099–1291), 94n109
Korean War (1950–1953), 115
kosher, 17, 73

language, 74–82, 104, 111–16, 120, 133, 138

Index of Subjects and Places

Latin (i.e., language), 75, 80
Latin American civilization, 10
laws of nature, 44
Lectures on the Philosophy of Religion (by G. F. W. Hegel), 48
Letter to America (by Osama bin Laden), 2, 3n11, 6
Leviathan (by Th. Hobbes), 44
lex, 41
liberty, 29
life, 28, 29, 31, 32, 40, 41, 50, 51, 72, 73, 86, 87, 89, 101, 106, 110, 111, 119, 123, 124, 134, 135, 138, 161, 162
life-style, 28
life-world, 19, 121
logic of terror, 12
love, 23, 24, 68
loyalty, 23
Lubna Hussain v. City of Omaha, Nebraska, 17
Lutheran church, 20

Mahabharata (Indian epic), 85
Marburg, 121
martyr(s), 91, 94n111
Marxist historical materialism, 53
Mecca, 73
mediation (mediations, mediating), 82, 102, 110
Medina, 73
Mexico, 9
Middle Ages (i.e., European Middle Ages), 16, 41, 42, 65, 110
Middle East, 1, 156
Mihna, 85n67
milchemet mitzvah/milkhemet mitzwah, 96–99
milites Christi, 93
milkhemet reshut, 97
milla, 55, 57, 131
Mishneh Torah (by Maimonides), 98, 100n135

misuse of language (*see also* abuse of language), 112–14
mock-dialogue, 111
Modern Religions (Japan), 40
Mongols, 69
Montenegro, 91n97
Moonies, 25
Morocco, 97
Moses, 80
Mosque(s), 73, 75
Mount Sinai, 73
mujahid (*mujahideen*), 90
Muslim(s) (*see also* Saracens), 15, 17, 26, 36, 43, 56, 62, 65, 66, 69, 71, 73, 80, 90, 136, 150, 153, 155

Nathan the Wise (by G. E. Lessing), 65
National Commission on Terrorist Attacks Upon the United States, 4
natural religion, 44, 46, 47, 142
nature, 137–38, 160
Nazi propaganda, 112
negotiation(s), 82, 109
Nestorianism, 43
New Age, 36
New Terrorism, 4
New Testament, 75, 87, 160, 161
New Zealand, 10
Niebelungs (by an anonymous author), 41
nihilism, 51
ningen, 120n40
Noble Eightfold Path, 114
Nonconformist (i.e., English), 63
North America, 10
North Korea, 9

Omaha, Nebraska, 17
On Religion, Doctrinal Opinions and Usages (by G. Herder), 46

Index of Subjects and Places

On Religion: Speeches to Its Cultured Despisers (by D. F. E. Schleiermacher), 47
open society, 20, 26, 29, 84
Order of St. Andrew the Apostle, 135n6
Order of St. John (Knights Hospitallers), 94n110
other (the Other), 117, 128, 152, 156

pacifist(s), 92
pain, 7
Pakistan, 3n16
Palestine, 65, 97, 155
Pali, 75
Parliament of the World's Religions, 15, 89
Parsi (Parsee, Parsees), 86
Parzival (by W. v. Eschenbach), 41
Paulo Freire Institutes, 71n33
Pauperes commilitones Christi Templum Solomonici (Templars), 94n110
peace, 21, 22, 64, 69, 92, 98, 106, 109, 115, 116, 129, 137, 153, 159, 163
Peace of Westphalia (1648), 9n
peacekeeping (i.e., proactive peacekeeping), 39
Pearl Harbor, 6
penultimate, the, 163
Persia (Iran), 4, 8, 80, 86
person (i.e., human person), 120n
Pew Forum on Religion & Public Life, 14n, 25
Peyote cult, 73
phenomenology, 116, 117
philosophy of encounter, 21, 103, 116–24, 128, 152
philosophy of religion, 54
pietas, 41, 42, 43
piety, 52
Pilgrim Fathers, 63
Pledge of Allegiance, 9

pluralism, 20
pluralism (pluralistic), 21, 35, 162
pluralistic relativism, 38
pluralistic theory of religion, 37, 148–51
politics, 8–10, 12, 27
post-modern(-ism), 24
The President's Interfaith and Community Service Campus Challenge, 13
Priest of war (*meshuach milchamah*), 98
Principality of Antioch (1098–1268), 94n109
Project World Ethos, 12n50
Promised Land, 3
Protestants (Protestantism), 25, 62, 75, 124
psychology of religion, 54
public discourse, 84
puja/pooja, 55, 61

Qur'an (Quran), 2, 36, 75, 89, 90

Rabbi(s), 96
rationality (*see also* critical rationalism), 116
reason (i.e., human reason), 70, 116, 133, 134, 138
reconciliation, 129
redemption, 34
Reformation (i.e., Protestant Reformation), 62
relativism, 20, 156
religio, 42
religion(s) (*see also* empirical religion(s)), 1, 5, 8–10, 12, 17, 20, 21, 23, 32–59, 60, 61, 75, 85, 122, 129, 130, 131, 138–41, 146
religion of reason, 46
Religion of Reason: Out of the sources of Judaism (by H. Cohen), 122

Index of Subjects and Places

Religion within the Boundaries of Mere Reason (by I. Kant), 47
religious competence, 9
religious diversity, 13, 141
religious illiteracy, 17, 156
religious literacy, 13, 17, 130
religious peace, 43
religious pluralism, 36, 129, 148
religious plurality (religious pluralism), 24
religious sentiments, 27
religious speech, 138
religious studies, 54
religious tolerance, 66
Renaissance (i.e., European Renaissance), 42
resurrection, 22, 36, 73, 87, 141, 156
retaliation, 8
retributive justice, 7
revelation, 35, 49, 90, 158
revenge, 6, 130
Ring Parable, 65–66
rock edit (rock edits of Ashoka), 61
Roman Catholic Church, 155
Rome (Roman Empire), 24, 62, 63, 92
roundtable talk(s), 82, 109, 110
Russia, 24, 91n97
Rwanda, 107

Sacred Scripture(s) (sacred text; *see also* Holy Scripture), 15, 79, 90
salvation, 34, 56, 114, 133, 146, 160
Sangha, 155
Sanhedrin, 97, 98
Sanskrit, 75
Saracens (Muslims), 42
security, 68
Seisen, 4n17
self-deception, 69
self-determination, 135
self-sacrifice, 24
Septuagint, 80

Serbia, 91n97
Shaktism, 55
Shiites, 155
Shintoism (*Kaminomichi*), 4
Shivaism, 55
Sikhs, 17, 18n68, 73
Silk Road, 16
Siva food, 73
Slavic-Orthodox civilization, 10
Social contract, 26
sociology of religion(s), 54
solipsism (solipsistic), 126, 127, 134
Soma sacrifice, 73
Sophist (also: Sophists), 113
Spain, 16, 62, 71, 80, 97
Sri Lanka, 119, 153
St. Bartholomew's Day Massacre (1572), 63n5
The Star of Redemption (by F. Rosenzweig), 121
state (i.e., as political entity), 65
Sudan, 107
Sufi(s), 89
Sunna, 90, 91
Sunnis, 92
Synagogue(s), 39, 49, 73, 75, 155
syncretism, 129
Syria, 80

Taliban, 89
Tanakh, 75
tear(s), 7
Templars. See *Pauperes commilitones Christi Templum Solomonici*
terror, 2, 5, 8, 84
terror prevention, 5
terrorism, 84, 100
terrorist(s), 8, 13, 130
terrorist attacks, 1, 84
Teutonic Knights, 94n110
theocracy, 26
theology (i.e., Christian theology), 20, 39, 93, 117, 124, 133, 154

Index of Subjects and Places

Theravada Buddhism (*see also* Buddhism), 119
Third Reich (Germany, 1939–1945), 112
Thirty Years War (1618–1648), 9
threat, 130
Tibet, 8, 15
Tipitaka, 75
Togo, 156
tolerance, 5, 21, 60, 74, 83, 84, 131
tolerance movement, 64
Torah, 75
true religion, 142
trust (ultimate and unconditional trust), 23, 24, 111, 115, 116, 128, 129, 131
truth (Truth), 8, 35, 133, 135, 145, 156, 157, 161, 162
Tucson, Arizona, 113
tulku, 8

U.S. Religious Landscape Survey, 25
Ulama, 56
ultimate authority (ultimate cause), 27, 100, 132
ultimate claims, 19, 37
ultimate commitment, 101
ultimate validity, 35, 145, 149
Ultimate, the, 21, 22, 34, 61, 133, 138, 153, 156
Ummah (Islamic Nation; *see also dar al-Islam*), 2, 73, 91n97, 155
uncertainty (i.e., final uncertainty), 30
United States of America (U.S.), 9, 14

Universal Declaration of Human Rights of 1948, 63

value(s), 18, 26, 34, 110, 137
Vedas, 75
vegetarianism, 17
violence, 114
virtue(s), 66, 93, 160
Vishnuism, 55
vulnerability (also: vulnerable), 21, 23, 27, 30, 34, 129, 162

Wahhabists, 91n96
war, 2, 6, 130
war demanded by God (also: war of God; see also "holy war"), 96–99, 98
War of the Cross, 2
war on terrorism, 1, 2, 6
Western civilization (also: Western world, Western culture), 27, 29, 56, 125
World Council of Churches, 154
world politics, 5
worldview (also: worldviews), 39, 79, 129, 137, 141, 142

yana, 55
Yellow Scarf Rebellion (Yellow Turban Rebellion), 3n15

Zend-Avesta, 87
Zionist(s), 99, 115
Zoroastrian(s), 87, 90
Zoroastrianism, 4, 86–87

www.ingramcontent.com/pod-product-compliance
Lightning Source LLC
Chambersburg PA
CBHW070324230426
43663CB00011B/2209